RARVM ORBIS TABVLA. *Auctore* IOANNE BLAEV.

❧ BLAEU'S ❧
THE GRAND ATLAS
OF THE
17th CENTURY WORLD

～ BLAEU'S ～
THE GRAND ATLAS
OF THE
17th CENTURY WORLD

INTRODUCTION, CAPTIONS AND
SELECTION OF MAPS BY JOHN GOSS
FORMERLY CARTOGRAPHIC ADVISOR TO SOTHEBY'S

FOREWORD BY PETER CLARK

KEEPER (1989-1992), ROYAL GEOGRAPHICAL SOCIETY LONDON

PUBLISHED IN CO-OPERATION WITH
ROYAL GEOGRAPHICAL SOCIETY LONDON

BARNES
&NOBLE
BOOKS
NEW YORK

ENDPAPERS:

Nova et Accuratissima Totius Terrarum Orbis Tabula

The concept of this new 1662 map is totally different, designed as an eye-catching ornament to serve as the frontispiece to a great atlas. Gone are the vignettes and cartouches of the old map. In their stead, Blaeu placed new representations of the four Seasons: from left to right along the bottom are Spring, Summer, Autumn and Winter. The two bust portraits in the upper left and right spandrels are the astronomers Galileo and Tycho Brahe respectively, the latter in honour of Joan Blaeu's father's teacher, with the figures of several Classical deities on cloud designs in between.

 As far as the geographical detail is concerned, features to note are the large island of California off the west coast of North America (copied from the map of North America by Joan Blaeu's rival publisher, Joannes Jansson – Blaeu himself never produced a separate map of North America to accompany that section of his atlas), and the inclusion of a remarkably accurate outline for the western portion of Australia. Here, Blaeu must naturally have drawn upon the archives of the VOC [*Verenigde Ooste-Indische Compagnie*, or United East-India Company] to which Joan Blaeu held the important appointment as cartographer.

This edition published by Barnes & Noble, Inc.,
by arrangement with Studio

1997 Barnes & Noble Books

M 10 9 8 7 6 5 4 3 2 1

ISBN 0-7607-0686-7

The original maps in *Blaeu's The Grand Atlas of the 17th Century World* first appeared in
Dr Joan Blaeu's *Atlas Major* published in Amsterdam in 1662. In this edition, the maps are reproduced at
between 80 and 90 per cent of their original size.

Typesetting by Behram Kapadia
Printed in Hong Kong

CONTENTS

FOREWORD

At the first meeting of the Geographical Society of London on 16th July 1830 (it was to receive its Royal appellation only later in the same year) Mr (later Sir) John Barrow, as chairman, expressed the hope that they would shortly be in a position to form 'a useful collection of maps and charts'; this hope was embodied in more formal terms in the objects of the new Society. What Barrow had in mind no doubt was to make available to explorers and travellers the latest geographical knowledge in cartographic form, as the starting point for further work of discovery with which the Society was to be principally preoccupied for the rest of the century. Thus began the collection that now forms the stock of the Map Room of the Society which, with its holding of some eight hundred thousand map sheets and over two thousand atlases, is believed to be the largest privately owned map collection in Europe.

Although the map collection was in the main directed towards practical applications and up-to-date maps, the Society's early concern for the history of mapmaking is seen in its commissioning in 1830-1831 of the copying, in manuscript facsimile, of the world map of Richard of Haldingham, the renowned Hereford Map. It was however mainly in the twentieth century that the Society built up the rich collection of early maps and, particularly, early atlases of which it is now possessed. The contribution of Edward Heawood, Librarian from 1901 to 1934, is of great importance; he took advantage of the relatively low prices in the antiquarian market of those days to make many valuable purchases, which have helped to make the atlas collection one of the major assets of the Society. However, the Society has benefited to an even greater extent perhaps from the generosity of Fellows, both in gifts and legacies. The copy of Joan Blaeu's *Atlas Major*, from which most of the plates in the present work were reproduced, was donated by the Earl of Northbrook in 1879, during his presidency of the Society. Its nine volumes in gilt-tooled vellum are a major treasure among the jewels of the Society's early atlas collection.

The Society has long endeavoured to make some of its important cartographic items more widely accessible by the publication of facsimile copies. In the past it was possible for the Society itself to undertake publication of rare works in its own series of reproductions of early maps. Beginning in the twenties at the initiative of Heawood and continuing after the war under the eminent scholarship of the Society's Librarian and Map Curator from 1945 to 1966, Gerald Crone, eight portfolios of maps from the collection were issued between 1927 and 1964, as well as an authoritative reproduction and memoir on the Hereford Map (1954); resources have unfortunately made it impossible to continue the series in more recent years. It is with particular pleasure therefore that the Society has collaborated with Studio in offering a selection of plates from this truly 'Great Atlas' to a wider public. In so doing, it is gratifying to be able to acknowledge the scholarship of John Goss, in preparing the introduction to the atlas and individual plates and to commend the high technical skills of Mr Gordon Roberton and his colleagues of A. C. Cooper Ltd. photographers, for the quality of the beautiful images which follow.

P. K. CLARK
Keeper (1989–1992)

INTRODUCTION

During the early hours of 23 February 1672 a fire broke out and engulfed premises on the Gravenstraat in the centre of Amsterdam. Such an event was nothing out of the ordinary, until we realize that the fire, to all intents and purposes, brought to an end the activities of one of the greatest map publishers of all time, Dr Joan Blaeu (1598–1673), publisher and printer of maps, atlases, religious and philosophical books. The fire was described in suitably vivid terms in the annual review publication, *De Hollandtse Mercurius*[1] for 1672–1673: '...the disaster occurred at 3.30 on the morning of 23 February because of the dryness of the timbers, or perhaps the carelessness of the apprentices; the magnificent establishment caught fire, and with it printing type, presses, plates and paper, were all burnt and sparks were sent flying as far as the Tol-heck [Toll-gate].' One report put the financial cost of the damage at *fl.*27,000 for the buildings, and some *fl.*355,000 for the plate-stock in the printing works and shop premises, to give a total estimated loss of *fl.*382,000 (or about *fl.*38,200,000 or nearly £11,000,000 in modern terms), together with some four or five thousand reams of paper, five or six thousand printed sheets, eighty-eight thousand kg. printing type, and so on.[2]

The fire precipitated the end of a publishing house established over forty years before, and very probably contributed to the death of its proprietor, Alderman Dr Joan Blaeu, a year later, effectively ending the reign of one of the greatest producers of printed maps and atlases in publishing history. Only ten years before, in 1662, the house had reached its zenith with the publication of its greatest achievement, the *Atlas Major* (to give it its Latin title) or 'Great Atlas'. In its turn, the atlas reflected many of the achievements of the so-called 'Golden Age' of the United Netherlands.

But how did this great enterprise reach such a height of fame? Not all of the history of the House of Blaeu has survived; indeed, we have very few records of any of the Amsterdam publishers and booksellers available to us today, fire and dispersal of their records having taken their inevitable toll over the years.

Alderman Dr Joan Blaeu was born at Alkmaar in the province of Noord-Holland in either 1598 or early 1599, to Willem Janszoon Blaeu and his wife, Maritgen Cornelisdochter. The eldest of seven children, from his earliest days Joan was surrounded by scientific and navigational instruments. Since before Joan's birth, Willem Janszoon Blaeu had been interested in mathematics and astronomy. To further this interest, he travelled, in 1594, to Denmark to study under the famous astronomer Tycho Brahe, becoming his assistant at the astronomical observatory on the small island of Ven in Öresund between Denmark and Sweden. Here he learned the art and science of instrument and globe-making.

Willem Janszoon returned to Alkmaar, and he and his family left for Amsterdam sometime during 1599, where he set himself up in business as a globe and scientific instrument-maker. In

---

[1] *Hollandtse Mercurius in den Jare* 1672. *tot* 1673 XXIII (Haarlem, Pieter Casteleyn, 1673), p. 14 [23 February 1672]: '...Het had nu al langh uyt den Oosten Gekoelt, het welck dappere koude en droogte veroorsaeckte: Men verhaeldt, dat d'Heer Schepen Johan Blaeuw tot Amsterdam, dese tijdt heeft gehad een der schoonste Druckeryen; ick voegh daer toe bij, dat sulcke gewijs is, 't ongeluck liet den Hemel toe, dat den 23 deser ten half vieren des nachts, door het droogen van het Kachel-hout, of immers wareloosheyt der Knechts, die soo heerlijcke Boeck-druckerye is ontvonckt, en met Letters, Parssen, Platen en Papieren (daer van de vlocken tot het Amsterd. Tol-heck quamen gevloogen) zijn verbrandt, geschroeyt, vernielt, en soo bedorven, dat men...jammer zijnde om de Platen van den Atlas, de Steden deser Landen, de Merchanise, en andere seer artificieuse Platen, Documenten, &c. die ten deele door den brandt geruineert en bedorven wierden.'

[2] See, for example, Jan van der Heiden, *Beschrijving der nieuwelijks uitgevonden en geoctroyeerde slang-brandspuiten en haare wijze van Brand-Blussen* (Amsterdam, 1690), p. 15.

1605 the family moved to an address 'op 't Water', which is now part of the west side of the Damrak in the centre of Amsterdam. Here, Willem Janszoon opened his shop and set up a printing-press under the sign called *in de Vergulde Sonnewijzer* ['at the sign of the gilded sundial'], where works on navigation (for example, *Het Licht der zee-vaert* (1608), which contained fifty-one sea charts with descriptive text), astronomy (the prime example being a revised edition of the astronomical treatise of Copernicus, *De revolutionibus orbium caelestium* (1617), edited by Blaeu's friend from Alkmaar, Nicolaeus Mulerius), literature (such as the works of another friend, the poet Joost van den Vondel), and related subjects such as theology, were printed and sold. We cannot now be sure what religion Willem Janszoon professed, but the few theological titles he is known to have issued from his press seem to indicate a certain tolerance of rival faiths. In later years, Joan himself seems to have had some leanings towards Roman Catholicism, to judge by the Jesuit missals (published under a false Cologne imprint), the series of plates illustrating the monastery-palace of the Escorial, near Madrid (the palace of Philip II, built in 1563–1582), or the series of Italian Townbooks which he began publishing in 1663, perhaps as a fond memory of his travels in Italy – his *geliefde Italië*[3] – during his earlier, student years.

Joan Blaeu studied Law at the University of Leiden, gaining his Doctorate in 1620. After this date, very little is known of his personal life except for a few brief mentions. He married, in 1634, Geertruida Vermeulen from Gouda (she survived him by about two years, dying in 1675). In 1651, Dr Joan Blaeu (as he liked to style himself) was elected to the *Raad en Schepen van Amsterdam* [Council and Aldermen of Amsterdam], the first printer in the history of the city to hold such an office and which meant that Blaeu was able to further the interests of the Amsterdam book trade.

However, it is not until about the year 1631 that the name of Joan Blaeu is met with in any real connection with his life's work, in the joint imprint with his father on the first of what was to be the long and celebrated series of atlases.

The business partnership of father and son began in 1630 with the publication of an atlas called *Atlantis Appendix, sive pars altera...nunc primum editas*, which contained sixty maps.[4]

The title is an allusion to an earlier atlas, published by the Amsterdam mapmaker Jodocus Hondius the younger, who published the later editions of the *Atlas* of Gerard Mercator until 1629. At the death of Hondius in that year, Willem Janszoon Blaeu bought several of his copper plates to add to his own then small plate stock with the intention of compiling and publishing an atlas of his own. In the preface to an early edition of his *Appendix* in 1631, Blaeu wrote: 'Abraham Ortelius, the celebrated geographer of Philip II, king of Spain, made a *Theatrum Orbis Terrarum*, in which are maps of different parts of the world, some representing the ancient state of things, and others the modern. Whatever praise and thanks that incomparable man may have merited by this work, and with whatever appreciation the educated public may have received it, nevertheless this *Theatrum* has its defects. Later the great mathematician Gerard Mercator began to prepare, with tremendous labour and at tremendous expense, the publication of his *Atlas*, but death overtook him [in 1595], so that he left his work incompleted. By that its value is very considerably decreased, because he was able to complete Europe only (with the exception of Spain).'[5]

Of the sixty maps in Blaeu's first atlas, thirty-seven came directly from the Hondius plate stock, a fact which did not escape either the notice or the criticism of his rivals in the Amsterdam map business, Henricus Hondius (1597–1651), brother of Jodocus the younger, successor-publisher of the Mercator-Hondius *Atlas* after his brother's death, and Joannes Janssonius

[3] See Herman de la Fontaine Verwey, *Uit de Wereld van het Boek III. In en om de 'Vergulde Sonnewyser'*, (Amsterdam 1979, p. 165).

[4] Six copies of this *Appendix* are known: two in The Netherlands, one in the British Library, London, one in Germany and one in Belgium. The sixth known copy, complete with sixty maps and formerly in the Bibliothèque des Fontaines, Chantilly, France, was sold at Sotheby's, London, 23 October 1986 (lot 29), and is now in a private collection.

[5] See J. H. Keuning, 'Blaeu's *Atlas*', in *Imago Mundi* XIV (1959), p. 76.

(1588–1664), calling Blaeu's *Appendix* 'a hotch-potch of old maps, which he [Blaeu] had altered, adapted, or copied from their atlas.'[6]

The term 'atlas' was first used to describe Gerard Mercator's *Atlas* of 1595 which, expanded by Jodocus Hondius the elder (1563–1612), had dominated the Amsterdam and, in effect, World map market since the last full edition of the Ortelius *Theatrum Orbis Terrarum* in 1612. Willem Janszoon Blaeu's use of the title *Appendix* or later on, *Atlantis Appendix*, was an astute commercial decision designed to link his new work with a well-established and well-respected work which was by then nearing the end of its effective commercial life following the death of Hondius the younger in 1629.

The first Blaeu atlas, then, to bear the joint imprint of father and son was the expanded *Appendix Theatri A. Ortelii et Atlantis G. Mercatoris,* containing ninety-eight maps. It was published in 1631. The young sapling was already growing rapidly, as it were. Blaeu's ambitions to produce a major World atlas were further advanced in 1635 with the appearance of the two-volume *Novus Atlas* or *Theatrum*, to give its alternative name, which housed up to two-hundred-and-eight maps. We can assume a great deal about Blaeu's ambitions with the publication of his *Novus Atlas* in 1635. Four separate editions in four different languages were published: German text (208 maps); Dutch text (207 maps); French text (208 maps); and Latin text (207 maps). The semi-official newspaper *Nieuwstijdingen bij Jan van Hilten* for 11 February 1634 recorded Blaeu's intentions as follows: 'At Amsterdam are now printed in Willem Jansz. Blaeu's office, the great book of maps, or 'Atlas', in four languages: Latin, French, High German and Low German [*i.e.* Dutch]. The High German will appear towards Easter, the Low German and the French in the month of May, or early June at the latest, and the Latin shortly thereafter. All on very fine paper, entirely revised with newly engraved plates and new, wide-ranging descriptions'.[7]

The rapid growth of the Blaeus' business meant that the premises 'op 't Water' had to be vacated in favour of a larger establishment. In 1637 therefore, the Blaeus moved to the Bloemgracht, quite nearby, where the foundation stone had already been laid by Joan Blaeu in 1636. It was here that the publishing house remained as the centre of the greater part of the Blaeus' operations. A French visitor to Amsterdam in 1646, Claude Joly, described the establishment as 'l'imprimerie la plus belle de toute l'Europe'.[8]

However, a description by Philip von Zesen, a German resident of some years' standing in Amsterdam, in his book, *Beschreibung der Stadt Amsterdam* (1664), gives a very good impression of the activity at the Bloemgracht premises:[9] '...On the Bloemgracht, at the third bridge and third by-lane, stands the world-famous printing house of Mr. Joan Blaeu, councillor and alderman of this city. The establishment is equipped with nine presses for letterpress printing, called after the nine muses, and six presses for printing copper-plates, and also with a type-foundry...The premises has a breadth of 75ft and extends 135ft. In front...is a room containing a number of cabinets in which are stored the plates which are used for the atlases, the Dutch and Walloon town atlases [*i.e.* the Townbooks of 1649 published in two volumes], and for the marine and other priceless books[10] ...Next-door is the room where the copper-plates are printed...Then comes the printing office proper in a long gallery, well provided with windows on both sides. At the far end

[6] J. H. Keuning, *op. cit.*, p. 77.

[7] *Nieuwstijdingen bij Jan van Hilten* (11 February 1634), quoted in M. M. Kleerkoper & W. P. van Stockum, *De Boek-handel te Amsterdam, vnl. in de 17e eeuw* ('s-Gravenhage 1914–1916), p. 1152: '...t Amsterdam bij Willem Jansz. Blaeu wordt teghenwoordighe ghedruckt het groot Landcaertboeck de 'Atlas', in vier Talen, Latijn, Fransch, Hoogh ende Nederduijtsche, de Hooghduijtsche sal uijtgaen teghen Paeschen, de Nederduijtsche ende Fransche in de maent May eerstcomende, or ten langhsten in 't eerst van Junio, ende de Latijnsche corts daerna: Alle op seer schoon papier, gheheel vernieut met nieuwe ghesnedene platen end nieuwe wijtloopighe Beschrijvingen'.

[8] See Claude Joly, *Voyage fait à Münster* (Paris 1670), p. 116.

[9] Quoted (in translation) in: C. Koeman, *Joan Blaeu* (Amsterdam 1970), pp. 17–18.

[10] For example, the plates for Antonius Sanderus's *Flandria Illustrata* which Blaeu purchased in 1641, or the maps and illustrations in Caspar Barlaeus's *Rerum per octennium in Brasilia* which Blaeu had published in 1647, and the Italian Townbooks series which began publication in 1663.

is a workroom where the type and other materials used in printing are kept. Before this room is a staircase leading to a room where on the next floor the corrector reads the proofs and revises and marks the errors made by the compositor. Here, too, there is a long ante-chamber or loft where, when the printing of the entire book is completed, the printed sheets are gathered into the order of appearance and also stored. At the very top...is the foundry where type for printing in several languages is cast...'.

A particular point of interest in von Zesen's description is that he makes no mention whatsoever of a bindery on the premises. In later years, it is known that the great binder Albert Magnus (*fl.* 1660s–1680) undertook the so-called 'ordinary' vellum atlas bindings as well as the elaborate morocco bindings in the French taste.[11]

Willem Blaeu died in 1638, just a few months after the death of his wife. Thereafter, Joan Blaeu took over the firm's activities, expanding the *Novus Atlas* to three volumes in 1640, four in 1645, five in 1654, six in 1655, and finally, the *Atlas Major* in from nine to twelve tall folio volumes, depending on the language of the printed text, in 1662–1663. Altogether, the *Atlas Major* contained some six hundred maps, and is believed to have been published in an edition of three hundred copies.

For a few years, from 1638 until 1644, Joan was in partnership again, this time with his younger brother Cornelis, whose name appears in the first edition of the German text edition of the *Novus Atlas*. That partnership lasted for only six or so years, for Cornelis Blaeu died in 1644, aged about thirty-four years. From then, until the fire in February 1672, Joan Blaeu was in sole charge of the business, the largest printing house in Europe, and effectively the largest in the World. He was helped later on by his own sons, Willem (*b.* 1635), Pieter (*b.* 1637), and Joan II (*b.* 1650). To maintain that position of pre-eminence entailed maintaining business contacts with fellow businessmen outside the United Netherlands. This he would do through such events as the Frankfurt Book Fair, which was and remains, the largest event of its kind in the World.

By the 1660s, such works as pilot-guides and sea chart atlases played a much less important role in the output of the publishing house. Other Amsterdam publishers had taken the lead here, for example Pieter Goos, or Hendrik Doncker, who issued folio atlases of sea charts on a much larger scale than the smaller format, old and largely obsolete chart atlases of Joan's father. Nevertheless, Joan Blaeu did continue the tradition of making globes of all sizes and types, from ten to sixty centimetres in diameter. He also continued to issue wall-maps, for example the great wall-map of the World of 1648, in twenty sheets, entitled *Nova Totius Terrarum Orbis Tabula*, on which the Dutch discoveries in the antipodes were shown.

In this respect, Joan Blaeu received a considerable incentive to further the development of his business now that he was in sole charge. It was an incentive that emphasizes the fact that he was an extremely competent mapmaker. On the death of his father in 1638, Joan 'inherited' the appointment of mapmaker to the *Vereenighde Oostindische Compagnie* [VOC, or United East-India Company, established in 1602 by the merger of several smaller pioneering trading companies in the East]. Since the VOC contributed in great measure to the wealth, prosperity and prestige of the United Netherlands, in particular to Amsterdam, it is highly unlikely that Blaeu would have merited, let alone held, such an appointment had he been ill organized and incompetent as a map publisher. He assumed the appointment in November 1638 with the duties of making manuscript charts and compiling sailing directions for the navigators and captains in the VOC, the map and chart stocks being kept at the *Oost-Indische Huis* [East-India House], established in 1606.

Although Joan Blaeu incorporated up-to-date information on discoveries on his manuscript charts and his large wall-maps, he seems to have made relatively little use of the information at his disposal in the VOC archives for his atlases.[12] His atlas maps of Asia and America date, for the most part, from about 1635. The discoveries of Abel Janszoon Tasman in what we now call

---

[11] See Herman de la Fontaine Verwey, *op. cit.*, p. 31.

[12] See, for example, the notes to map 85, which is the map of the East Indies.

Tasmania, New Zealand and Western Australia in 1642–1644 were incorporated in his wall-map of the World in 1648, but the relevant maps in the *Novus Atlas* were never revised as such. Furthermore, although his fellow map publishers, such as Hendrik Doncker or Pieter van Alphen, did incorporate relatively recent information in their sea atlases, Blaeu did not, or perhaps could not, take advantage of his privileged position with the VOC in order to issue such an atlas to match his other atlas publications. This helps to explain why some surviving sets of Blaeu's *Atlas Major* and others are complemented by a sea atlas, bound uniformly with them, by one or other of his publishing rivals, or occasionally a copy of Andreas Cellarius's *Atlas Coelestis; seu Harmonia Macrocosmica* (1660) published by Blaeu's arch-rival Joannes Janssonius. This celestial atlas, as it transpired, remained the only atlas of its kind published in The Netherlands until the nineteenth century.

And so we come to the *Atlas Major*, 'Great Atlas' itself. The literature on the history of cartography is full of superlatives when mentioning or describing this work.[13] While many of these could be repeated here, it will serve you, the reader, better if you are allowed to decide for yourself after having read the text before you and studied the plates that follow this introduction.

---

[13] H. de la Fontaine Verwey's comment, *op. cit.*, p. 195 suffices admirably and is quoted here at the head of this introduction.

PRESENTATION OF THE ATLAS

Most of the surviving copies of the atlas are bound in what might be termed a 'standard' binding, in other words, uniform cream-coloured vellum with gilt tooling and lettering. Wealthy clients for the atlas could commission a binder to bind their sets in morocco or even velvet, embellished with their crests or other decorative devices. Such bindings were carried out by the celebrated binder Albert Magnus, who flourished in Amsterdam from the 1660s to 1680. As it appears that Joan Blaeu had no bindery on his premises, it is very likely that Magnus also bound copies in the 'standard' binding.[1]

Colour was also a very important consideration. Although the atlas could be bought in black and white (without applied hand colouring), many clients buying the atlas for display in their houses preferred their copies illuminated with rich hand colouring and gold highlighting. This of course was considerably more expensive, and there were in Amsterdam at the time artists who carried out such work. One of these was Dirk Janszoon van Santen who coloured and gilded maps and atlases to order, examples of which have survived and may be seen in institutional collections.

Blaeu's atlas was the most expensive printed book in the seventeenth century. Blaeu's catalogue of 1670, his *Catalogue des Atlas, Théâtre des Citez*, quoted prices for the twelve-volume French-text edition of the atlas at *fl*.450 for a coloured set, and *fl*.350 for a black and white set, the prices including the 'standard' vellum binding. Koeman,[2] writing in 1970, translated these figures into current values at that time, using a multiplication factor of 100, so that in 1970, a twelve-volume coloured set of the atlas would have cost the equivalent of *fl*.45,000 (or about £5,500) from publishers, which also equates quite well with auction prices for the atlas at that time. More recently, copies of the French-text edition have sold for as much as £100,000.[3]

After the fire in February 1672, Blaeu's printing establishment was forced to close, but his atlases and plates remained in demand. Many of the plates were rescued and these, together with unsold sets of the atlases and other books in Blaeu's stock were sold by public auction, beginning in 1674. Many of the plates were bought up by Amsterdam publishers, for example Abraham Wolgang who was in partnership, or consortium with the booksellers Boom, van Waesberghen en van Someren. Following Wolfgang's death in 1694, the plates of Blaeu's atlas that still survived were disposed of again by auction, to the publishers Pieter Mortier (who bought the plates of the Italian Townbooks) and Frederick de Wit (who bought the plates of the Townbooks of The Netherlands). The fate of the atlas map plates is not known, although occasionally one finds composite atlases of the first half of the eighteenth century compiled in Amsterdam or in Germany containing impressions of a few of the Blaeu plates. For example, in 1978, the writer found a composite atlas issued by the heirs of Johann-Baptist Homann, a German mapmaker of Nürnberg, which contained some very faint or worn impressions of a few of Blaeu's plates showing parts of Germany. The atlas is thought to have been compiled in about 1735 and contained one-hundred-and-twenty maps. It is now in a private collection.

---

[1] See H. de la Fontaine Verwey, *op. cit.*, p. 31.

[2] See C. Koeman, *Joan Blaeu* (1970), p. 47.

[3] See Sotheby's sale catalogue, *Topography, Travel, Prints and Natural History*, 23–24 October 1986 (lot 237), for example.

ARRANGEMENT OF THE ATLAS

Any study, article or commentary on the Blaeu atlases must rely to a great extent on the work of Prof. C. Koeman, whose great bibliography of Netherlands-published atlases contains detailed collations of all the editions of, *inter alia*, the *Atlas Major*, or 'Great Atlas'.[1]

Described below is a map and plate content of the atlas. The plates that follow are, with one or two exceptions, maps and plates in the Dutch-text edition of the atlas held by the Royal Geographical Society, London. Broadly speaking, although this edition is in nine volumes instead of ten, eleven or twelve of the Spanish, Latin or French-text editions respectively, the arrangement of text, maps and plates is more or less the same, except for the last two volumes of the Dutch-text edition, *i.e.* Volumes VIII and IX, in which the American section is placed immediately after Africa in Volume VIII instead of after the Asian division in Volume IX. In all other editions, the Americas come last in the binding order reflecting the traditional arrangement of an atlas going back at least as far as Ptolemy in the second century AD where, in his *Geographia*, he placed Europe first immediately following the then known World, followed by Africa and then Asia. Only in the post-1500 editions of Ptolemy illustrated with maps was there, naturally, any indication of the New World of the Americas. The New World was therefore placed towards the end of books of maps and this is an arrangement still followed by many atlas publishers to the present day in Europe.

As it is physically the largest edition, we shall take the twelve-volume French-text edition as the basis for a simplified comparison of the contents of the Blaeu atlas, pointing out where necessary how this compares with the Dutch-text editions.

The title of the nine-volume Dutch-text edition of 1664 runs: *Grooten Atlas, oft Werelt-Beschrijving*, omitting the wording *Cosmographie Blaviane* (or other language equivalent) of French-text and Latin-text editions. No particular reason for this has been put forward but, since the largest sales of the atlas would have been either French, Latin or Spanish editions (these being the languages of diplomacy, the educated classes, and of the Roman Catholic rulers of the Southern Netherlands), a grander presentation of the title in the form of a 'Blavian Cosmography' was deemed proper. Such an embellishment of the title implies also a fuller treatment of the World and of the Universe to include unrealized volumes covering the oceans and seas, the Solar System and the Universe, perhaps.

In the collation notes and index that follow, the number preceding the bracketed numbers and letters is the number of the colour illustration following this introductory text. The numbers in brackets [ ] (*e.g.* [V D 3; VI F 3]) indicate the map number in the nine-volume Dutch-text edition of 1664, followed immediately by its corresponding position and numbering in the French-text edition in twelve volumes of 1662. For example, 1 [I D 1; I F 1], which is the general map of the World, indicates that this map is to be found in Volume I as map 1 in the Dutch-text [D] edition, and in Volume I as map 1 in the French-text edition also.

VOLUME I

Grooten Atlas...Eerste Stuck der Aerdrycks-Beschryving, welck vervat de Landen onder de Noordpool, en de Noorderdelen van Europa

Dutch text, containing ninety maps, including the World (ill. 1), the Arctic Regions (ills. 2 and 3), Norway (ills. 5 and 6), Denmark (ill. 7), Slesvig (ill. 8), Sweden (ills. 5, 9 and 10), Russia (ill. 11)

---

[1] See C. Koeman, *Atlantes Neerlandici I* (*Aa-Blaeu*) (Amsterdam 1967), pp. 73–292.

and Poland (ills. 12 and 13). Volume I of the French-text edition contains sixty maps: Sweden, Russia and Poland occur in Volume II of that edition.

In addition to the maps, Volume I of the Blaeu atlas contains a suite of eleven plates that describe and illustrate Tycho Brahe's astronomical observatory on Ven island in Öresund, built with funds from Frederik II of Denmark in 1576, and where Willem Janszoon Blaeu had studied in 1595–1596. The plates, which show the Uranienborg observatory and the various instruments, are based on corresponding woodcut illustrations in Tycho Brahe's own astronomical work, *Astronomiae instauratae mechanicae*, published in 1598 from his own presses set up at Wandsbeck, near Hamburg. It is worth noting here that, since Tycho Brahe demanded and exacted high standards from his students, receiving them at Ven only by invitation or by special recommendation, we may assume that Willem Blaeu had achieved a high standard of competence in his chosen career before he embarked for Ven, and that these plates were included by Joan Blaeu in his atlas as a tribute to both his father and his father's teacher. Twenty-one plates from a work on Slesvig and Holstein by Johannes Mejer and Caspar Danckwerth published in 1652 are included in the maps in this volume (see the notes to ills. 8 and 15).

The maps illustrated from Volume I are:

1   *Nova Totius Terrarum Orbis Geographia ac Hydrographica Tabula* [World map] [I D 1; I F 1]
2   *Regiones sub Polo Arctico* [The Arctic Regions] [I D 2; I F 2]
3   *Tabula Islandiae* [Iceland] [I D 9; I F 9]
4   *Europa* [Europe general map] [I D 10; I F 10]
5   *Suecia, Dania, et Norvegia* [Sweden, Denmark and Norway] [I D 11; II F 1]
6   *Norvegia regnum* [Norway] [I D 12; I F 11]
7   *Dania regnum* [Denmark] [I D 19; I F 18]
8   *Ducatus Sleswicum sive Iutia Australis* [The Duchy of Slesvig] [I D 41; I F 41]
9   *Suecia regnum* [Sweden] [I D 62; II F 2]
10 *Magnus Ducatus Finlandiae* [The Grand Duchy of Finland] [I D 68; II F 8]
11 *Urbis Moskvae* [The City of Moscow] [I D 76; II F 13]
12 *Polonia regnum* [Poland] [I D 80; II F 19]
13 *Prussia* [Prussia] [I D 83; II F 22]

VOLUME II

Tweede Stuck der Aerdrycks-Beschryving, 't Welck vervat Duytsland, en d'Aengegrensde Landtschappen

Dutch text, containing one-hundred-and-seven maps, all relating to Germany and immediately adjacent territories (ills. 14–20) and including the balance of the Mejer-Danckwerth maps of 1652 (see the notes to ills. 8 and 15). Forty-two of the maps in this volume were printed for the first time in the 1662 edition of the Blaeu atlas.

The maps illustrated from Volume II are:

14 *Nova Totius Germaniae Descriptio* [The German Empire] [II D 1; III F 1 (replaced by *Germania, vulgo Teutschlandt*)]
15 *Nova & Accurata Ducatuum Slesvici et Holsatiae* [The Duchies of Slesvig and Holstein] [II D 16; III F 41]
16 *Ducatus Bremae et Ferdae* [The Duchy of Bremen-Verden] [II D 30; III F 41]
17 *Danubius, Fluvius Europae Maximus* [The Rhine] [II D 84; III F 76]
18 *Rhenus Fluviorum Europae celeberrimus* [The Rhine] [II D 84; III F 76]
19 *Austria Archiducatus* [The Archduchy of Austria] [II D 73; III F 2]
20 *Helvetia, cum finitimis regionibus confoederatis* [The Swiss Confederation] [II D 88; III F 31]

VOLUME III

Derde Stuck...Welck vervat De Nederlanden

Dutch text, containing sixty-five maps, all relating to The Netherlands and the United Netherlands. Thirty of the maps are new to the atlas, many of which come from Antonius Sanderus's *Flandria Illustrata* (1641), the rights for which Blaeu had bought up from Henricus Hondius in 1641 for *fl.*11,000. The majority of the plates are among the oldest printed by the Blaeus (see the notes to ill. 21), copied from the maps of Hondius in his editions of the *Atlas* of Gerard Mercator, or after Michiel Florisz van Langren (*c.* 1630), and others.

The maps illustrated from Volume III are:

21 *Novus XVII Inferioris Germaniae Provinciarum Typus* [The Seventeen Provinces] [III D 1; IV F 1]
22 *Tertia pars Brabantiae* [The Third Quarter of Brabant] [III D 5; IV F 5]
23 *Caerte van de Scher-meer* [The Schermer Polder] [III D 53; IV F 49]
24 *Brabantia ducatus* [The Duchy of Brabant] [III D 2; IV F 2]

VOLUME IV

Vierde Stuck...Welck vervat Engelandt

Dutch text, containing fifty-eight maps of England and Wales, including general maps of the British Isles as well as county and regional maps, most of which take their geographical detail from the maps in John Speed's *Theatre of the Empire of Great Britaine* (1611, but in their post-1623 states in order to show Roman and tribal names), with descriptive texts after William Camden's *Britannia*. This atlas first appeared as a single entity in 1645, but Joan Blaeu's name appears on only four of the maps.

The maps illustrated from Volume IV are:

25 *Britannia prout divisa fuit temporibus Anglo-Saxonum* [The Anglo-Saxon Heptarchy] [IV D 2; V F 2]
26 *Oxonium Comitatus* [Oxfordshire] [IV D 16; V F 16]
27 *Wallia Principatus* [The Principality of Wales] [IV D 36; V F 36]
28 *Comitatus Caernarvoniensis . . . et Mona Insula* [Caernarfon and Môn] [IV D 45; V F 45]
29 *Cumbria* [Cumberland] [IV D 54; V F 54]
30 *Sarnia Insula . . . et Insula Caesarea* [Channel Islands] [IV D 58; V F 58]

VOLUME V

Vyfde Stuck...Welck vervat Schotlandt en Yrlandt

Dutch text, the Scotland and Ireland volume, containing fifty-four maps. The French-text volume VI has fifty-five maps (the extra map being one of Aran). Of all the parts which comprise the complete Blaeu atlas, it is the Scotland and Ireland volume which is the best documented concerning its compilation history. There is a considerable body of surviving documentary evidence as well as original information and drafts supplied by surveyors and cartographers who supplied Joan Blaeu (or Willem Janszoon Blaeu in earlier years) with his materials. This has been examined in great detail and discussed by the late R. A. Skelton in his *County Atlases of the British Isles* (1970), C. Koeman in *Joan Blaeu* (1970), and most recently by J. C. Stone in *The Pont Manuscript Maps of Scotland* (1989).

An outline of the history of the maps of Scotland based on the surveys of Robert Gordon and Timothy Pont is given in the notes to maps 31–35 which follow. Parts of the survey date back some fifty or more years before Blaeu's publication of the atlas for the first time in 1654, particularly those maps based on the work of Pont. This must have been known to at least some of the Amsterdam mapmakers since the early years of the seventeenth century, since Jodocus Hondius the elder had engraved a map of the Lothians and the Firth of Forth for Andrew Hart in Edinburgh, but it was not until 1630 that it appeared in Henricus Hondius's edition of the Mercator *Atlas*. The six maps of Ireland at the end of this volume copy their geographical detail from the corresponding maps of John Speed (see the notes to Volume IV above).

The maps illustrated from Volume V are:

31   *Scotia regnum* [The Kingdom of Scotland] [V D 3; VI F 3]
32   *Skia vel Skiana* [The Isle of Skye] [V D 45; VI F 46]
33   *Praefectura Renfroana* [Renfrewshire] [V D 26; VI F 27]
34   *Hibernia regnum* [The Kingdom of Ireland] [V D 49; VI F 50]
35   *Ultonia* [Ulster] [V D 54; VI F 55]

VOLUME VI

Seste Stuck...Welck vervat Vranckryck

Dutch text, containing sixty-six maps of France and parts of Switzerland brought together in one volume in contrast to the two volumes of the French-text edition which contains sixty-seven maps in all. It is interesting to compare this with, for example, the ninety-seven maps of the German Empire bound into one large volume in the French edition: perhaps it was a particular sales policy on the part of Joan Blaeu. It is only in the French-text editions that Blaeu divided his coverage of Louis XIV's France into two volumes, much of which dates back to the 1630s and the early editions of the *Novus Atlas*. Nevertheless, a copy of the atlas, with a dedication in Blaeu's own hand to Colbert, *Conseil Royal des Finances* to Louis XIV, survives and is now in the collection of the library of the University at Amsterdam.

The maps illustrated from Volume VI are:

36   *Gallia* [The Kingdom of France] [VI D 1; VII F 1]
37   *Ager Parisiensis* [L'Isle de France] [VI D 11; VII F 5]
38   *Le Pais de Brie* [Brie] [VI D 12; VII F 13]
39   *Lacus Lemanni* [Lac Léman or Lake Geneva] [VI D 27; VIII F 28]
40   *Normandia Ducatus* [The Duchy of Normandy] [VI D 43; VII F 20]
41   *Gouvernement de La Guienne & Gascogne* [Guyenne and Gascogne] [VI D 52; VIII F 6]

VOLUME VII

Sevende Stuck...Welck vervat Italien en Griecken

Dutch text, containing sixty-seven maps covering Italy and Greece, the Greek maps being brought back here from Volume II of the French-text edition. Most of the maps in this volume stem originally from the *Theatrum* volume of 1640, itself copying Giovanni Antonio Magini's *Italia* maps published in 1620. In this area, Blaeu's real originality was reserved for his famous set of the Italian Townbooks, covering *Città del Vaticano; Roma;* and *Napoli & Sicilia*, the first edition of which, with Latin text, was published in 1663. The work was expanded posthumously by Joan Blaeu's heirs from 1682, remaining in print until 1726.

The maps illustrated from Volume VII are:

42   *Nova Italiae delineatio* [Italy] [VII D 1; IX F 1]
43   *Corsica Insula* [Corsica] [VII D 10; IX F 9]
44   *Dominio Veneto nell' Italia* [The Venetian Dominions in Italy] [VII D 19; IX F 18]
45   *Stato della Chiesa con la Toscana* [The Papal States and the Grand Duchy of Tuscany] [VII D 33; IX F 32]

VOLUME VIII

Achtste Stuck...Welck vervat Spaenjen, Africa, en America

Dutch text, containing sixty-four maps shared between Spain, Africa, the West Indies and America. Here, the American division is brought forward from the final, XIIth, volume of the French-text edition of the atlas.

Most of the Iberian coverage dates from about 1630 to 1640 with the exception of the architectural views of the Escorial itself (see ill. 57) which appeared for the first time in 1662. No documentation on these impressive plates is known to have survived, but is it possible that Joan Blaeu had in mind a Townbook for Spain in parallel with The Netherlands volumes of 1649, or those of 1663 for Italy? For Africa, Blaeu's atlases up to 1662 contained only five maps, dating from about 1617 for the general map of the continent (see ill. 59), to the 1630s. Seven new regional maps appeared in the 1662 atlas (see, for example, the notes to ills. 60, 61, 64 and 66).

Volume VIII concludes with twenty-three maps of the West Indies and the American continent. These, again, range in date from about 1617 (the continental map, see ill. 67) to 1662, many based on maps by Johannes de Laet, and the series of maps of Brazil which Joan Blaeu had first published in 1647 in Caspar Barlaeus's *Rerum per octennium in Brasilia* (see the descriptive notes to ills. 67–83).

The group of maps of the (by then former) Dutch colonies in Brazil is quite unlike anything else in the Blaeu atlas, as remarkable in its own way as are the Mejer-Danckwerth maps of Slesvig-Holstein in the Scandinavian and German sections of the atlas. The Brazilian maps provide a memorable visual record of the Dutch in Brazil. As one commentator[2] put it, the maps and views constitute 'the most extensive and varied collection of its kind that was formed until the voyages of Captain Cook'. The regional maps are after parts of the nine-sheet wall-map *Brasilia qua parte paret Belgis* by Georg Markgraf (1657) which Joan Blaeu issued together with the plates and views of the 1647 work of Barlaeus. The pictorial vignettes of the Markgraf map, as well as Blaeu's own atlas maps, were taken from illustrations done by the painter Frans Janszoon Post (*c.* 1612–1680) who was in Brazil with Johann Maurits, and give a vivid impression both of the natural history as well as of the commercial activity of the Dutch settlements in the first half of the seventeenth century.

The maps illustrated from Volume VIII are:

---

[2] See R. Joppien, 'The Dutch Vision of Brazil', in: *Johann Maurits van Nassau-Siegen, 1604–1679* ('s-Gravenhage 1979), p. 296 and P. J. P. Whitehead and M. Boeseman, *A Portrait of Dutch 17th century Brazil* (Amsterdam, Oxford and New York 1989).

VOLUME IX

Negende Stuck...Welck vervat Asia, en Sina in 't selve gelegen

Dutch text, containing Asia, China and Japan, twenty-eight maps in all, being the final volume of the Dutch-text edition of the atlas. This is really two atlases in one, the second part consisting of the maps of China and Japan under the title *Novus Atlas Sinensis*. Like the Scottish division of the atlas, this too is well documented as far as its compilation history is concerned. The notes to ills. 94–100 give this in some detail, with maps based on Chinese surveys together with Jesuit researches. Blaeu's contribution to the cartography of Asia as a whole was slight, most of his maps dating from about 1617 (see ill. 84, the general map of the continent) to the 1650s. Nevertheless, his one great contribution was his publication of the first European atlas of China, and this alone must outweigh any defaults in his coverage of the rest of the continent.

In 1670, the foremost French cartographer of the day, Nicolas Sanson, wrote a commentary on the various maps of China then available. His note on the Martini maps, published by Blaeu, in respect of their accuracy is no small tribute. Comparing the faults of latitude and longitude on the map of another Jesuit mapmaker in China, Sanson wrote that Martini 'knew better than the others the proportion between the Latitudes and Longitudes, or because his maps had been engraved and printed in Holland where there are persons who have handled too many Maps not to know this proportion...F. Martinius describes China on several Maps in order to facilitate their inclusion in a book. The first is a general one, divided into her fifteen or sixteen Provinces; then he describes these fifteen or sixteen Provinces on fifteen or sixteen other sheets, each sheet to its Province; each of his Provinces is subdivided into several smaller parts or Jurisdictions; in his Discourse he enumerates the biggest Cities, the medium, and the small which are in the Jurisdiction of the bigger ones. Besides the *Fu*, and *Chou*, and the *Hsien*, he also places the Towns for the Militia and for the Officers which he traces on his Map, and which in his Description are called Fortresses...'.

The maps illustrated from Volume IX are:

84 *Asia noviter delineata* [Asia general map] [IX D 1; XI F 1]

85 *India quae Orientalis dicitur* [The East Indies] [IX D 2; XI F 8]

86 *Magni Mogolis Imperium* [The Moghul Empire] [IX D 3; XI F 9]

87 *Moluccae insulae* [The Moluccas or Spice Islands] [IX D 4; XI F 10]

88 *Tartaria* [Tartary or North-eastern Asia] [IX D 5; XI F 11]

89 *Persia* [Persia] [IX D 6; XI F 7]

90 *Turcicum Imperium* [The Turkish Empire] [IX D 7; XI F 2]

91 *Cyprus Insula* [Cyprus] [IX D 8; XI F 4]

92 *Terra Sancta* [Palestine or The Holy Land] [IX D 10; XI F 5]

93 *Arabia* [The Arabian Peninsula] [IX D 11; XI F 6]

94 *Imperium Sinarum nova descriptio* [The Chinese Empire] [IX D 12; XI F 12]

95 *Pecheli sive Peking* [Hebei Province] [IX D 13; XI F 13]

96 *Xensi* [Shaanxi Province] [IX D 15; XI F 15]

97 *Xantung* [Shandong Province] [IX D 16; XI F 16]

98 *Nanking, sive Kiangnan* [Nanjing, or Jiangnan Province] [IX D 21; XI F 21]

99 *Fokien* [Fujian Province] [IX D 23; XI F 23]

100 *Iaponia regnum* [The Japanese Empire] [IX D 28; XI F 28]

THE MAPS

Nova Totius Terrarum Orbis Geographia ac Hydrographica Tabula

Willem Blaeu's magnificent World map prefaced atlases published by the Blaeu establishment from 1630 until it was superseded by a twin-hemispherical design in 1662. The map illustrated shows the World drawn on Mercator's projection, perhaps the most familiar of all map projections since it is still in use today after about four and a half centuries as a means of plotting navigational courses by straight lines on a plane surface. This map is also perhaps the best known of all early maps, containing as it does virtually everything of aesthetic appeal to the collector. It is celebrated as one of the supreme examples of the map-maker's art. Since it was the first map in an atlas of anything up to perhaps six hundred individual mapsheets, it was perforce an engraving by which the skills, genius and technique of the publisher himself could be judged in the eyes of the prospective purchaser.

Although the map contains a wealth of geographical detail, and such decorative features as sea-monsters, sailing ships, polar insets and decorative cartouches, it is perhaps the elaborate border designs that first draw the attention of the eye, designs for which Blaeu's work remains unsurpassed. The upper border is a frieze of allegorical vignettes representing the Moon, Mercury, Venus, the Sun, Mars, Jupiter and Saturn. The side borders comprise at the left, four vignettes representing the four physical elements (Fire, Air, Water and Earth) and at the

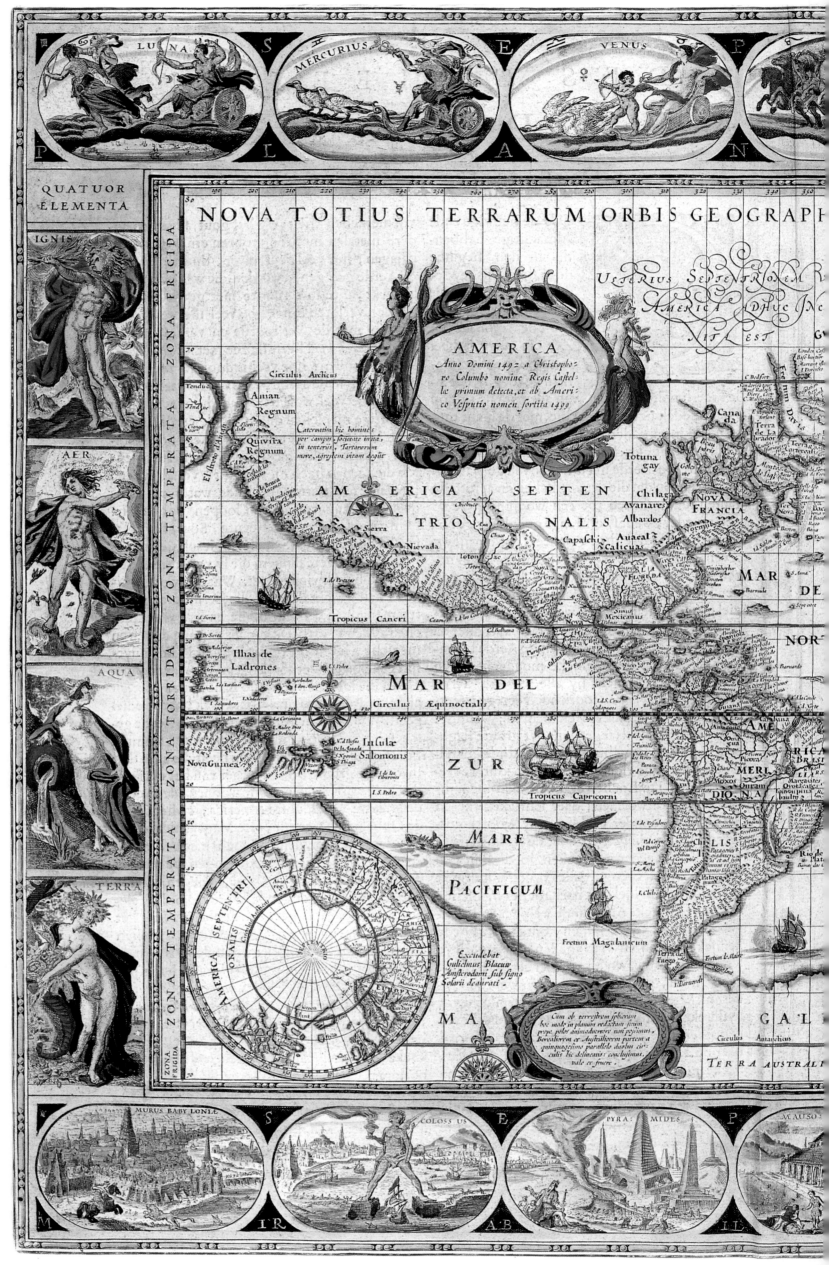

right, four vignettes representing the four seasons (Spring, Summer, Autumn and Winter). The lower frieze shows vignettes of the Seven Wonders of the World: the Hanging Gardens of Babylon, the Colossus of Rhodes, the Pyramids (barely recognizable as such!), the Mausoleum of Halicarnassus at Caria, the Temple of Diana at Ephesus (in a very Flemish style), the Jupiter of Olympia, and the great Pharos or Lighthouse of Alexandria.

The example illustrated is a particularly good sample of the quality of hand-colouring found in Blaeu's atlases. More often than not, such atlases sold on account of their rich colouring and embellishment, purchased by wealthy clients in a desire for ostentation. There could have been few better ways to show off a library or to impress rivals than by having a volume of Blaeu's atlas open – at the World map, for example – and if it was also heightened with gold, as is the example shown, then so much the better.

No doubt Robert Burton was right when, in his *Anatomy of Melancholy* published at Oxford in 1621, he wrote: 'Methinks it would please any man to look upon a geographical map…to behold, as it were, all the remote provinces, towns, cities of the world, and never to go forth of the limits of his study, to measure by the scale and compass their extent, distance, examine their site…'.

Regiones sub Polo Arctico

Willem Blaeu's map of the circumpolar regions, first published in 1635, was one of the best atlas maps available during the first half of the seventeenth century.

Where his predecessor Gerard Mercator had, in 1595, shown the North Pole surrounded by four landmasses, Willem Blaeu leaves a blank, unmapped area, omitting Mercator's famous 'black magnetic rock' which was thought to represent the magnetic pole.

Blaeu's is one of the prototype maps of the Arctic, incorporating the discoveries made by Captain Thomas James of Bristol along the southern and western shores of Hudson Bay during his expedition of 1631–32. James Bay today commemorates this voyage. Captain James was of the opinion that the Northwest Passage did not exist, declaring to his fellow navigator, Captain Luke Foxe, in the search for the sea route to the Far East, 'you are out of the way to Japon, for this is not it'.

Elsewhere, the Arctic shores of Russia reproduce much of the information derived from the voyage of Willem Barentsz in 1596–97, while Spitsbergen [Svalbard] is shown as laid down according to James Hall, pilot of the Danish expeditions of 1605–1607. However, Blaeu corrects the mistake made by Hall, and later copied by Samuel Purchas in 1625, in labelling Spitsbergen as Greenland, perhaps not an unforgivable mistake since on most early maps both islands appear remarkably similar in outline!

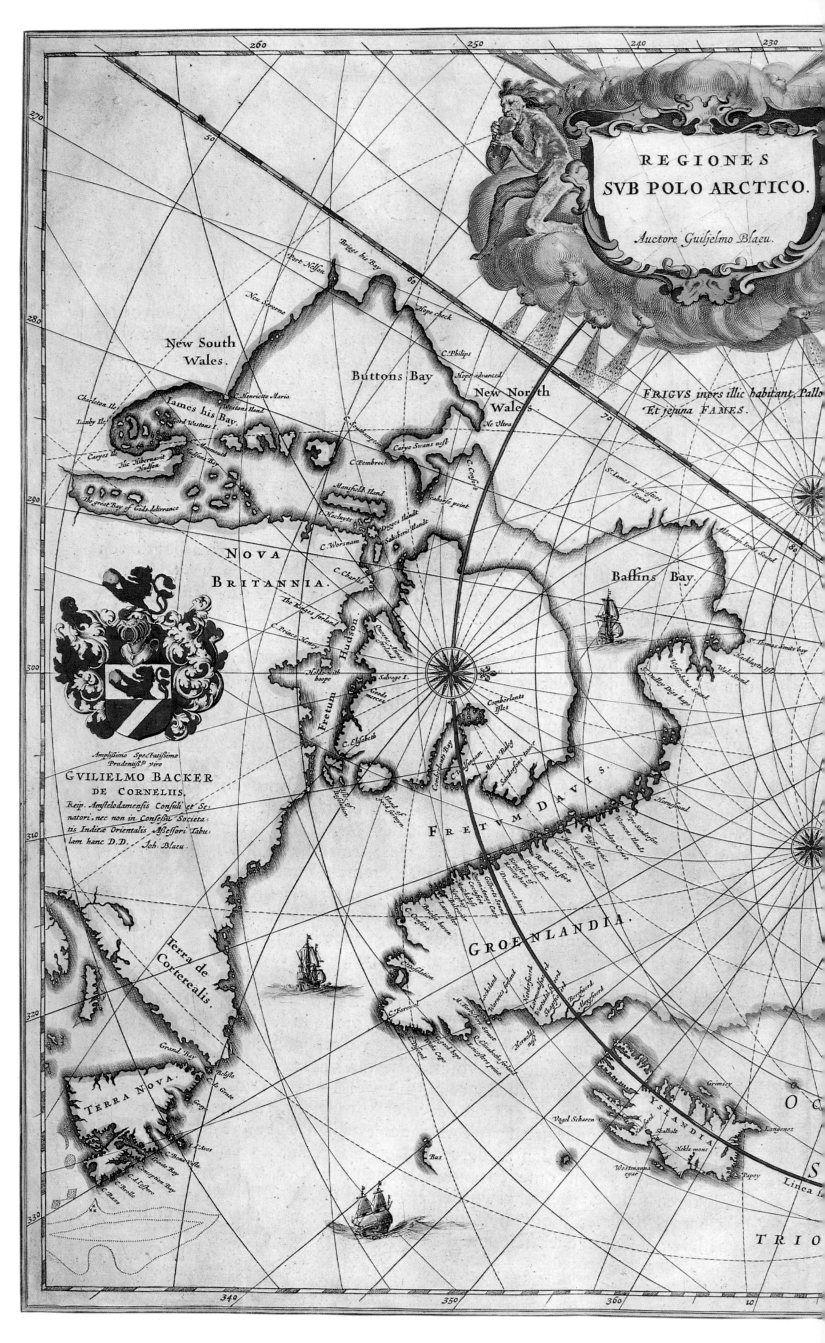

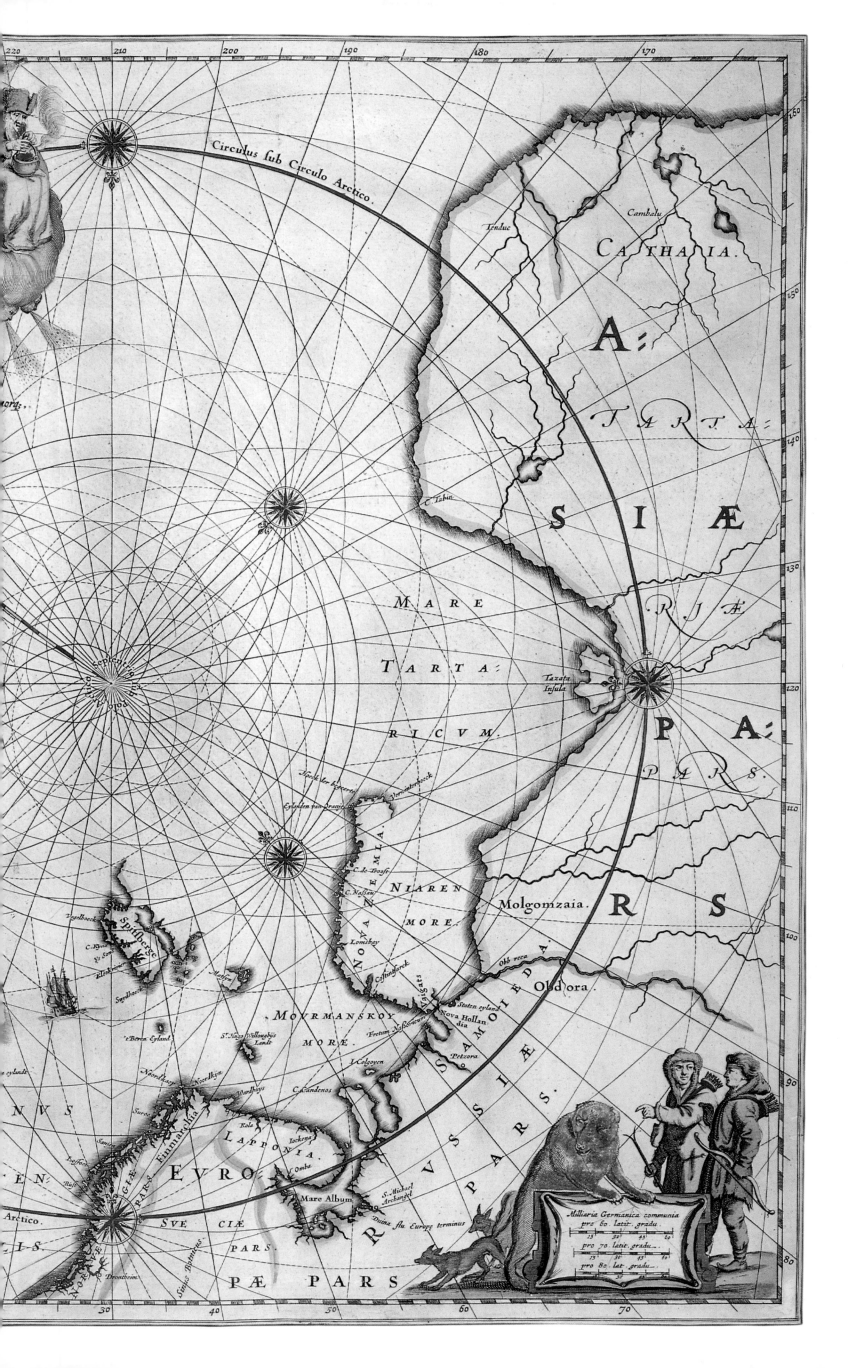

Tabula Islandiae

This map of Iceland is perhaps the most familiar of all the outlines of the island ever published. The author is stated to be one Joris Carolus, a Dutch navigator from Enkhuizen, whose map was first engraved and prepared by Jodocus Hondius the Younger in 1628, whose plates were bought by Willem Blaeu in 1629. Iceland bears the imprint of Willem Blaeu who issued it in his *Appendix* of 1630.

The Carolus map was copied by virtually all mapmakers throughout the rest of the seventeenth century and well into the eighteenth. Some of the information is derived from a map made famous by the Flemish cartographer Abraham Ortelius, the *Islandia* of Gudhbrandur Thorláksson (1541–1627), Bishop of Hólar, who had studied mathematics and astronomy as well as theology, while other information, such as place names, is derived from Gerard Mercator's map of 1595.

Willem Blaeu reprinted the map without change in his subsequent atlas editions, as did Joan after him, including the great atlas of 1662. In the southern part is shown a lively impression of Hekla in full eruption, described as *mons perpetuo ardens*, while immediately to the west, the Bishopric of Skálholt is marked. To the south, a note by *Eiapialla hokel* [Eyjafjallajökull] states that here may be found *falcones albi* or white falcons, presumably referring to the *gyr* falcon.

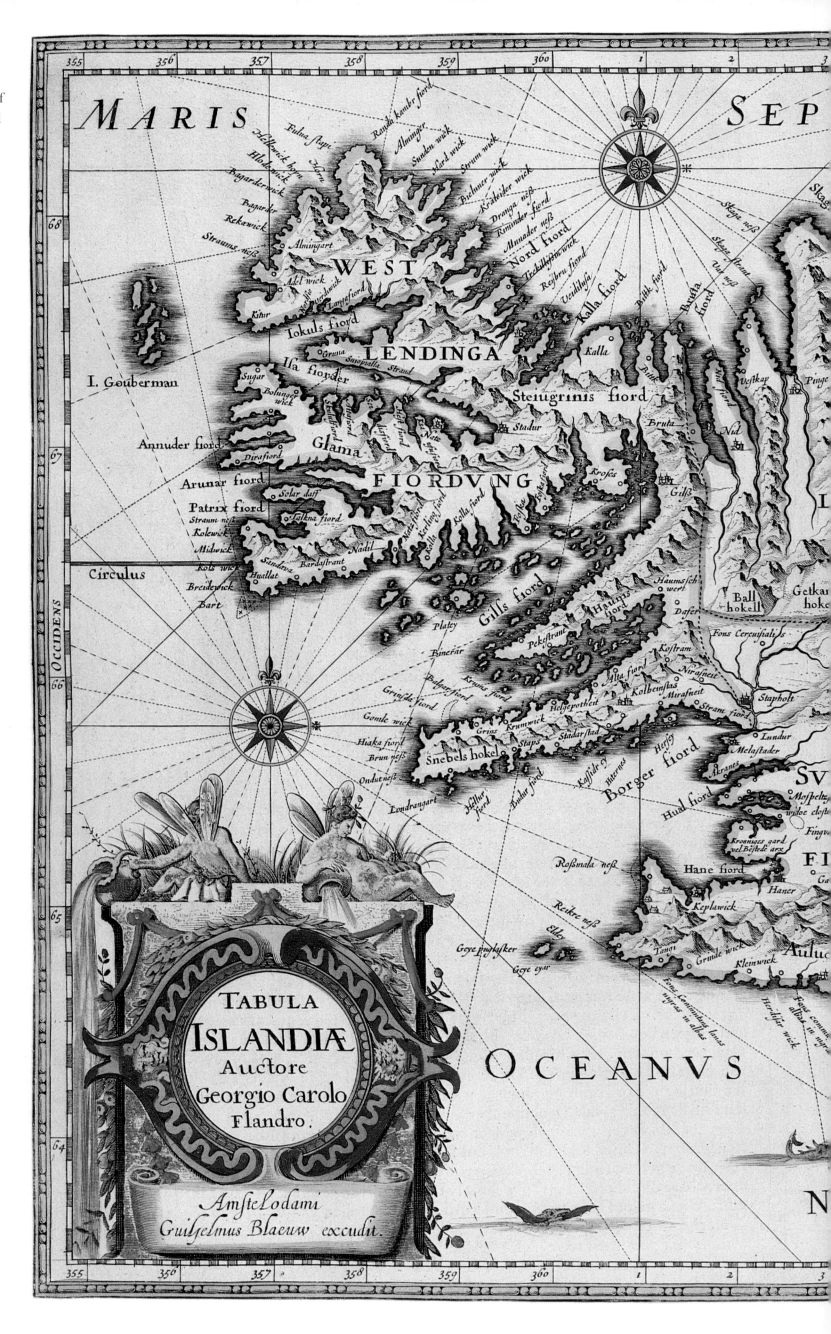

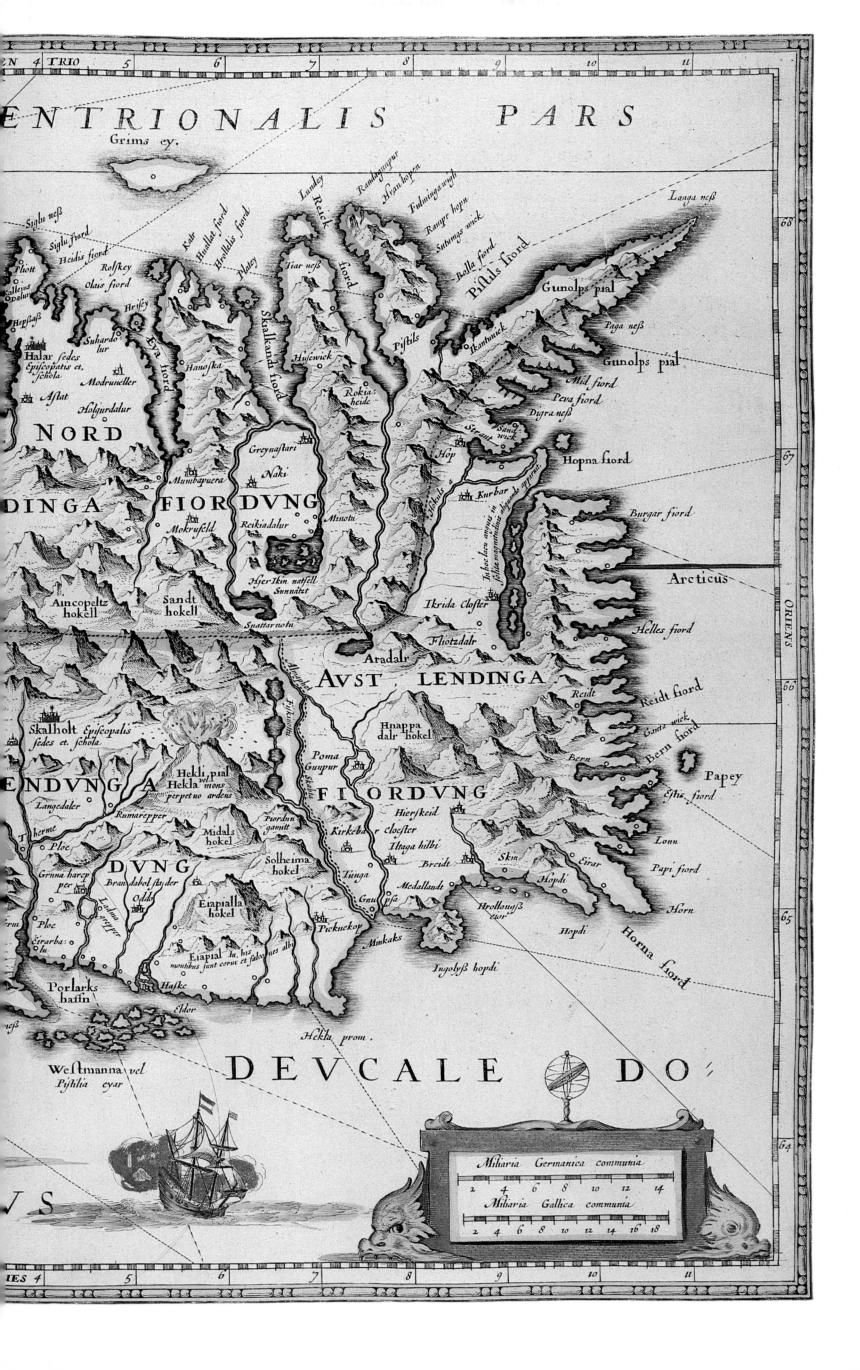

ENTRIONALIS PARS

Grims ey.

Langa neſs

Siglu neß
Siglu fiord
Heidis fiord
Flott
Kalleus
Dalur
Heßaß

Rolskey
Olas fiord

Suhardo
lur
Hrisey

Katle
Huallat fiord
Hrollelis fiord
Platey
Eya fiord
Hanoska

Skalkanda fiord

Landey
Reick

Ramlauugur
Hean hopen
Fulninga wigh
Raupr hopn
Suhuugs wick
Bolla fiord

Piſtils fiord

Gunolps pial

Tiar neſs
Husewick

Piſtils

Paga neſs

Gunolps pial

Halar ſedes
Epiſcopatis et.
ſchola
Aſlat

Modruneller

Holgurdalur

Rokia
heide

Mid fiord
Peva fiord
Digra neß

NORD

DINGA   FIOR

Greynaſtari
Naki

Mumbapuera

DVNG

Mokruſeld

Reikiadalur

Minotu

Hop

Kurbar

Hopna fiord

Burgar fiord

Arcticus

Helles fiord

Aincopeltz
hokell

Sandt
hokell

HſerIkin natſell
Sunnätzt

Snattarnoti

Ikrida Cloſter

Fliotzdalr

Aradalr

AVST LENDINGA

Reidt

Reidt fiord

Ganta wick

Skalholt Epiſcopalis
ſedes et. ſchola

ENDVNGA

Langedaler

therme

Ploe

Grnna harep
per

Ploe

Eirarba
lu

Hekli pial
Hekla vel mons
perpetuo ardens

Rumarepper

Midals
hokel

DVNG

Brandabol ſtayder
Oddo
Lathan orepper

Erapialla
hokel

Fiordun
gamtt

Poma
Gunpur

Hnappa
dalr hokel

Bern

Papey

Eſtis fiord

FIORDVNG

Kirkeba
cloeſter

Iltaqa hilbi

Hierſkeid

Breidt

Skin

Hopdi

Lonu

Papi fiord

Eirar

Solheima
hokel

Tunga

Gnul ſa

Medallandt

Erapial la. his
monthus ſunt corui et falcoues albi

Picknekop

Minkaks

Hrollauyſ
ewr

Ingolyß hopdi

Hopdi

Horn

Horna fiord

Porlarks
haffn

Eldor

Hekla prom.

Weſtmanna vel
Piſtilia eyar

DEVCALE   DO

Miliaria Germanica communia

2   4   6   8   10   12   14

Miliaria Gallica communia

2   4   6   8   10   12   14   16   18

Europa recens descripta

The atlases compiled and published by the Blaeus and other mapmakers as a rule included general maps of the then known continents: Europe, Asia, Africa and America, usually conceived as a uniform group. This is Willem Blaeu's map of the continent of Europe which dates back to 1617, although the date was removed from later printings prior to the inclusion of the map in the first of a long series of World atlases that began to appear in 1630. That date marks the first atlas publication of this and other continental maps (see maps 59, Africa; 67, the Americas; and 100, Asia).

Uniform in both style and layout with the other continental maps, Europe is embellished with ornamental borders: the side borders showing costume vignettes representing England, France, The Netherlands, Castille, Venice, Germany, Hungary, Bohemia, Poland and Greece. The upper frieze shows nine town views, respectively Amsterdam, Praha, Constantinople, Venezia, Roma, Paris, London, Toledo, and Lisboa.

PARIS · LONDON · TOLEDO · LISBONA

MYRMANSKOY MORE

EVROPA
recens descripta
à
Guilielmo Blaeuw.

RVSSIA

ASIÆ

TARTARIÆ
PARS

PARS

DVCATVS
SEVERIENSIS

Tartaria
Præcopensis

PONTVS EVXINVS

ASIA MINOR
nunc
NATOLIA

Cyprus

GRÆCIA

HVNGARIA

Candia ol. Creta

MARE MEDITERRANEVM

MARMARICA

ÆPARS

ALGYPTVS

Germani

Hungari

Bohemi

Poloni

Græci

31

Suecia Regnum

This general map of
Sweden was first published
in the Blaeu atlas of 1662
and, like many of his maps
of Scandinavia, was based
on his surveys of Anders
Bure de Boo (see the
description to map 9).

The map shows what
could be called a Baltic
Empire, a Sweden covering
900,000 km^2 with a
population of some three
million. Despite the fact it
appeared only two years
after the Treaty of
Copenhagen of 1660,
which effectively curtailed
Swedish expansion, Blaeu's
map has a few historical
inaccuracies, particularly in
the south of Sweden, where
he shows the southernmost
provinces as parts of
Denmark, Bohuslän as part
of Norway and so on. The
easternmost part, the
Grand Duchy of Finland
(see map 10), shows Finland
at its greatest extent, but the
Baltic provinces of Estonia,
Ingermanland and Livonia
are coloured as though they
were not part of the
Empire. Oddly enough,
Sweden's possessions in
northern Germany,
Pomerania and Bremen-
Verden are omitted entirely.

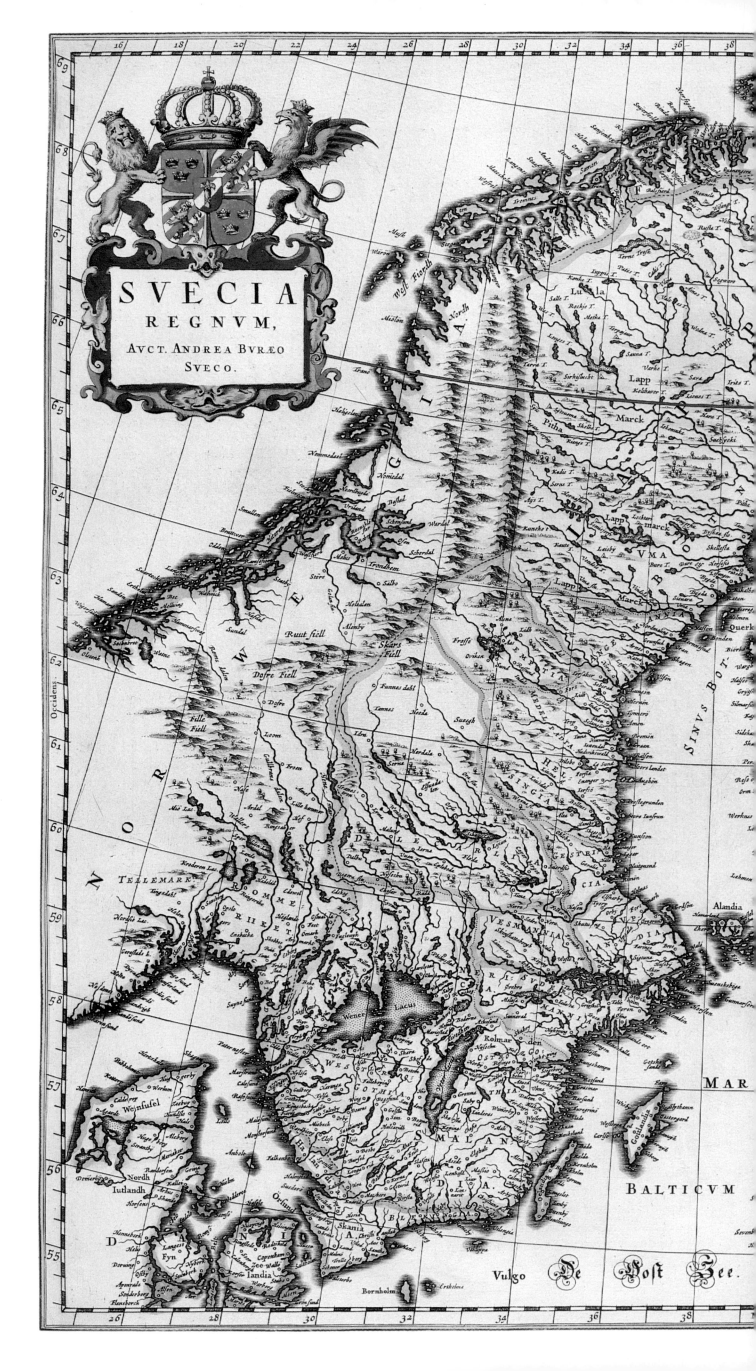

MARCHIA

Mare Album

D. CAROLO GVSTAVO,
SVECORVM GOTHORVM VANDALORVMQ:
REGI AC PRINCIPI HEREDITARIO,
Magno Duci Finlandiæ, Comiti Palatino Rheni,
Duci Eſthoniæ, Careliæ, Iuliæ, Cliviæ, ac
Montium, Comiti in Veldentz, Marcæ &
Ravensburgi, Domino Ingriæ & Ravenstein, &c.
Tabulam hanc D. D.
J. Blaeu.

Orient:

Onega Lac.

Onega ozero

Ladoga Lacus
Ladesko Ozero

MEGRINA.

Europe

SINVS   FINNI   CVS

INGRI

BESETSCH PETIN.

Sinus
Livonicus

ESTHONIA

LIVONI

CVRLANDIA.

SAMOGI TIA. LITV-
NIA.

Scala Milliarium.

Milliaria Dalica 7½ uni grad.
Milliaria Weſtrogothica 8½ uni grad.
Milliaria Vplandica Weſmannica Sudermannica et Oſtrogothica 12 uni grad.
Milliaria Germanica et Smalandica 15 uni grad.
Milliaria Fenonica Cajanica et Livonica quorum 18 uni grad. reſpondent
Milliaria Helsinica Botnica et Lapponica quorum 22 uni grad. reſpondent

Norvegia regnum, vulgo Nor-ryke

Joan Blaeu's map, issued for the first time in the atlas of 1662, is one of the few early, separate maps of the country.

It portrays a country very little known in the mountainous interior. It is coloured to show the boundary between Norway and Sweden – *Iemptia* [Jämtland] (acquired in 1645) – indicating a date of origin of about 1658, or perhaps even of 1660, when Trondheim was awarded to Norway by the Treaty of Copenhagen. This is despite the fact that Blaeu dedicated his map to Christian IV of Denmark who reigned from 1588 to 1648. His impressive Royal arms are shown at the lower right-hand corner.

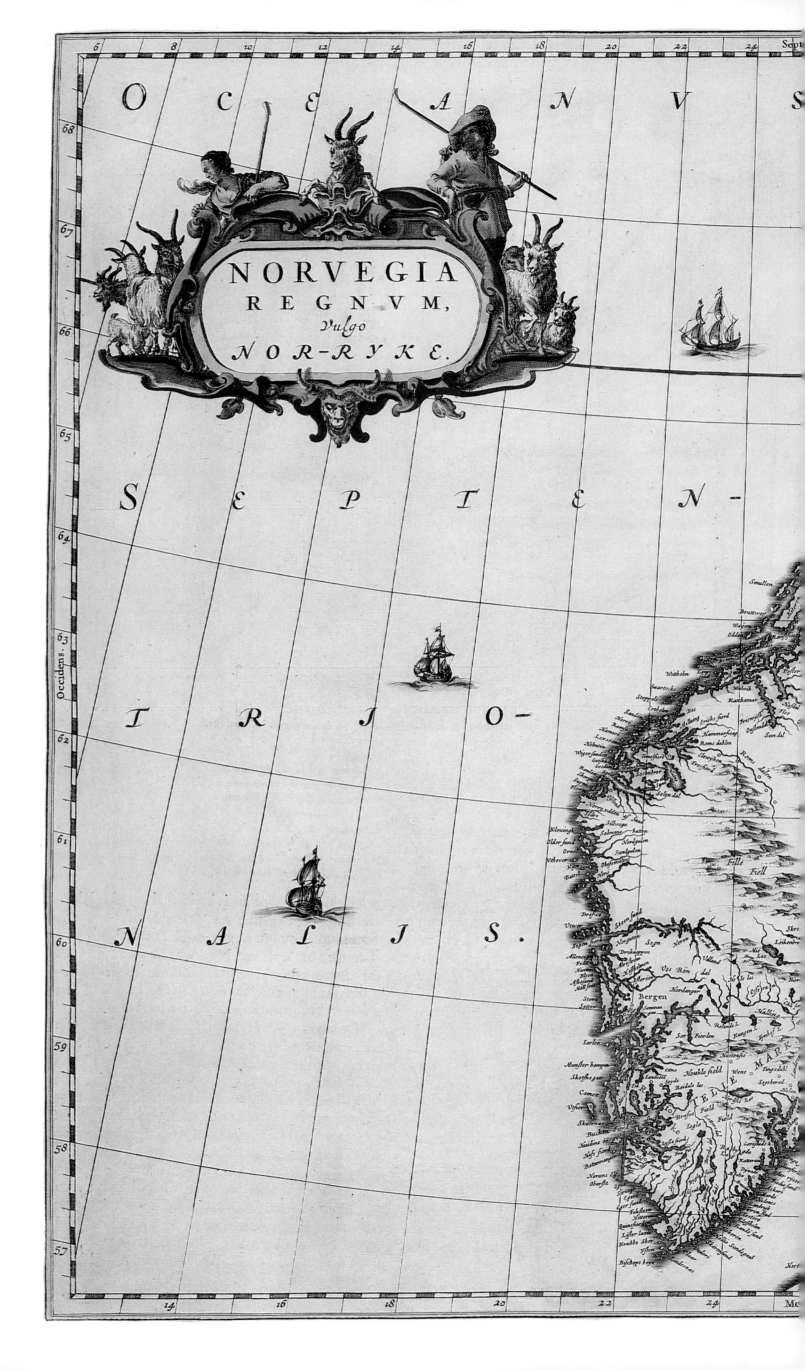

LAP-

PONIÆ

PARS.

REGNI

SVECIÆ

CONFINIA.

West Fiorth

Miolon

Noffladen
Burgenes
Beflad
Streenker
Wardal
Schonland
Leefwangen
Profiten
Ofen
Scherdal
Geuinghoos
Trondhem
Hommahugh
Salbo

Holtalen
Menby
Skars Fiell

Ruut
Fiell

Funnes dahl!
Needa
Susegh
Tannes
Dalecarlia
Idra
Nordala

Froon
Ofer
Iolla
Kammer
Amol
Elixerism
Nof
Rowers
Rings
aker
Lenkou
Dalba
Maloker

Hadeland
Ringerike
Na om
Speinberg
Ber

MEKET
ME

Brevig

Pater nofter
Marftrand
Westrogothia

Cale sund

Angermannia.

Iemptia.

Medelpadia.

Helfingia.

Lyma
Fiell
Lyma
Ierna
Malung
Serna
Transforen
Ofce
Sätum
Lufen
Rottuyk
Room

Geftricia.

Vestmannia.

Nericia.

Wener
Lacus

Suatrilia
Scare

Jertom
Gamlobio
Indahl

GOTHIÆ PARS.

Gotheborg
Alfbors

Oriens

SERENISSIMO PRINCIPI
CHRISTIANO,
DANIÆ, NORVEGIÆ,
VANDALORVM, GOTHORVMQ̃ PRINCIPI,
Duci Slefvici, Holfatiæ, Stormariæ, & Ditmarfiæ,
Comiti in Oldenburgh & Delmenhorft.
Tab. hanc D. D. D.   I. Blaeu.

Dania regnum

Unsigned, Willem Blaeu's general map of Denmark first appeared in 1635 and marks a considerable advance on the then available published mapping, particularly with regard to the topography of such areas as Limfjord in Jylland, but paying little regard to administrative divisions of the country.

However, by the time this printing of the map was included in the atlas of 1662, certain changes had indeed taken place, notably in the southern part of Sweden. Here, the provinces Halland, Blekinge and Skåne are coloured as though they were still Danish territory, when in fact Sweden had acquired them some years previously, in 1658 after the Treaty of Roskilde. This treaty ended the war of 1650–1658 between the two countries for control of the Baltic, thereby giving Sweden permanent control over strategically vital provinces.

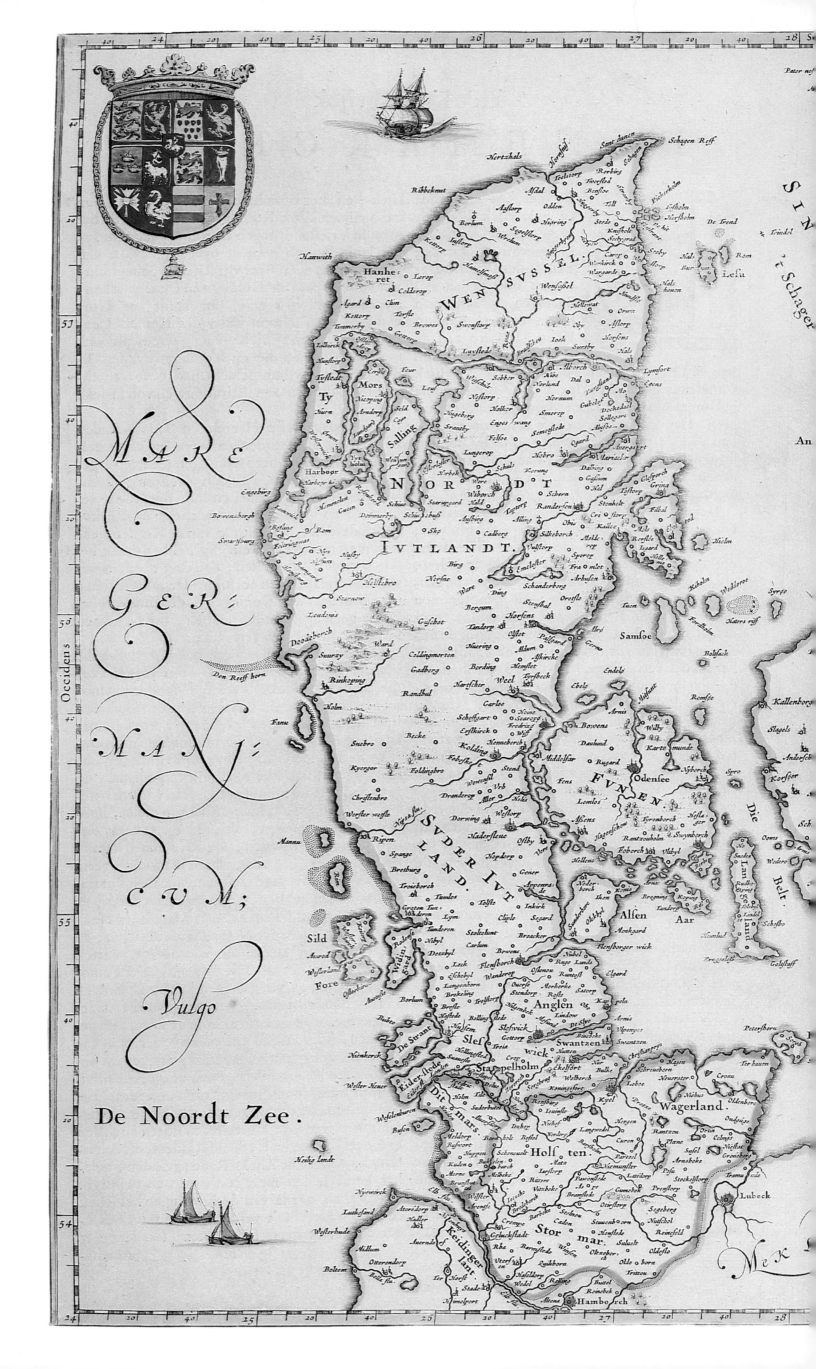

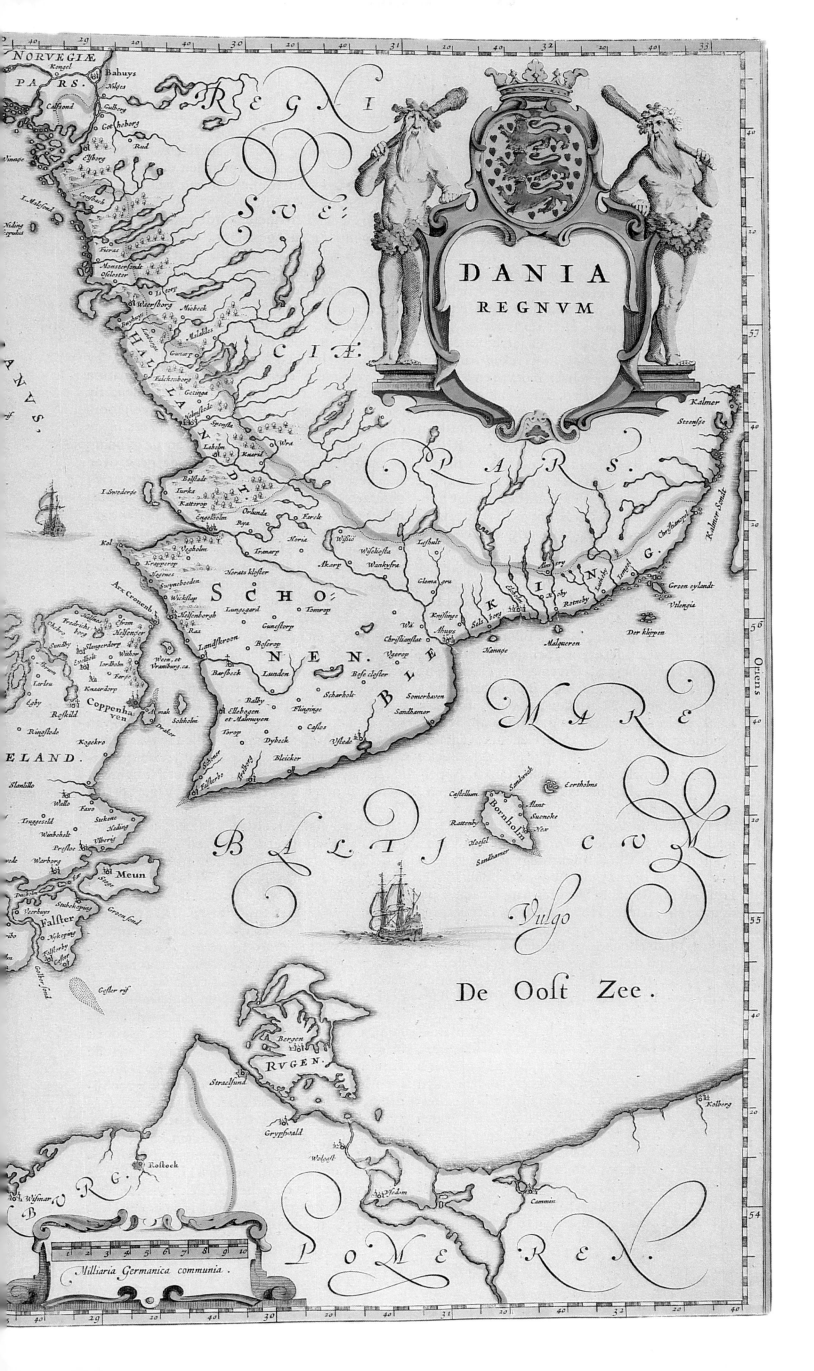

NORVEGIÆ
PARS.

REGNI

SVE:

CIÆ.

DANIA
REGNVM

HALLANDI.

PARS.

Kalmer
Steenſpe

Kalmer Sonde
Chriſtianop

SCHO
NEN.

BLE
KIN
G.

Groen eylandt
Vilengia
Der klippen

Opiens

Arx Cronenb.

Coppenha
ven

Roſkild

ELAND.

MARE

Caſtellum
Rattenby
Moeſel
Sandhamer

Smdwick
Bornholm
Alant
Suenoke
Nex
Eertholms

BALTI CV

Meun

Falſter

Ooſter rif

Vulgo

De Ooſt Zee.

Bergen

RVGEN.

Straelſund

Kolborg

Gryphſſvald
Woloſt

Cammin

Roſtock

RG.

Wiſmar
B

POME

REN.

Milliaria Germanica communia.

37

Ducatus Sleswicum sive Iutia Australis

Joan Blaeu published this map of southern Denmark, the provinces of Sønderjylland and Schleswig, in the atlas of 1662 reprinting one of the plates from a work published in 1652 by Johannes Mejer and Caspar Danckwerth entitled *Newe Landesbeschreibung der zweij Herzogthümer Schleswich und Holstein.*

The history of Blaeu's acquisition and use of those plates is given in the description of map 15, the general map of Schleswig-Holstein.

The area shown on this map is now almost equally divided between Denmark in the north and Germany in the south. The present boundary runs just to the north of Flensburg following the settlement by plebiscite in 1920, along the linguistic boundary from Tønder to Flensburg, between Danish and German-speaking inhabitants.

When the map was published, Sønderjylland was a region of sparsely settled heaths and moors, of which reclamation as pastoral and arable farmland only began in the 1750s under the auspices of Frederik V of Denmark.

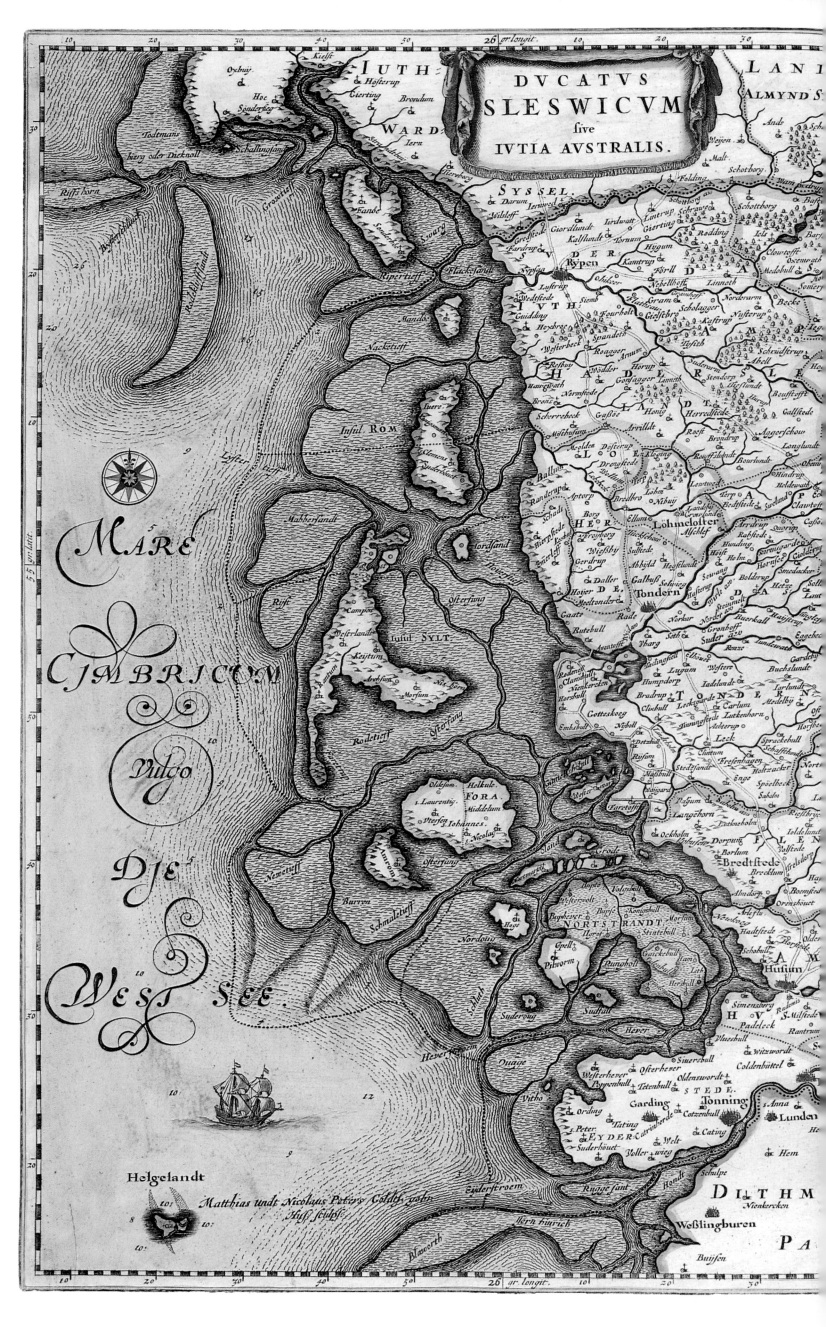

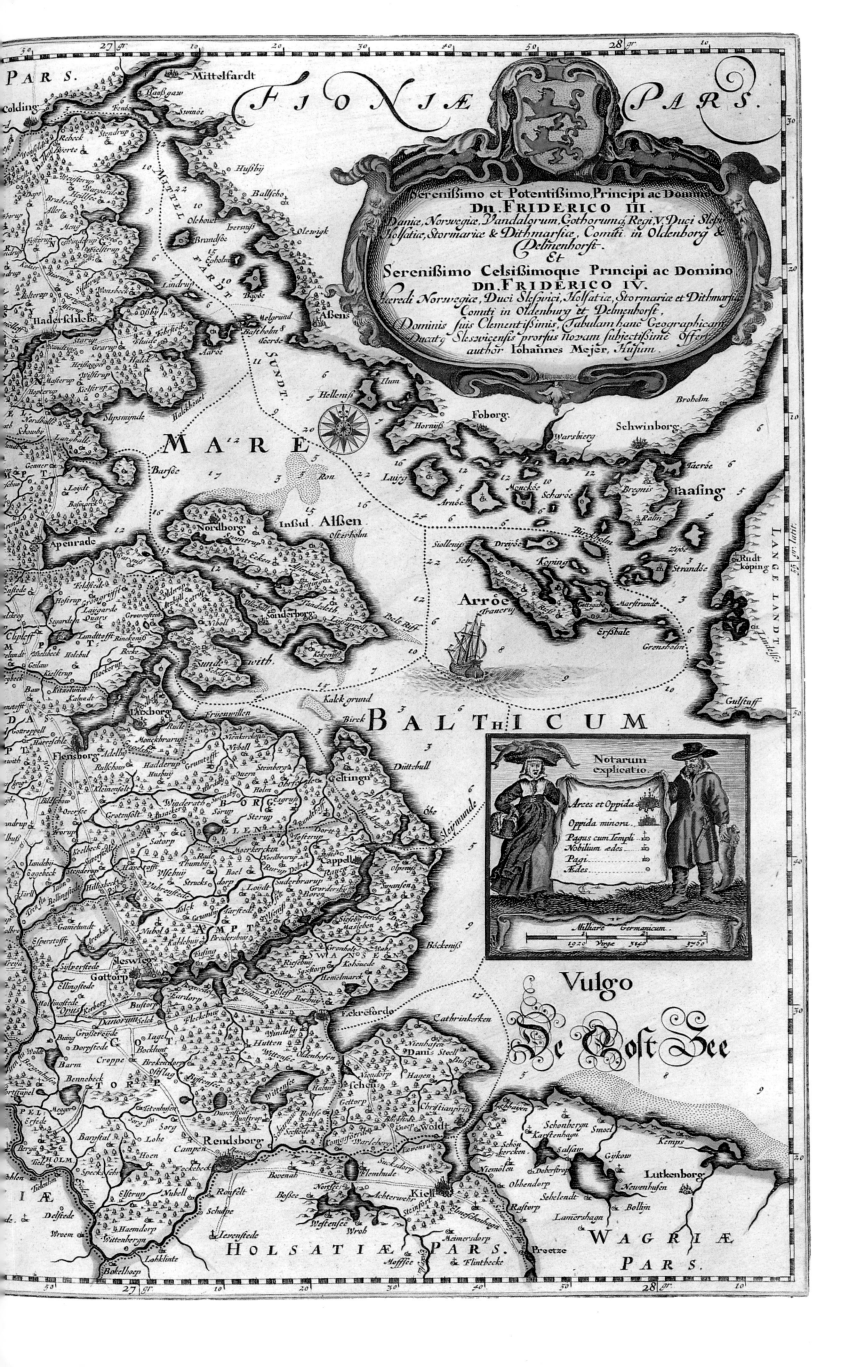

Suecia, Dania, et Norvegia, Regna Europae Septentrionalia

Willem Blaeu's handsome general map of Scandinavia was based on the work of the Swedish mapmaker, Anders Bure de Boo (1571–1646) whose map, *Orbis Arctoi nova et accurata delineetio*, published in six sheets in 1626, is regarded as the corner-stone of Scandinavian mapmaking.

Bure wrote an historical geography of Sweden in 1626, and in 1628 instituted for Gustaf II Adolf a land survey of Sweden, the *Svenska Lantmäteriet*, of which Bure remained head, laying the foundations and guidelines of land surveying that lasted throughout the first two hundred years of its history.

Blaeu's map shows the Swedish Empire at about its greatest extent, including all of the Grand Duchy of Finland, the Baltic provinces of Estonia and Livonia (acquired at the Treaty of Altmark in 1629) and the southern provinces of Halland, Blekinge and Skåne which Denmark ceded to Sweden in 1658 at the Treaty of Roskilde. Blaeu does not, however, include the North German territories in Pomerania, Bremen and Verden which Sweden acquired in 1648 at the Treaty of Westphalia and by which she gained the important port city of Stettin.

Blaeu's map includes the Royal arms of Sweden, Denmark and Norway in his title cartouche. Several of Blaeu's regional maps of Scandinavia owe their origins to the prototype work of Anders Bure.

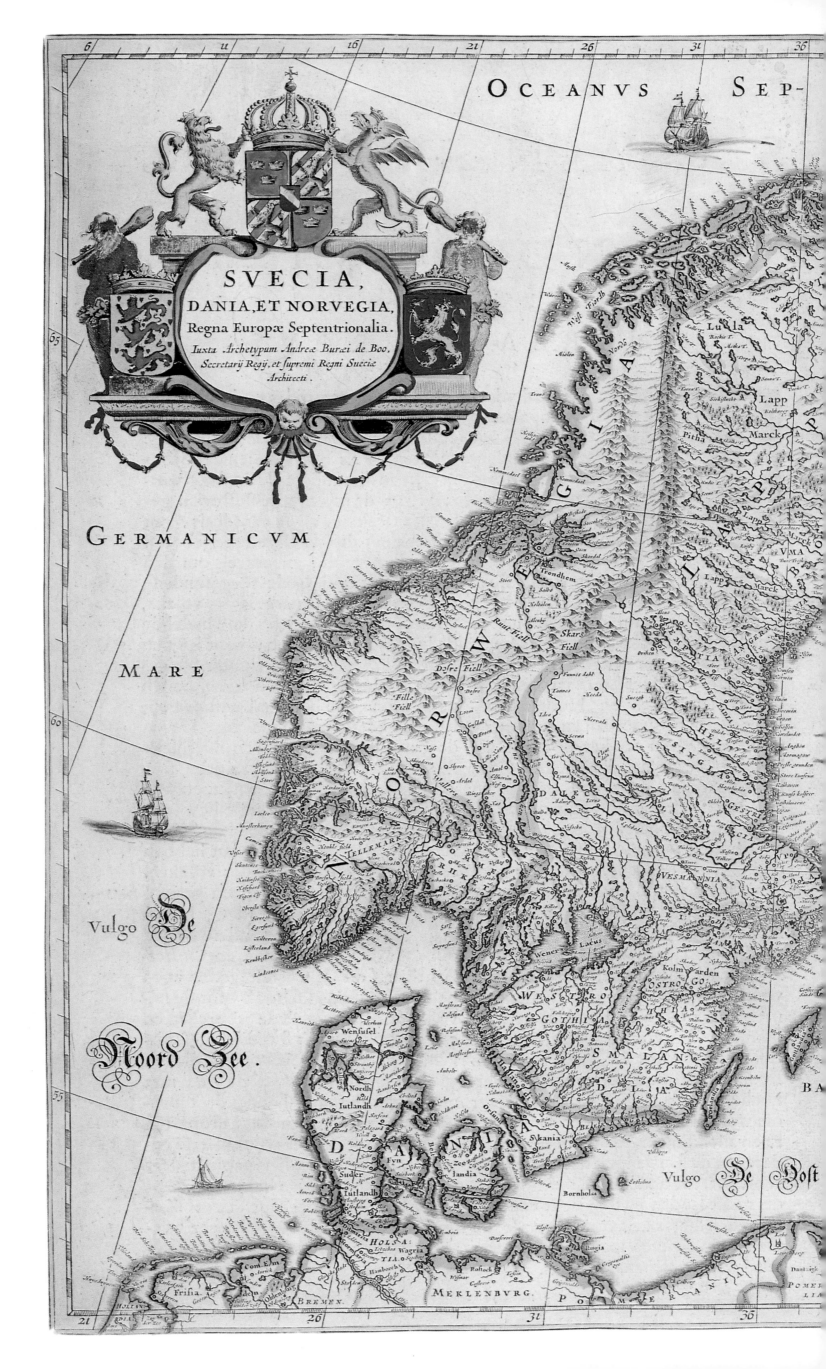

Mare Album

Onega Lacus

Onega Ozero

Ladoga Lacus

Ladelko Ozero

Sinus Finnicus

BOTNICVS

CVRLANDIA

ESTHONIA

LIVONIA

LETTEN

PRVSSIA

Koningberg

Dago

Osel

Biela osera

Novogorodt

MEGRINA

BESETCHI PETIN

DONE SCHI PETIN

SELON SCHI PETIN

Scala miliarium.

	5	10	15	
Miliaria Dalica.				
Westrgothica.	5	10	15	7
Oplandica Wfmannica Su dermannica et Ostrogothica.	6	12	18	24
Germanica et Smaland.	5 10	15 20	25	30
Finnonica, Cajanica et Livonica.	6 12	18	24	30 36
Hellinsica, Botnica et Lapponica.	10	20	30	40 46

Magnus Ducatus Finlandiae

This remarkably accurate-looking map was published by Joan Blaeu in 1662, and is the first printed map of the Grand Duchy of Finland, taken from the Scandinavian maps of Anders Bure.

At the time of publication, Finland was a Grand Duchy of the Swedish Empire, with most of its settlements concentrated in the south and south-west, still an area with a large Swedish-speaking minority, particularly in *Finlandia*, *Nylandia*, *Caiania* and *Tavastia*. The south-eastern frontier region, around Lake Ladoga [Ladozhskoye Ozero today] shows two boundaries, one to the west, the other to the east, coloured with a double green and yellow line. The green represents the boundary established at the Treaty of Täysinnä in 1595 by which the Grand Duchy received all of the territory to the north-west of the lake shown then as Savolax. The yellow line is the more recent boundary determined at the Treaty of Stolbovo which ended the Russo-Swedish War of 1610–1617. Most of this territory was ceded back to Russia after the USSR-Finnish War of 1940.

Blaeu's title piece incorporates the arms of the provinces of the Grand Duchy: *Caiania* [Oulu and Vaasa], *Finlandia* [Turku and Pori], *Finlandia Septentrionalis* [Lappi], *Savolaxia* [Kuopio and Mikkeli], *Tavastia* [Häme], *Nylandia* [Uusimaa], and *Carelia* [Karjala]. In the opposite corner, Blaeu gives a dedication to Gustav Horn (1592–1657) of Björneborg [Pori], who was governor of the south-

eastern regions of Kexholm and Ingermanland, giving a date of origin of Blaeu's map between 1651 (when Horn was made a Count) and 1657 (the year of his death). The arms of Finland were also relatively recent in origin, being first used in the 1580s.

CAIANIA · FINL.MERI · FINLANDIA · FINL.SEPT · SAVOLAXIA

TAVASTIA · NYLANDIA · CARELIA

MAGNVS DVCATVS
FINLANDIÆ
Auct. Andrea Buræo Sueco.

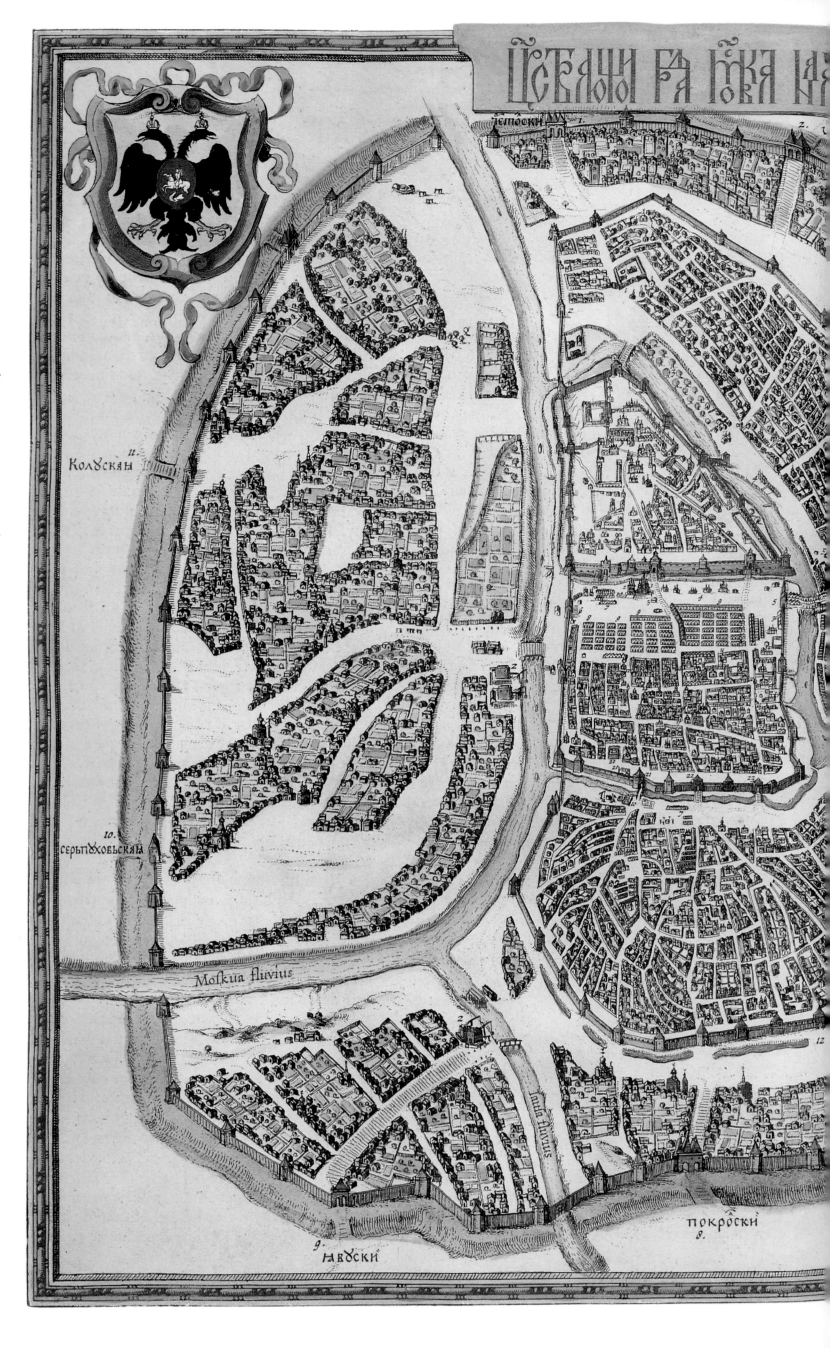

Tsarskoi grad Moskva...Urbis Moskvae

Aside from this and a plan of the Kremlin, Blaeu published no town plans in his atlas: he had already issued an atlas of plans of towns of The Netherlands in 1648, and at the time of the preparation of the 1662 atlas, he was also compiling an atlas of town plans devoted to Italy.

This most impressive plan of Moscow [Moskva] appeared in Blaeu's atlas for the first time in 1662. However, it is believed to pre-date even the embryonic *Appendix* of the 1630s, stemming from a Russian original survey prepared at the orders of Boris Fyodorovich Godunov (*c.* 1551–1605), Tsar of Muscovy since 1598. The original Russian plan has apparently not survived, and Blaeu may have used a copy made in 1610 for King Sigismund III of Poland.

The plan, as published by Blaeu, shows the old city which surrounds the Kremlin and the *Kitai Gorod* (or fortified city). The name Kremlin first appeared as *Kreml'* (or High Town) in an account of the fire in the town in 1331. It was founded in 1147 at the junction of two rivers, the Moskva and the Neglinnaya, the latter forming a moat on the north and east flanks of the Kremlin.

Until 1367, when construction of the masonry walls began, the settlement was called *gorod* (or fenced-in town) protected by a wooden palisade. As Moscow grew, the Kremlin became the royal, religious and secular heart of both the city and the expanding dominions of Muscovy. For nearly four

hundred years, until Tsar Peter I transferred his seat of government to his new city of St Petersburg in 1713, Moscow was the capital of Russia, the seat of the Orthodox faith, the custodian and guiding centre of Russian literary and artistic life, and the principal commercial metropolis of the realm. Moscow again became the capital following the Revolution in 1917.

During the earlier part of Moscow's history, outside the moat formed by the Neglinnaya, there was a traders' quarter protected, like the Kremlin, first by a palisade, and later by a masonry wall built in 1534–1538, which led to the renaming of the district as *Kitai gorod* (called *Kitaygrad* on the plan illustrated). This became the active centre of commerce, the richest and most crowded part of Moscow.

Then, beyond the walls of *Kitai gorod*, another section grew up, called *Belgorod* (or White City), enclosed in 1584 after the death of Tsar Ivan IV 'The Terrible' by a wall some nine kilometres in length and with twenty-eight towers. In 1591, the outer peripheral belt shown on this plan, protected by a wooden wall was built, called *Zembiyanoy gorod* (or Earthen City). This was the home of craftsmen of the two-hundred-and-fifty distinct crafts and trades that existed in Moscow in the sixteenth century, each occupying its own area.

Blaeu's beautifully presented plan includes a key to the numbered features, quarters and buildings shown on the right-hand side, each list divided by the four major quarters of Moscow.

Polonia Regnum, et Silesia Ducatus

Blaeu's map of the Kingdom of Poland and the Duchy of Silesia dates from 1634, the Polish arms appearing at the upper right and the Silesian crest at the lower left.

The map itself was based on an older map published during the latter half of the sixteenth century in the atlases of Abraham Ortelius and of Gerard Mercator, based on the work of Waclaw Grodecki in the 1560s. It shows Poland almost encircled in the north and west by German territory in Prussia, Pomerania and Silesia.

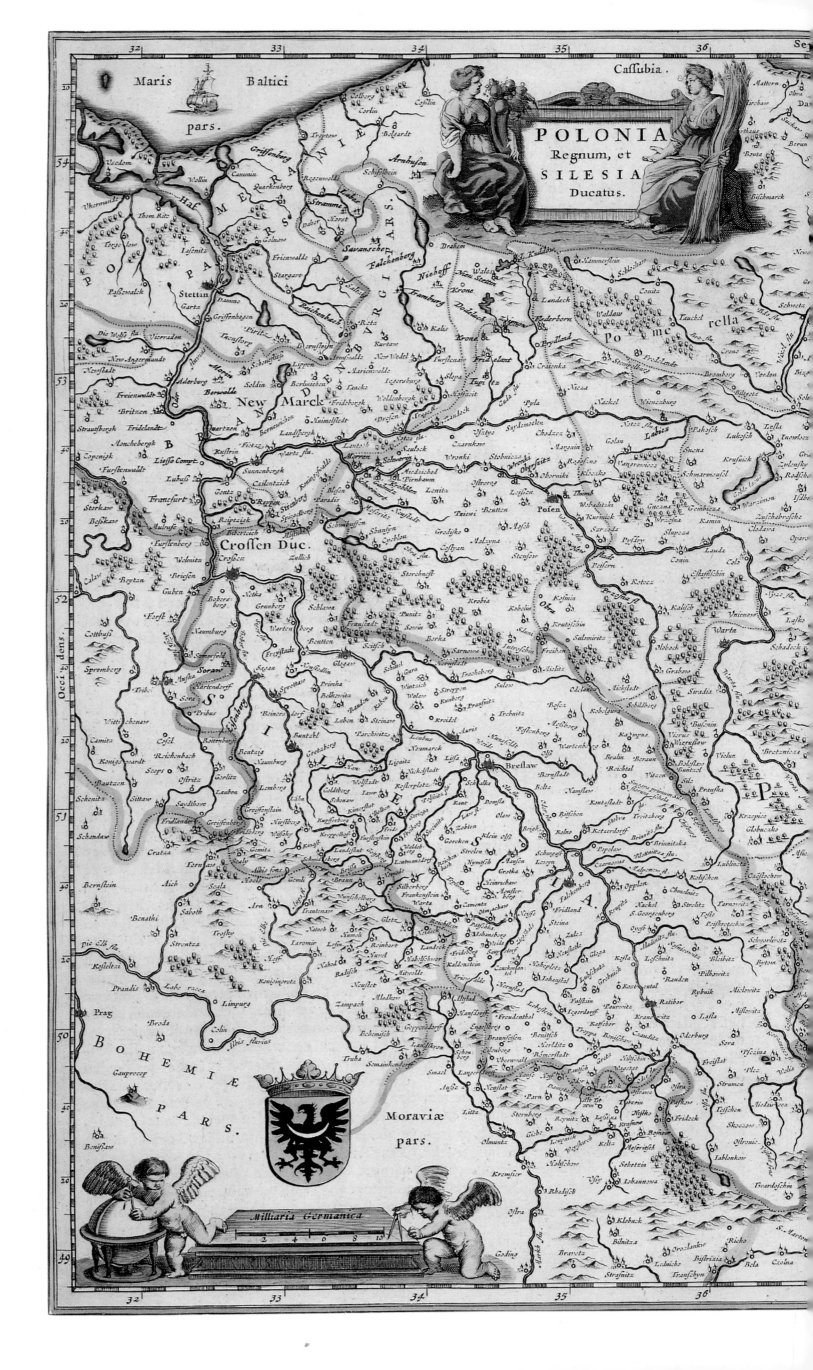

Prussia accurate descripta

Willem Blaeu's detailed
map is based on a prototype
by Gaspar Henneberg
(1529–1600).

Prussia had been an area
of German settlement from
about 1280 in the wake of
the campaigns of the
Teutonic Order which,
from its headquarters at
Marienburg (now called
Malbork, in Poland),
controlled the eastern
Baltic, conquering
Pomerania and large areas
of present-day Poland. The
Order was secularized as
the Duchy of Prussia in
1525.

Several German-settled
cities were founded under
the auspices of the Order,
such as Königsberg
[Kaliningrad] in 1286,
Elbing [Elblag] in 1237,
Marienwerder [Kwidzyn] in
1233 and the Cistercian
monasteries of Oliva
[Oliwa] and Pelplin.

The agricultural wealth
of Prussia is symbolized in
the very decorative title
cartouche. Note that Blaeu's
name appears in its old
Latin form as *Guiljelmus
Jenss: Caesius.*

Nova Totius Germaniae Descriptio

This is Willem Blaeu's general map of the German Empire, dating originally from the 1630s.

Although the way in which the map was coloured does not show it in great detail by the time it was issued in 1662, Germany was divided into as many as two-hundred-and-thirty-four distinct territorial units, fifty-one free cities and innumerable estates of Imperial Knights. Germany was kept weak by both religious division and dynastic rivalry – a 'geographical expression', as it were. The western part was extraordinarily fragmented, often into very small territories, while the eastern marches consisted of very large principalities which had grown up as a result of the colonizations of the thirteenth and fourteenth centuries. It was the eastern provinces of Prussia and Austria that were to play the predominant role in the eventual unification of Germany some two hundred years after the publication of Blaeu's atlas.

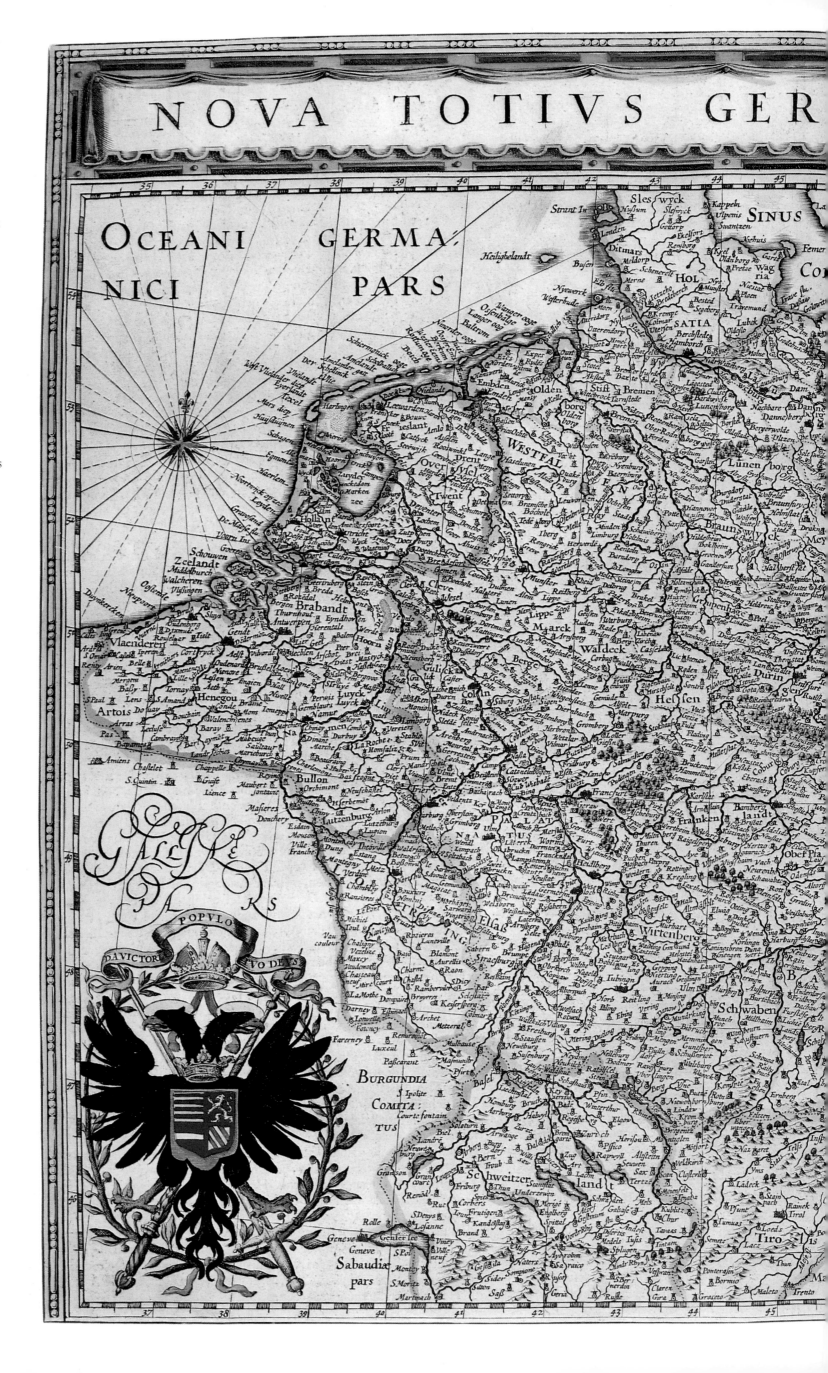

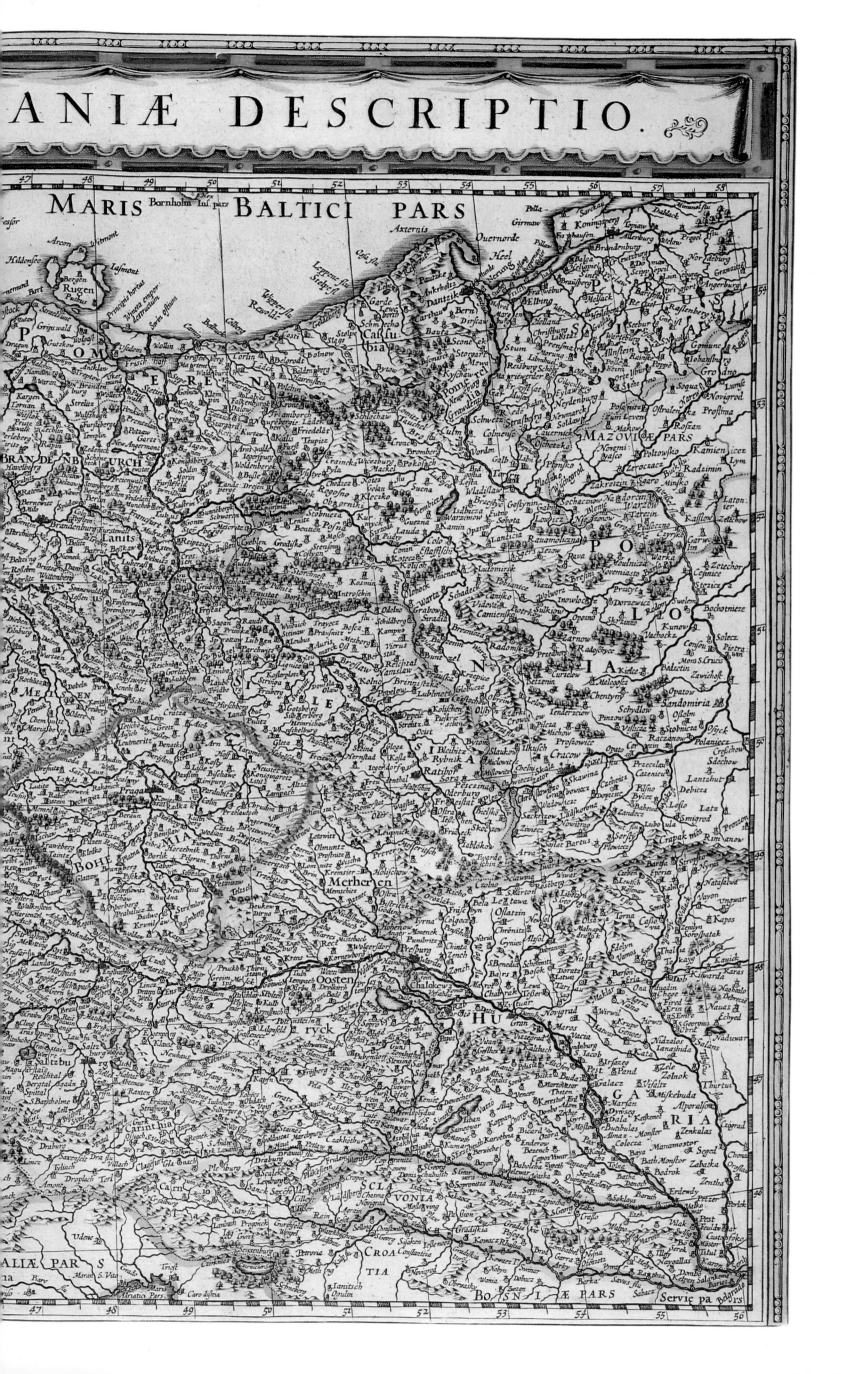

Nova & Accurata Ducatuum Slesvici et Holsatiae Tabula

This map was made by Johannes Mejer (1606–1674), Royal Mathematician to Christian IV of Denmark, later to Frederick III, and a former pupil of the astromomer Tycho Brahe, under whom Joan's father, Willem, had studied for a time during the 1590s. Mejer compiled an extremely detailed and remarkably accurate survey of Schleswig-Holstein under the patronage of Frederick IV, Duke of Schleswig-Holstein between 1648 and 1652.

Most of the original survey materials are now lost, but Mejer's work provided the basis for the regional maps in a work which he published with Caspar Danckwerth (d. 1672), entitled *Newe Landesbeschreibung der zweij Hertzogthümer Schleswich und Holstein*, published in 1652. The maps, of which we show a fine example here, were engraved by the Husum goldsmiths Matthias and Nicolaus Petersen, with assistance from the engravers Anders and Christian Lorensen. The book contained forty maps and plans, the most detailed published up to the time of the frontier region between Denmark and Germany. Only one edition was published.

Unfortunately the book was not a commercial success, partly because of ducal disapproval and partly, no doubt, because of the then very limited appeal of the work. However, the plates remained intact and undamaged – they could so easily have been melted down or sold for scrap – and they were bought sometime later in the 1650s by Joan Blaeu himself

through the good offices of the diplomat and traveller Adam Oelschlager (otherwise known as Olearius, who had been Frederick's ambassador in Persia during the 1630s) for the sum of 300 *thaler* (equivalent to about £40 at the time). Blaeu subsequently reprinted thirty-four of the plates in volumes I and III of his 1662 atlas, unchanged in detail but with the titles now recut from the original German into Latin. The original Petersen imprints were retained also.

The side borders of the map comprise eighteen miniature town plans, among the earliest printed plans issued for some of these towns. They are: Rijpen [Ribe, in Denmark], Sleswieg [Schleswig, in Germany], Flensborg [Flensburg, in Germany], Haderschleben [Haderslev, in Denmark], Husum [in Germany], Tondern [Tønder, in Denmark], Sonderborg [Sønderborg, in Denmark], Apenrade [Åbenrå, in Denmark], Eckernförde [in Germany], Tonning [Tönning, in Germany], Hamburg, Kiel, Rendßborg [Rendsburg in Germany], Itzehoe [in Germany], Oldesloh [Bad Oldesloe, in Germany], Krempe [in Germany], Gluckstadt [Glückstadt, in Germany], and Plöen [Plön, in Germany].

Ducatus Bremae & Ferdae

This shows the area of north-western Germany between Hamburg and Bremen bounded by the Elbe and Weser rivers. The orientation is north to the left-hand side of the plate.

This regional map appears for the first time in the 1662 atlas as one of a number, some forty-two in all, of maps new to the German division of the Blaeu atlas. The map was based on the work of two mapmakers: a Captain Johannes Gorries of the Swedish army, and a Joannes Christoph, both of whom apear to be otherwise unknown. That a map by a Swedish military officer should be the main source of Joan Blaeu's map may at first seem rather strange, but it is less so when it is realized that most of the area shown, which is the Archbishopric of Bremen and the Bishopric of Verden, became Swedish territory in 1648 by the Treaty of Westphalia which finally ended the Thirty Years War. Bremen and Verden remained in Swedish possession until 1721.

The greater part of the region appears as a sparsely settled marshy heathland with a few woodland clearings as settlements. The only towns of importance were Hamburg, Bremen and Stade on the fringes of the territory. Even such an area as this was subject to division and administration from outside: the northern tip at Ritzebüttel (where Cuxhaven now stands)

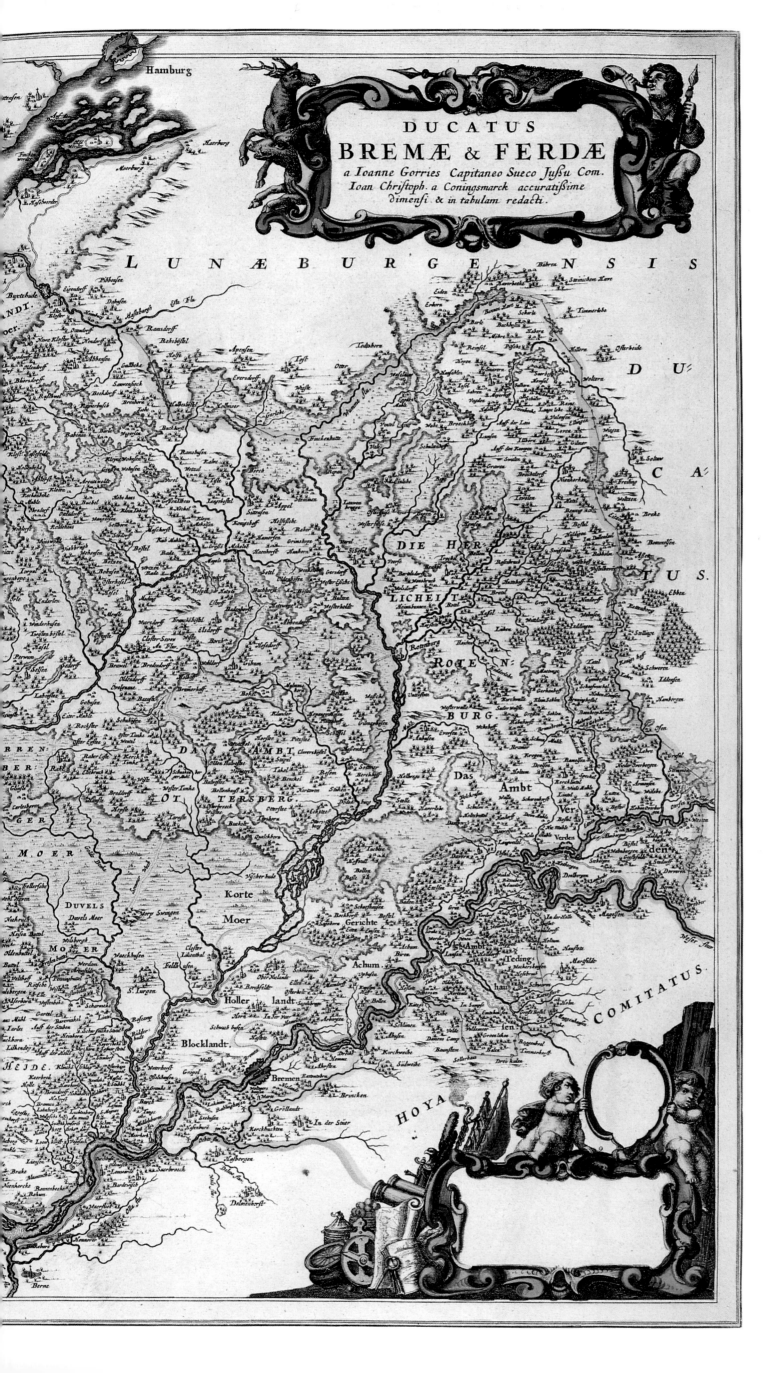

belonged to Hamburg, while Bremen and Hamburg were themselves Imperial City States. In the case of Bremen, the scale of the map allows for an outline of both the old and new town, the latter having been founded in the 1620s, to be shown.

Danubius, Fluvius Europae Maximus, a Fontibus ad Ostia, Cum omnibus Fluminibus, utroque latere, in illum defluentibus

This and the following map of the Rhine were first produced in 1635 by Willem Blaeu to replace maps composed of sections cut up from older maps, in this instance from Rumold Mercator's large map of Europe dating from 1595.

The large title cartouche symbolizes the great river at once uniting and dividing two empires and two religious faiths: on the one hand, the Holy Roman Empire represented by the figure of the Emperor Ferdinand III himself, defending Christendom against the Ottoman Turks represented by the figure of the Bey on the other. An ornate vignette at the lower left is an allegory of the Danube and its major tributaries.

One of the largest maps in Blaeu's atlas, it measures 412 by 965mm., and was printed from two plates.

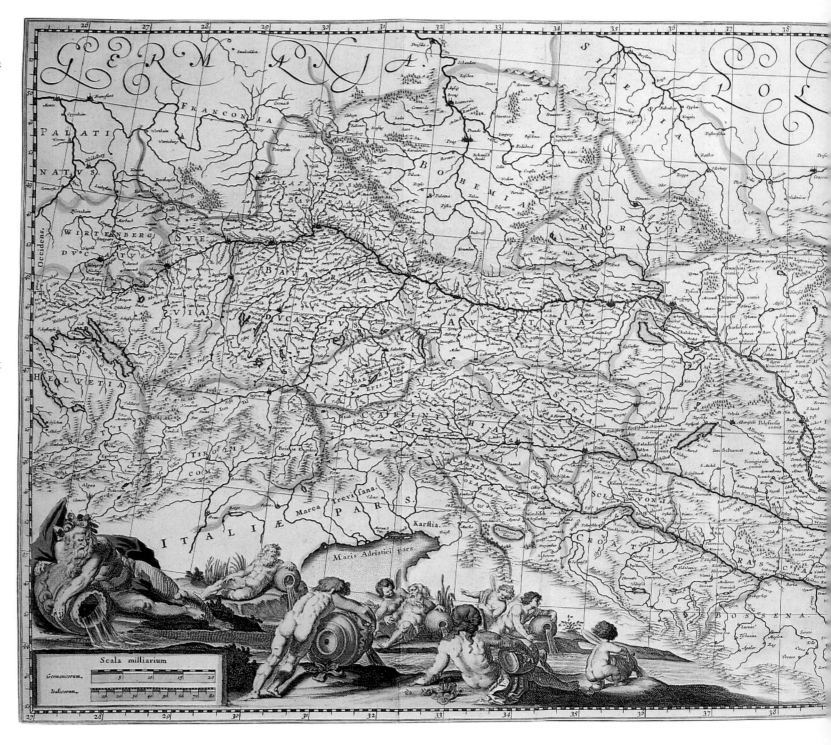

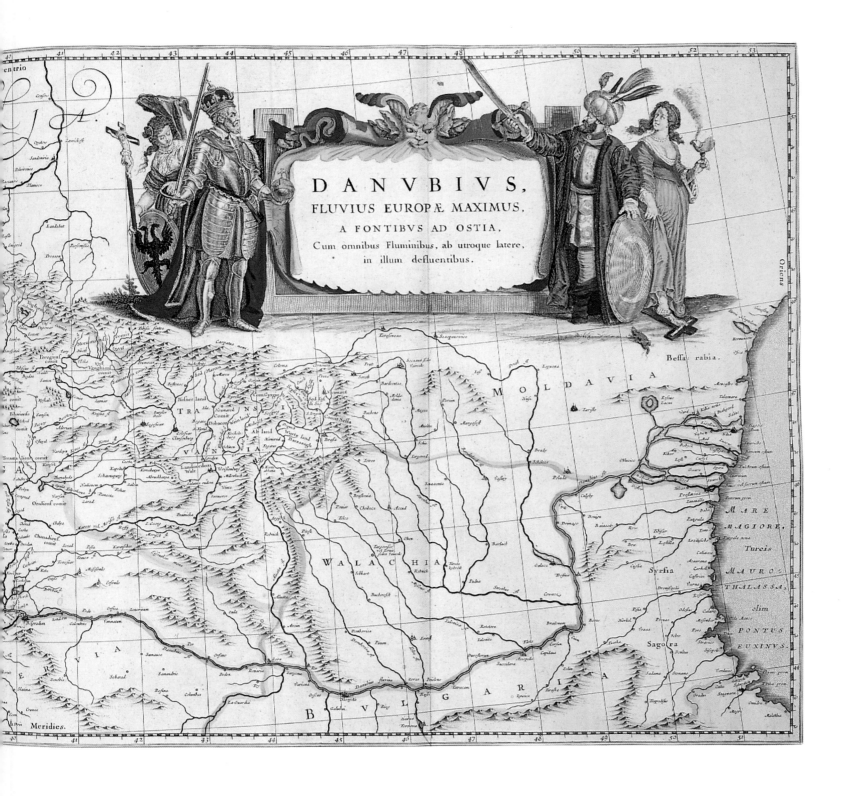

Rhenus Fluviorum Europae celeberrimus, cum Mosa, Mosella, et reliquis, in illum se exonerantibus, fluminibus

Willem Blaeu's large and impressive map shows the entire course of the Rhine, from its source in Switzerland to its North Sea delta in The Netherlands. Like the Danube (the subject of map 17), the river both unites and divides. The territories through which the river flows are represented by means of their crests which appear at the upper left: Switzerland, Alsace, the Rhineland Palatinate, the Archbishopric of Köln, Kleve, Gelderland, Utrecht, and Holland. The title is placed within an allegorical tableau symbolic of the river from its source to the sea, with the various river gods pouring their tributaries (the Maas and the Mosel) into the main stream.

One of the largest maps in the Blaeu atlas (it measures 410 by 940mm.), it was printed from two plates and first issued in 1635.

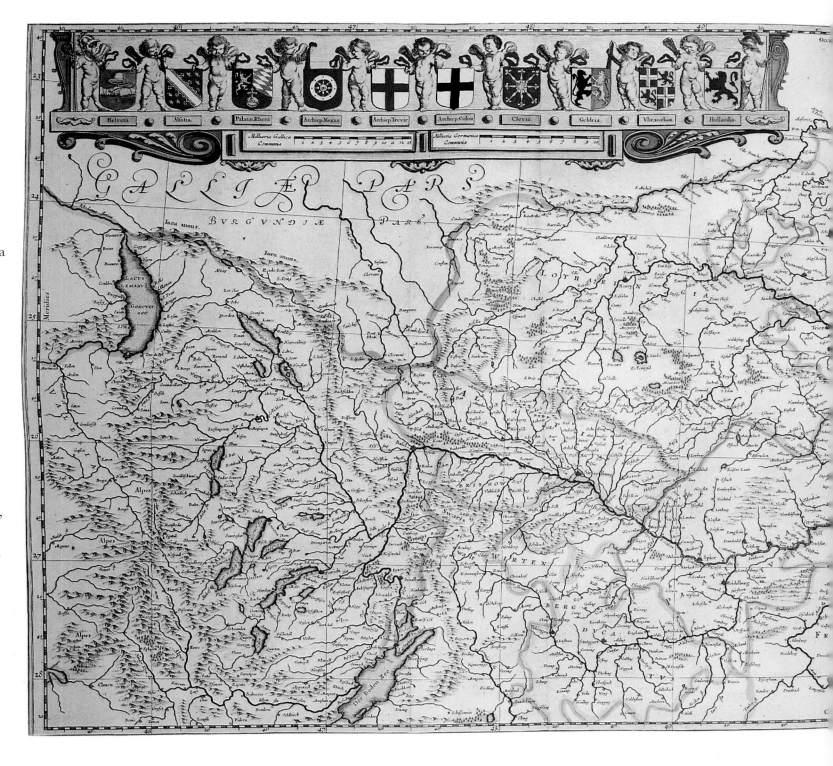

RHENVS
Fluviorum Europæ celeberrimus,
cum MOSA, MOSELLA, et
reliquis, in illum se exonerantibus,
fluminibus.

Austria Archiducatus

Ober- and Niederösterreich, or the Danube valley from Linz to Wien, is the subject of this map, an area formerly known as the Archduchy of Austria, which, at the time of publication in the atlas, was a province of the Holy Roman Empire.

Willem Blaeu's map of 1630 is taken from maps drawn by the Hungarian Wolfgang Lazius (1514–1565). A particular point of interest is the key which shows feature categories such as cities, towns, religious houses, castles, villages and vineyards. Although sixteenth century in origin, Lazius's maps were still copied by mapmakers over a century later, as attested to by Blaeu's use of it as late as the 1660s.

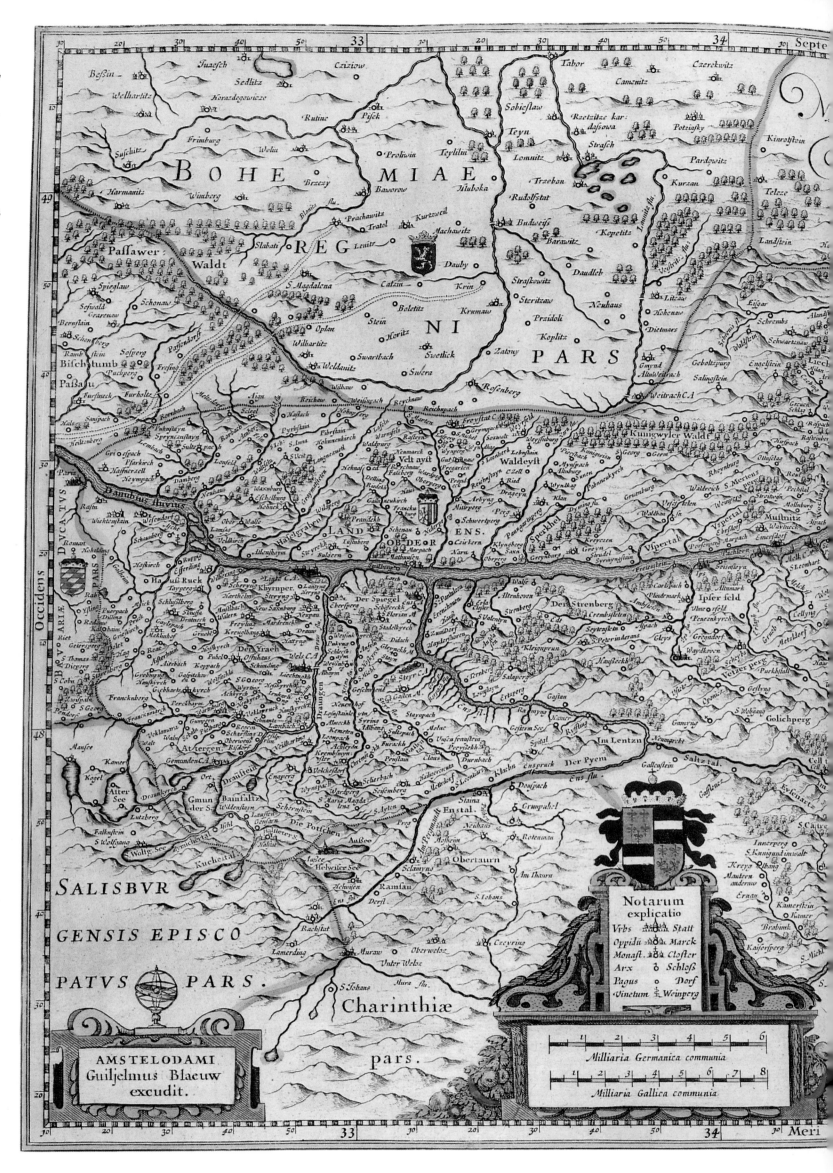

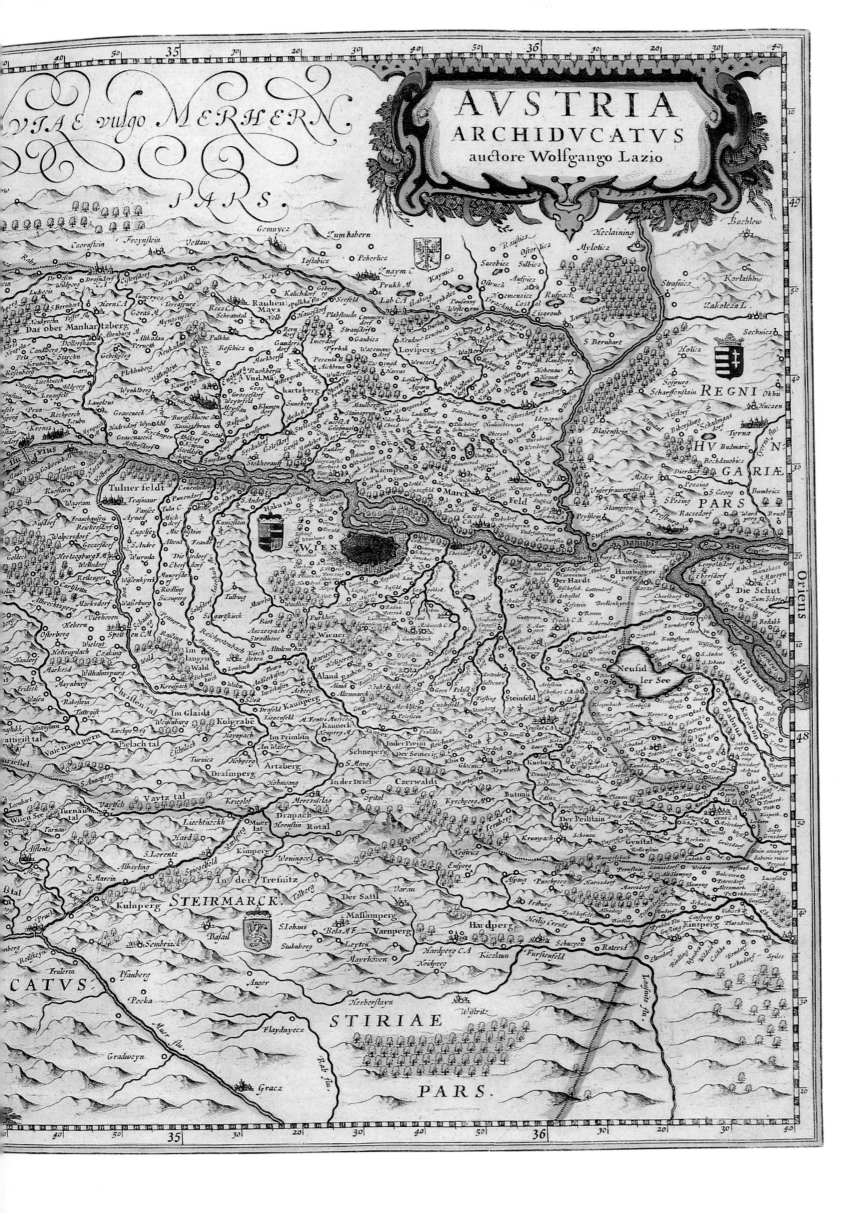

AVSTRIA
ARCHIDVCATVS
auctore Wolfgango Lazio

Helvetia, cum finitimis regionibus confoederatis

Willem Blaeu's general map of Switzerland, although first issued in 1634, acknowledges the work of his great predecessor Gerard Mercator who died in 1595. Mercator's survey was first published in 1585.

Except for the westernmost extremity of Switzerland at Genève and the easternmost part of the canton of Graübunden, Blaeu's map shows the Swiss Confederation more or less as we know it today.

Whether by accident or design, the prominence of river valleys on this map underlines the difficult nature of the terrain, even though mountain ranges are only hinted at in the traditional manner as lines of 'molehills'. Despite the barriers posed by mountains, the valleys and passes were then, as now, used as trade routes between northern and southern Europe. Then, trains of mules were the means of transport; now road and railway lines carve through the mountain passes or bore beneath through long tunnels.

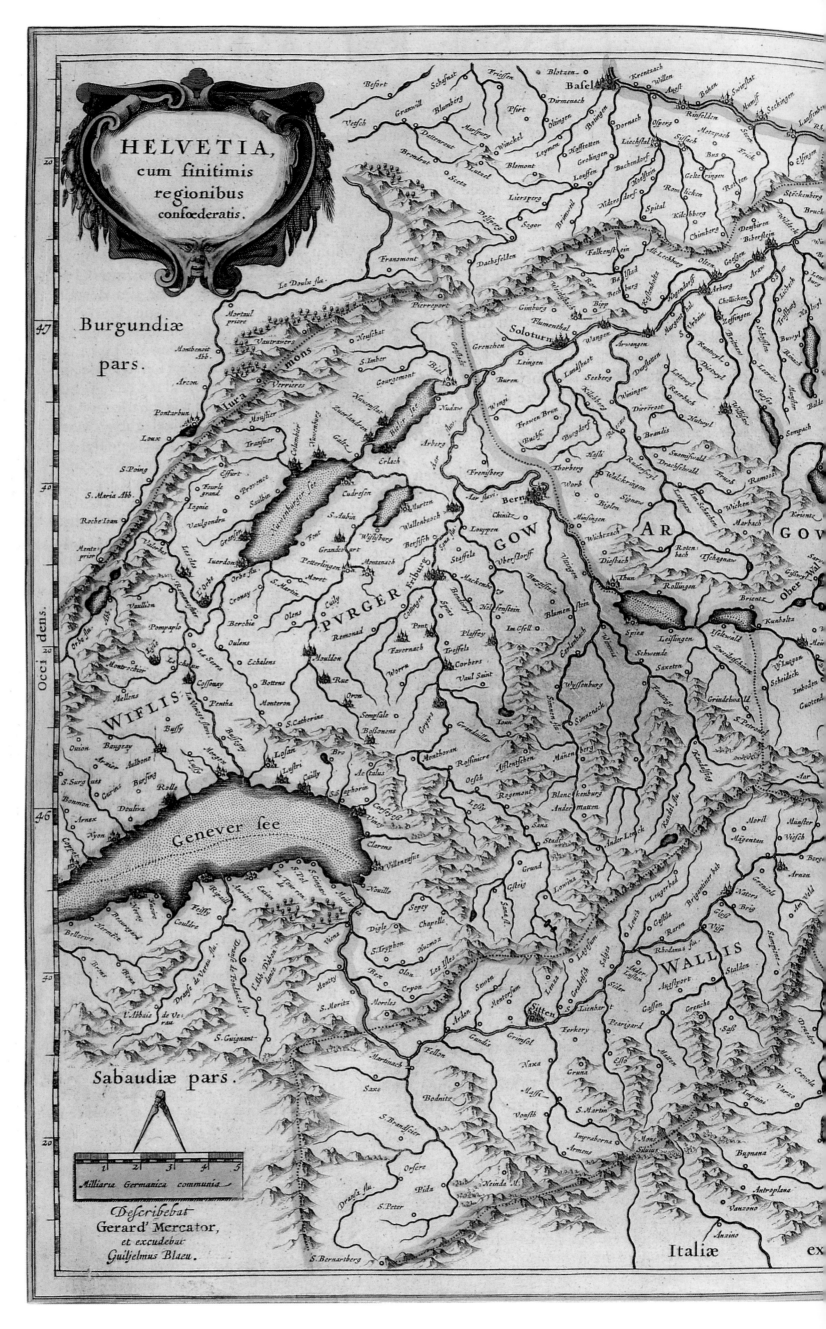

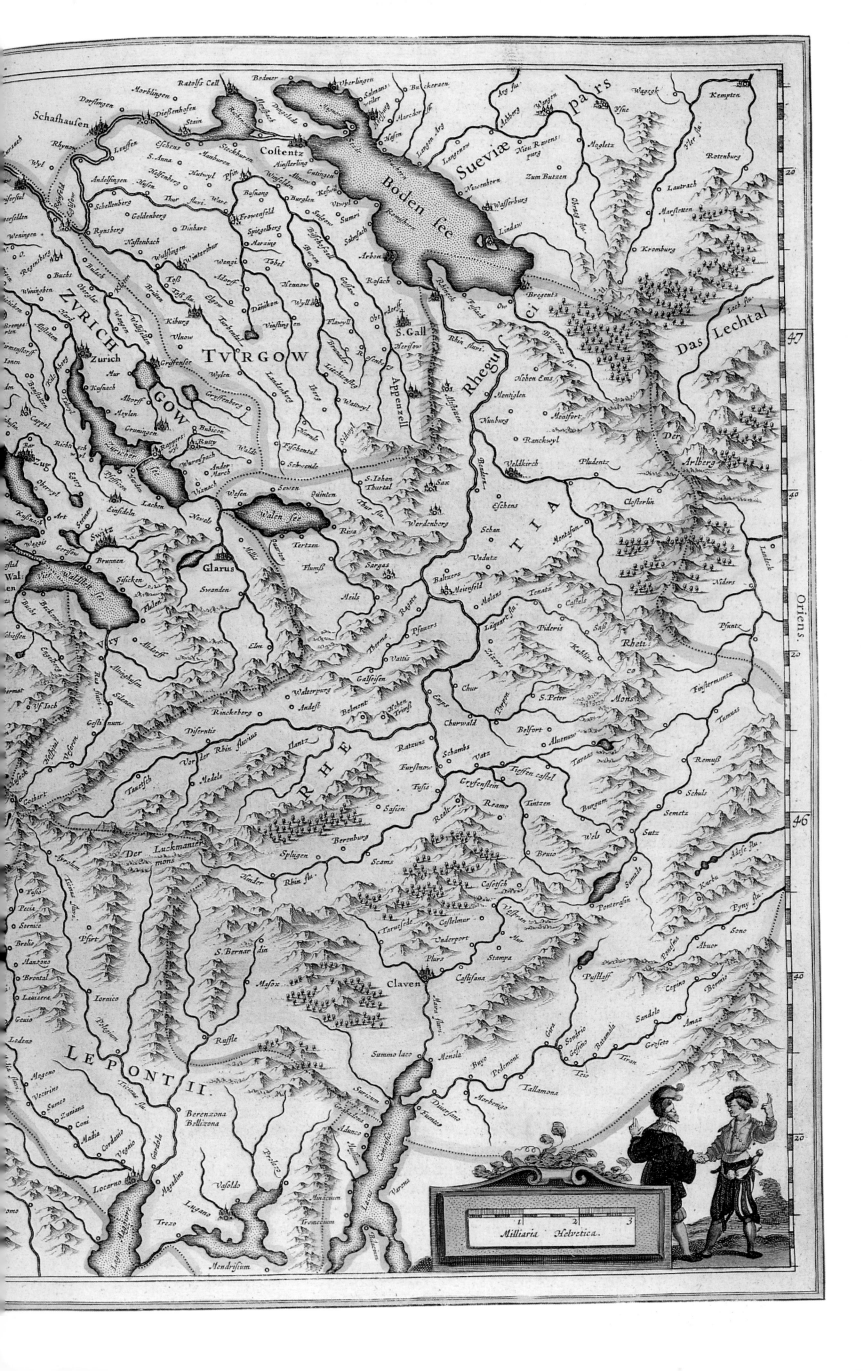

Milliaria Helvetica.

63

Novus XVII Inferioris Germaniae Provinciarum Typus

The origins of this impressive general map of the Seventeen Provinces, the first map of the volume covering The Netherlands, go back to the early days of Willem Blaeu's career as a mapmaker in 1608, when it was issued as a separately published map with decorative borders. In that form (the map originally measured 510 by 670mm.) it would have been rather too large as an atlas map, so the plate was cut down prior to its use for the first *Appendix* atlas of 1630.

Broadly speaking, Blaeu's map covers an area more or less equivalent to the modern Benelux. Several features associated with old maps are here: the elaborate decoration of the title cartouche with its allegorical figures, the fine illustrations of sailing ships that symbolize the maritime power of The Netherlands, and the large compass rose placed in the sea off the west coast.

The section covering The Netherlands contains some sixty-three maps in all, only thirty of which were new to the atlas of 1662. Writers on cartographic history have commented that The Netherlands volume is a good example of the opportunist methods of Joan Blaeu as an atlas publisher, for a considerable number of the sixty-three maps were printed from often very old plates. It remains a curious fact that, where his native land was concerned, Blaeu was content to put up with obsolete materials.

It is not unlikely that Blaeu, in catering for clients who may have bought his atlas more for display purposes than for

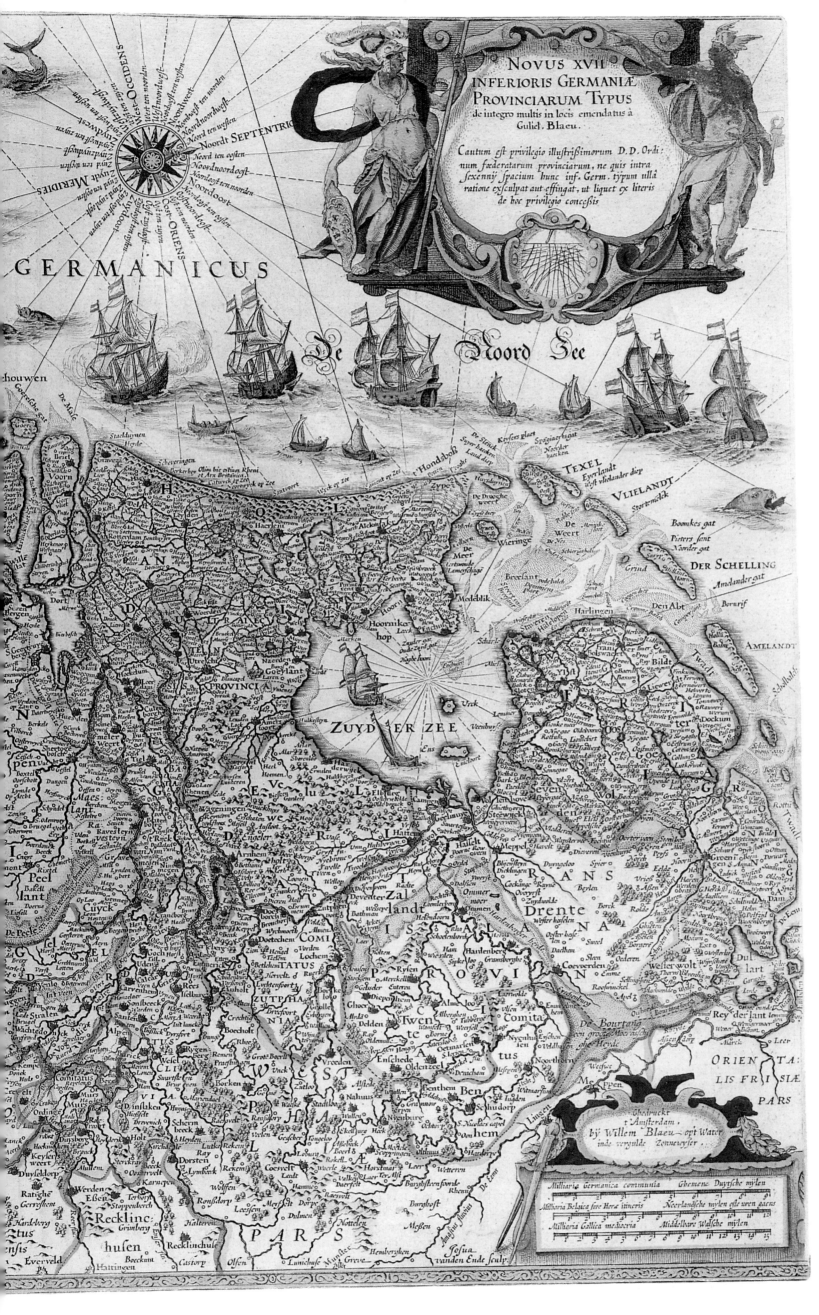

cartographic accuracy, sought to give them quantity rather than quality. Another possibility is that he did not necessarily have the time or the resources to commission more up-to-date material for all of his regional maps. Certainly, his atlas issued in 1662 would have looked very odd without a volume devoted to his home country!

This map, oriented west to
the top of the sheet, shows
the Third Quarter of the
province of Brabant. This
quarter is now more or less
equally divided between
Belgium and The
Netherlands. It is shown as
stretching from the Biesbos
in the north to just north of
Aarschot and includes the
great city of Antwerpen,
the crest of which
surmounts the title
cartouche. In this crest can
be seen two severed hands.

Many studies have been
made into the etymology of
the name Antwerpen
(sometimes seen as
Hantwerpen on old
engravings). One
assumption is 'aan de
werven' (at the quays), but
the most colourful story is
that of Brabo and Antigoon
(or Druoen). Antigoon was
a giant who cut off the
hands of those
bargemasters who refused
to pay the toll, throwing the
severed hands into the river.
Brabc met Antigoon in
combat on the Schelde, the
river on which the city is
situated. In the fight, Brabo
triumphed over the giant.
The severed hands
appeared for the first time
in 1230 on the crest of
Antwerpen.

Blaeu's map, first
published in 1635, was
based on a large-scale
survey of Brabant by
Michael Florisz van
Langren (*d.* 1675),
appointed mathematician
and astronomer to the King
of Spain in 1628.

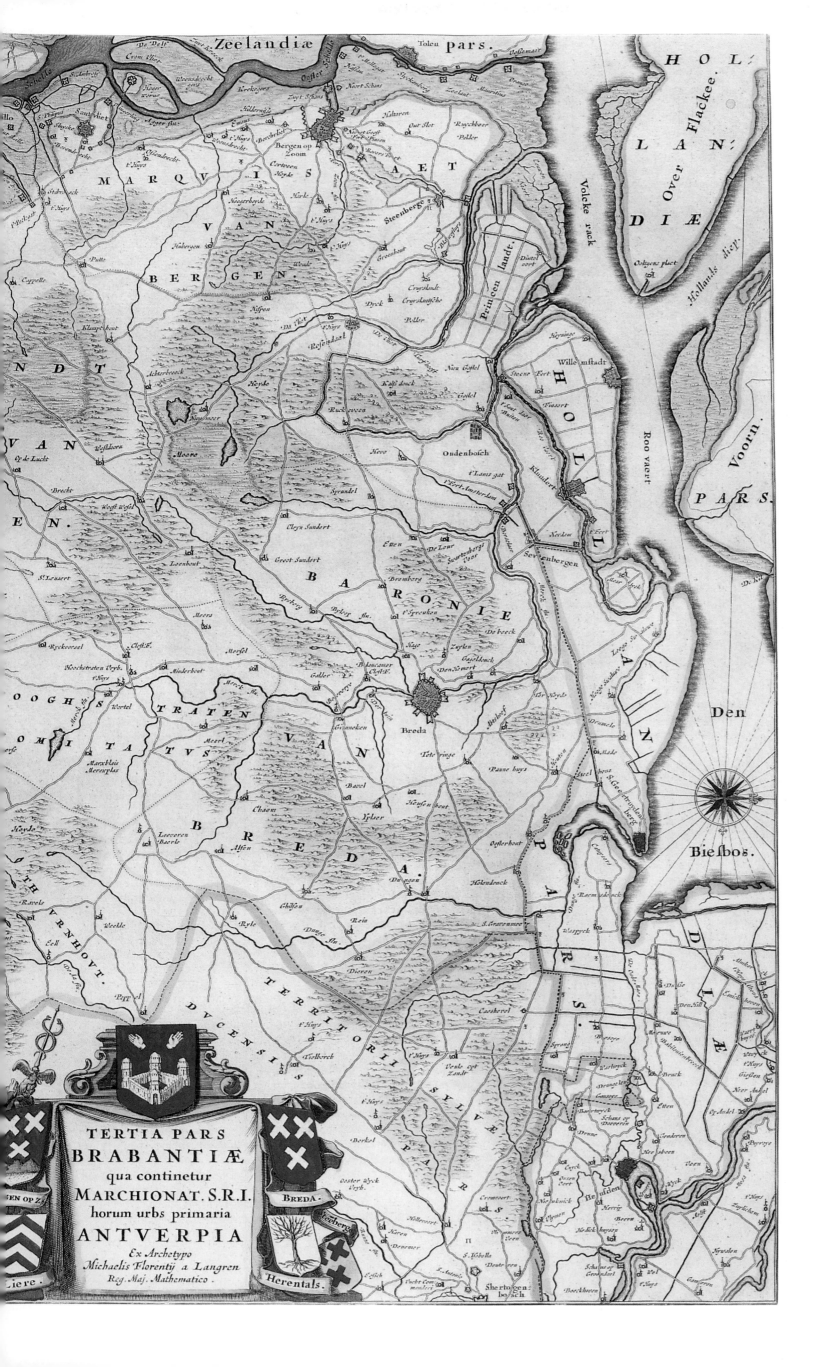

Caerte van de Scher-meer, Alsoo de selve is Bedyckt, ende by Cavels van 15 morgen suyver landt door lotinge uytgedelt, op den 25 October Anno 1635, ende aldus met groote verbeteringe int licht gegeven

Since about 1550, there had been a marked growth in the population of The Netherlands and this, combined with the destruction and uncertainty of food supplies during the long war with Spain, as well as an increase in the areas of land given over to peat workings, had led to an increase in the price of staple foods. So, the best soils were turned over to the plough and the reclamation of shallow lakes and sea inlets in the north of the country became a worthwhile proposition. Under the leadership of wealthy patricians from Amsterdam and other towns, some twenty-seven lakes to the north of Amsterdam were drained by 1640. The area shown on this map was one such lake, the Schermer, which lay immediately east of Alkmaar in the province of Noord-Holland. This drainage technique, known as *droogmakerijen*, was carried out by constructing dykes around the waterbody to be drained and then pumping it dry using pumps powered by windmills.

Drained between 1631 and 1635, the Schermer was the most successful of several similar projects in Noord-Holland during the first half of the seventeenth century. It took some forty mills to drain a lake nearly 4 m. deep in places and the drained land, or *polder*, is still in use today as an area of particularly rich farmland. The map shows

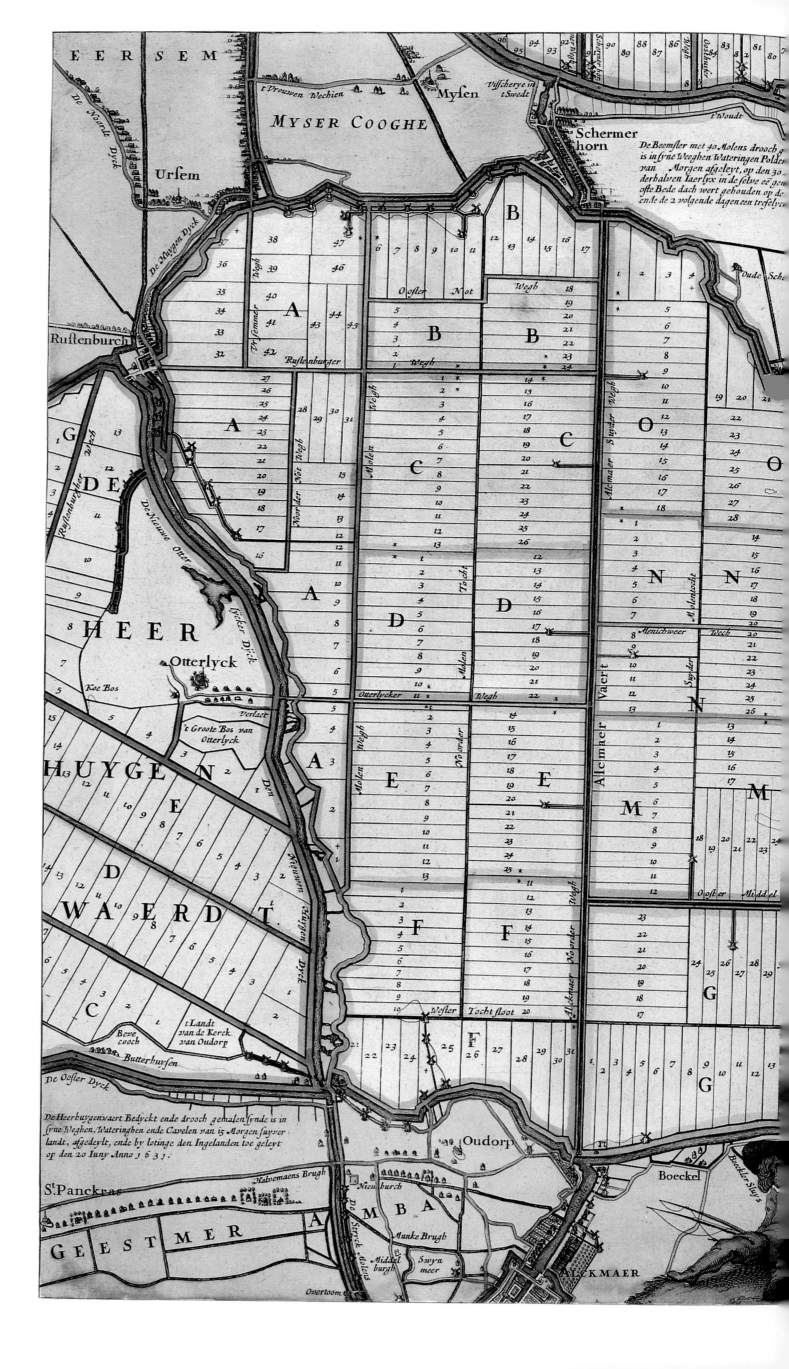

the several parcels or *kavels* of land 15 *morgen* in area (a little over 812 ha.) as declared in October 1635.

The author of the map is not known. It first appeared in Joan Blaeu's atlas in 1662, forming one of a small group of six similar maps of the seventeenth-century polders, some of which were derived from maps published as long before as 1617. That apart, it could be taken as a matter of pride that the relatively small Dutch Republic could muster the resources to carry out such ambitious and necessary projects in the centuries-long struggle against the sea.

Willem Blaeu's map of
Brabant (today divided
between Belgium and The
Netherlands) was first
published in an atlas in
1631. Oriented west to the
top of the plate, it shows
the course of the Maas (also
called the Meuse) in a great
U-shape, emptying into the
sea in the delta region of
the western Netherlands.

The design of this map
recalls that of several earlier
mapmakers, such as
Cornelius de Jode
(1568–1600) of Antwerpen,
or Jodocus Hondius
(1563–1612) of Amsterdam,
on whose work Blaeu
appears to have based much
of his information. The
provincial crest of Brabant
appears above the title
cartouche at the lower left-
hand corner.

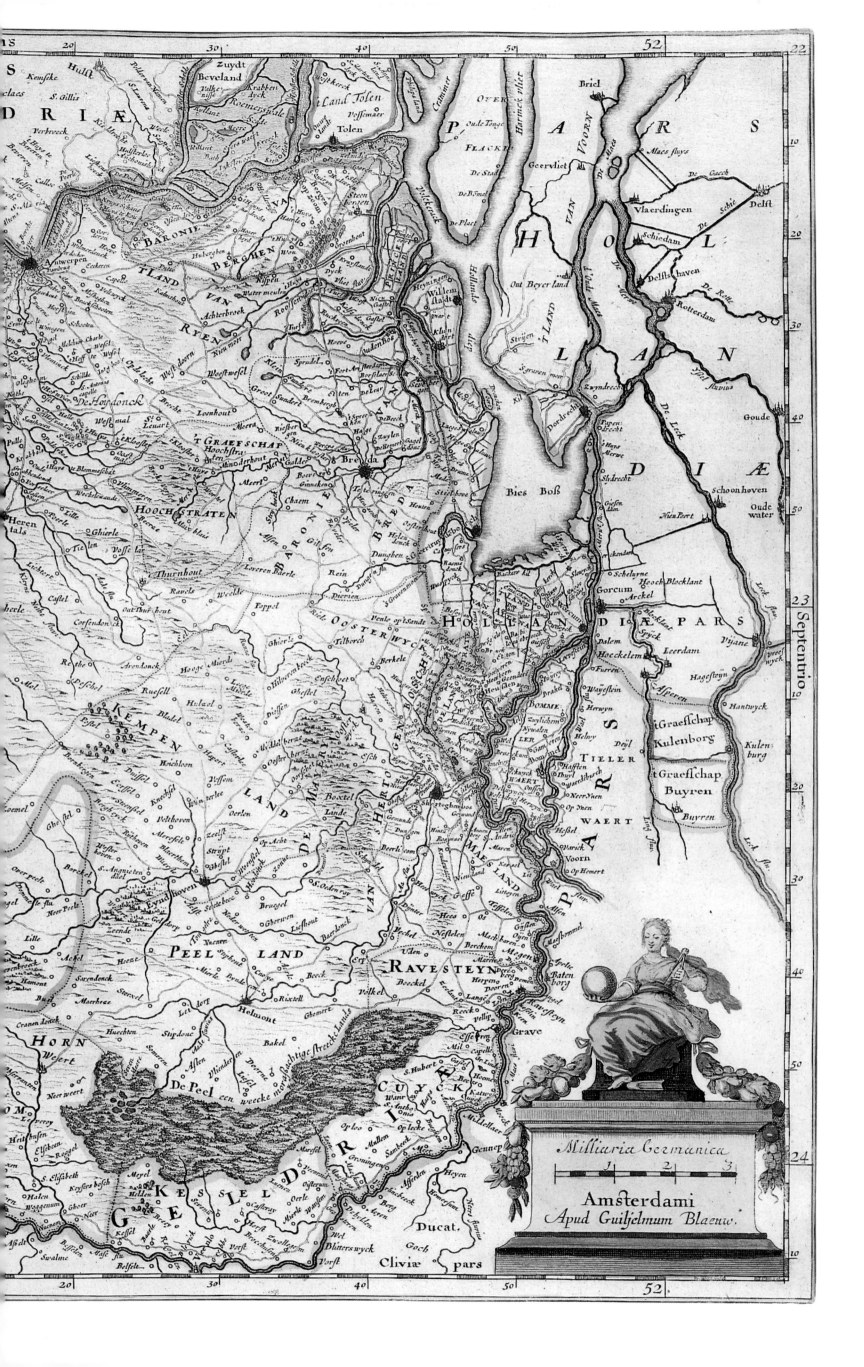

Milliaria Germanica

Amsterdami
Apud Guiljelmum Blaeuw.

Britannia prout divisa fuit temporibus Anglo-Saxonum praesertim durante illorum Heptarchia

This extremely decorative historical map of the British Isles first appeared in 1645, in the atlas volume devoted to the counties of England and Wales. An almost identical map was also issued by Blaeu's great rival publisher Joannes Jansson.

This dramatic piece shows the ancient divisions of the kingdom, the idea for which Blaeu took from a map in John Speed's *Theatre of the Empire of Great Britaine* of 1611. Here, Blaeu's unknown engraver has re-created Speed's side border vignettes as typically contemporary Dutch scenes to show the figures of seven Anglo-Saxon kings down the left-hand side to represent Kent, Sussex, Wessex, Essex, Northumberland, East Anglia and Mercia, while the vignettes at the right-hand side depict incidents from the turbulent history of the period.

Such elaborate maps as this required the abilities of the best colourists and, when coloured in the best contemporary tradition, Blaeu's historical map can often rank as one of the most decorative of all printed maps available to the modern collector.

OCEANVS

GERMANICVS;

Murray

Anglis

THE

GERMAN-

SEA.

BRITANNIA
prout divisa fuit temporibus
ANGLO-SAXONVM
praesertim durante illorum
HEPTARCHIA.

KINGDOME OF CLEVE LAND

YORKE

THE KINGDOME OF

MERCIA.

EAST ANGLES KINGDOM

EAST SAXONS KINGDOME

London

THE KINGDOM OF KENT

SOUTH SAXONS KINGDOME

Wight Iland

MARE BRITANNICUM.

GALLIA.

KENT
Ethelbert
595.

EAST
SAXON
Sebert
604.

EAST
ANGLE
Erpenwald
624.

NORTH
VMBER-
LAND
Edwin
627.

WEST
SAXON
Kengils
635.

MERCIA
Peada
650.

SOVTH
SAXON
Ethelwolfe
661.

73

Oxonium Comitatus, vulgo Oxford shire

Figures in academic robes to symbolize the University of Oxford support the title cartouche of Blaeu's county map.

In the side borders are shown the crests, with dates of foundation, of sixteen colleges, beginning with University College and concluding with Jesus College.

The map first appeared in Blaeu's atlas in 1645.

Wallia Principatus vulgo Wales

Aesthetically, this general map of the Principality, published by Joan Blaeu in 1645, is perhaps one of the most pleasing of all in his large cartographic output.

In common with most of Blaeu's English and Welsh maps, the detail is copied from John Speed's map of 1611, but instead of the severe strapwork ornamentation of the earlier model, Blaeu introduces an almost rococo flavour with his ornate cartouche, *putti*, beribboned coats of arms and the dedication within a cartouche composed of swags of fruit. Note also that Wales is drawn in a remarkably accurate outline.

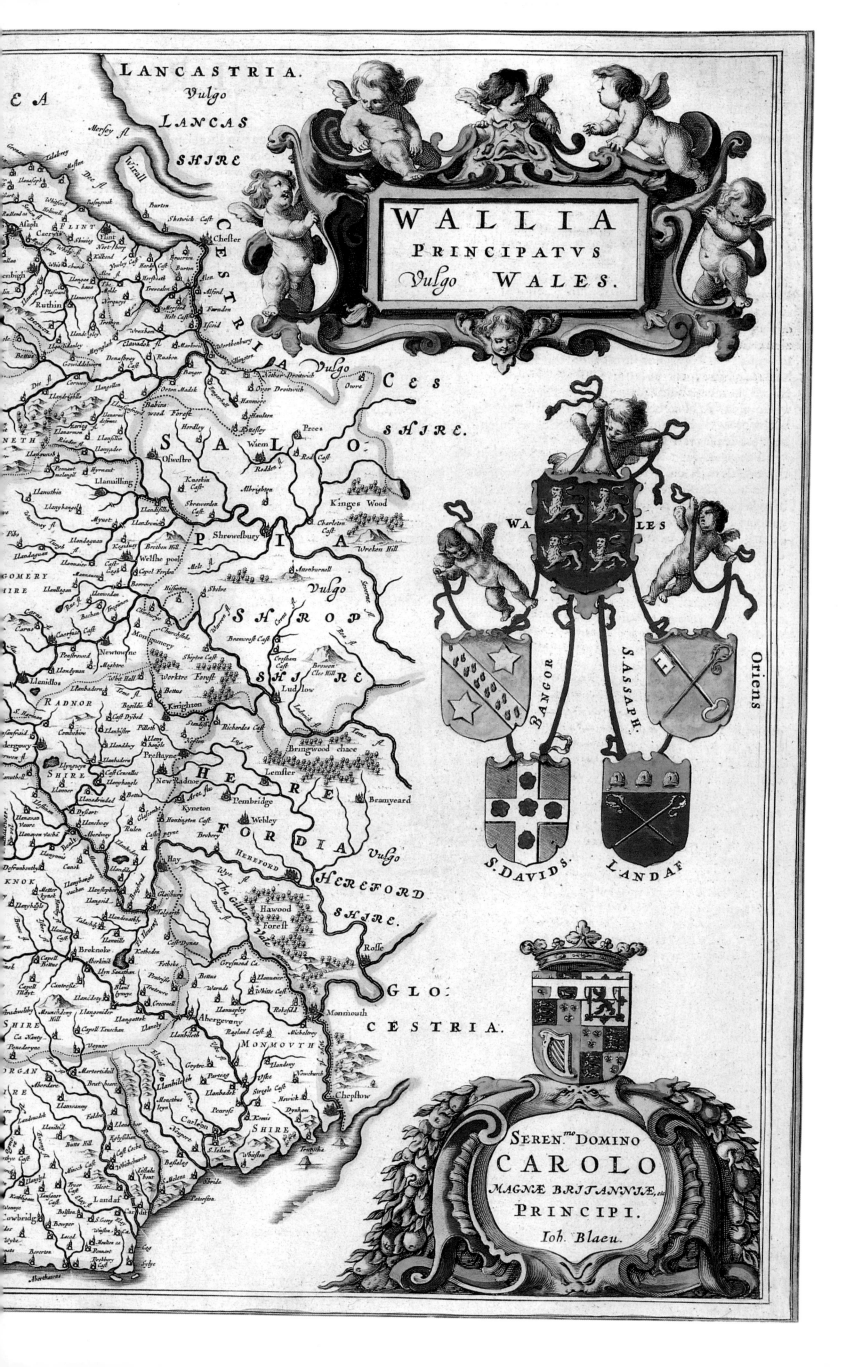

LANCASTRIA.
Vulgo
LANCAS
SHIRE

WALLIA
PRINCIPATVS
Vulgo WALES.

CESTRIA

CESHIRE.

Vulgo

SALO-

PIA

Vulgo

SHROP

SHIRE

Kinges Wood

Wreken Hill.

Shrewelbury

Ludlow

RADNOR

Bringwood chace

Lemfter

HERE

FORDIA

Vulgo

HEREFORD

SHIRE.

Rofle

GLO-

CESTRIA.

MONMOVTH

SHIRE

Chepftow

LANDAF

WA LES

BANGOR   S. ASSAPH.   Oriens

S. DAVIDS.   LANDAF

SEREN.mo DOMINO
CAROLO
MAGNÆ BRITANNIÆ, etc.
PRINCIPI.
Ioh. Blaeu.

77

This map of the north-western part of Wales, showing part of present-day Gwynedd and Môn is one of a group of ten in Blaeu's England and Wales atlas volume covering the old counties of Wales. The crest of the Prince of Wales is shown on the right-hand side above the title cartouche to symbolize Caernarfon as the place of investiture of the Princes.

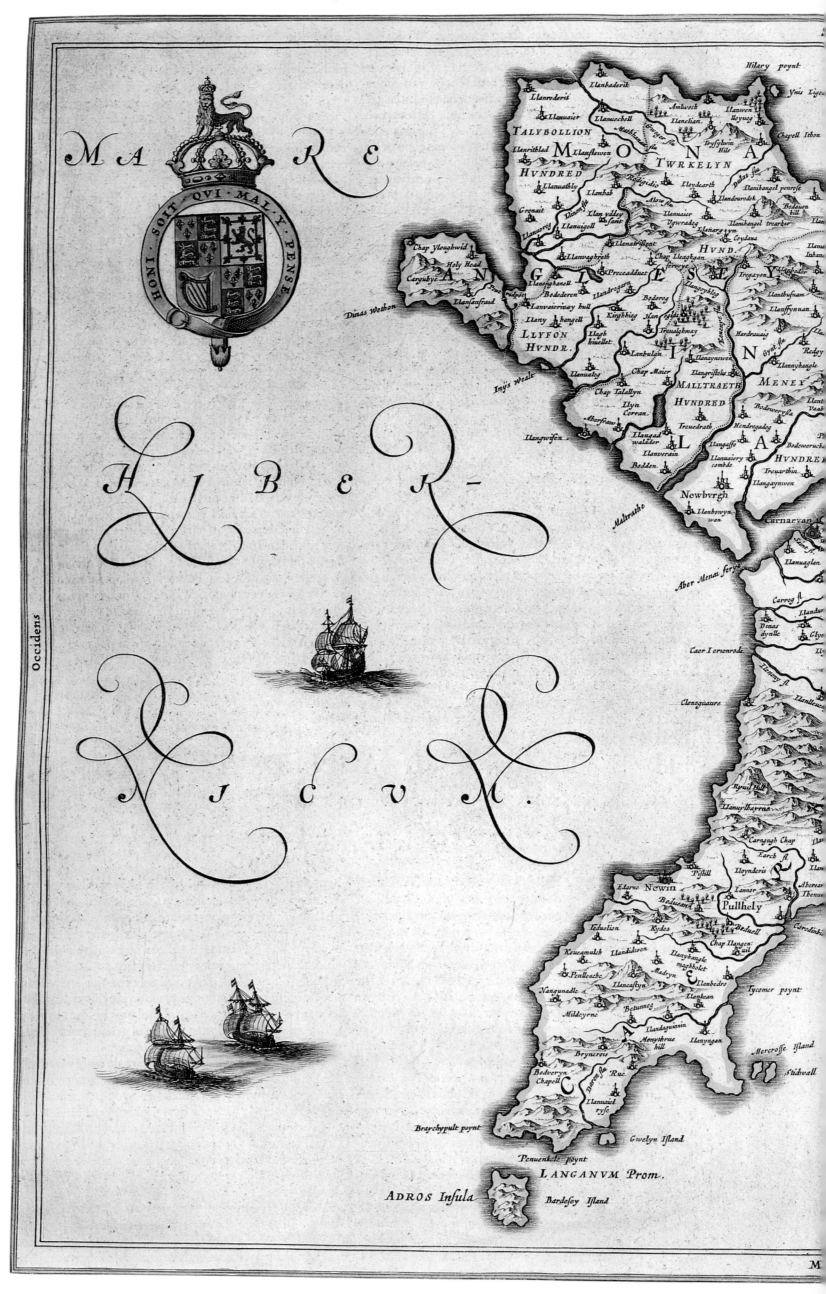

THE IRISH SEA.

CONOVII FLV. OSTIVM

DENBIGIENSIS

COMITATVS PARS;

PART OF

DENBIGH SHIRE.

MERVINIÆ COM=

TATVS PARS;

PART

OF

MERIO=

NETH

SHIRE.

COMITATVS
CAERNARVO=
NIENSIS;
Vernacule
CARNARVON-SHIRE.
et
MONA INSVLA
Vulgo
ANGLESEY.

Milliaria Anglica quorum quatuor æquip. 1 German.

Oriens

CHE DIENE

Cumbria, vulgo Cumberland

Joan Blaeu's map of Cumberland first appeared in 1645. Like many of his county maps, this includes some charming decorative detail: the cartouche at the lower right-hand corner includes illustrations of such pastoral and rural occupations as sheep-rearing on the fells, ploughing and broadcasting seed. Although the topographical content was copied from Speed, Blaeu succeeds in giving the impression of an entirely new map by the use of his carefully balanced decoration.

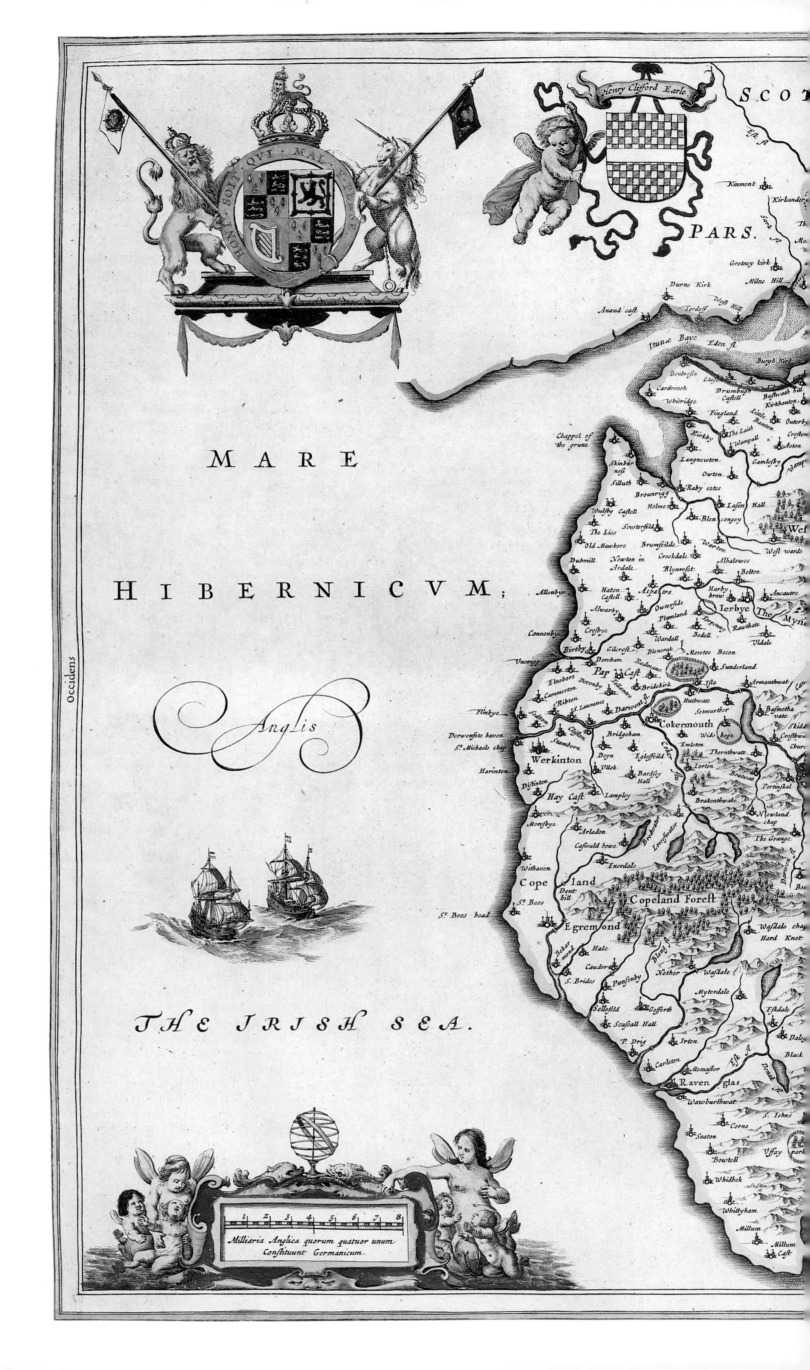

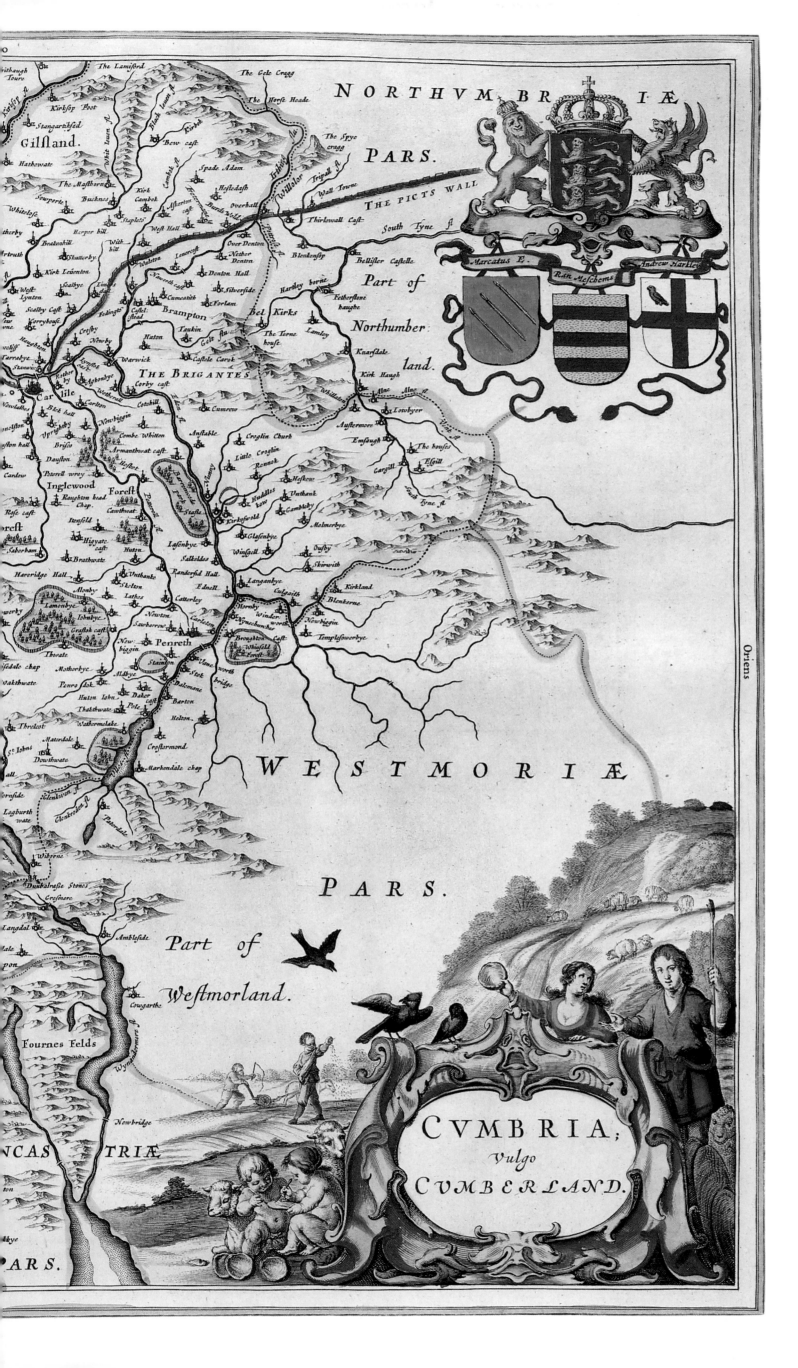

NORTHVMBRIÆ

PARS.

THE PICTS WALL

Gilsland.

South Tyne fl.

Part of

Northumber·

land.

THE BRIGANTES

Oriens

WESTMORIÆ

PARS.

Part of

Westmorland.

Fournes Felds

NCASTRIÆ

PARS.

Marcatus E.   *Ran Mescheus*   *Andrew Harkley*

CVMBRIA;
vulgo
CVMBERLAND.

Sarnia Insula, vulgo Garnsey; et Insula Caesarea, vernacule Iarsey

For this map of the Channel Islands, Blaeu used the map published by John Speed in his atlas of the British Isles published in 1611 for such features as place name detail and topography. The decorative features are, however, Blaeu's own, almost giving the map the appearance of a sea chart, with its finely engraved sailing vessels and the distinctly marine aspect of the scale cartouche shown at the upper right.

The map appeared for the first time in Joan Blaeu's England and Wales atlas volume in 1645.

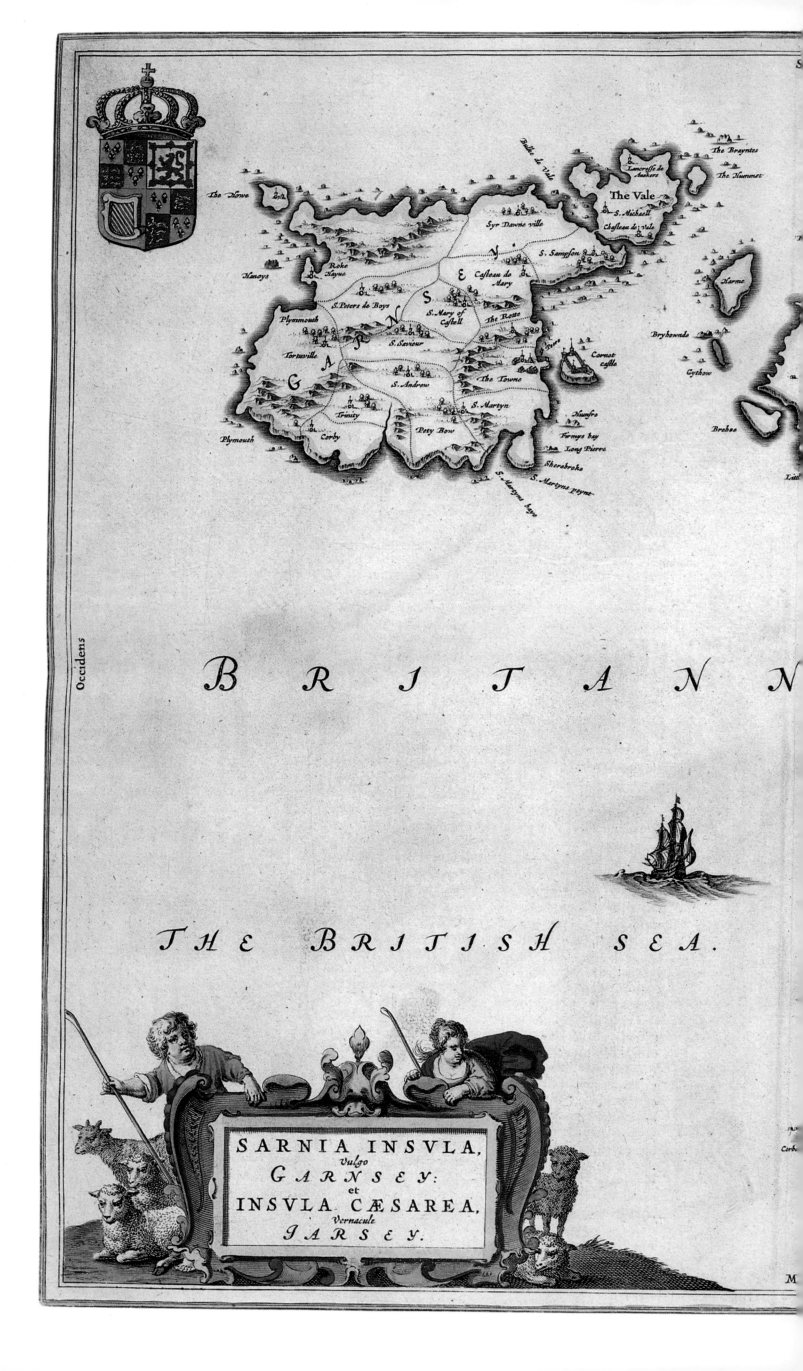

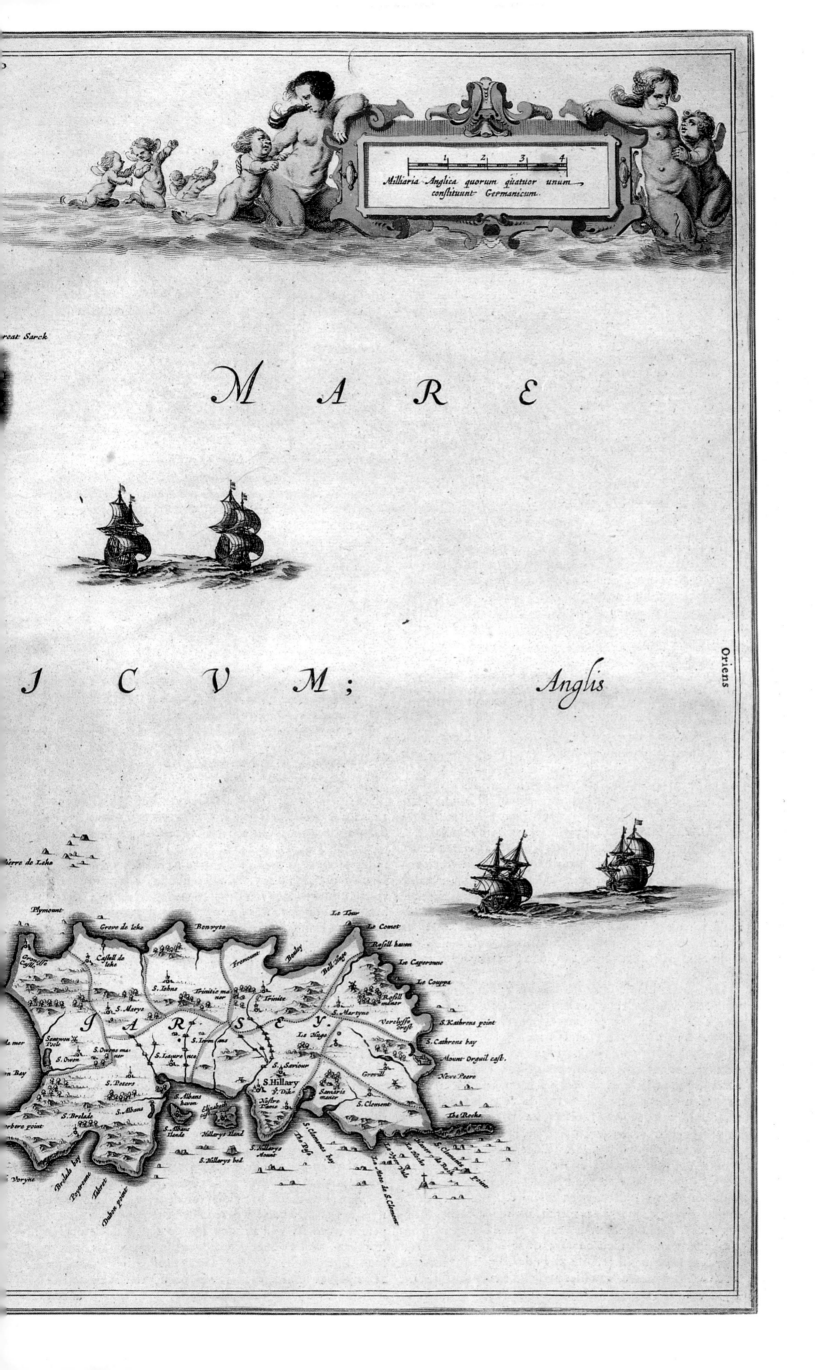

MARE

Oriens

JCVM;   Anglis

reat Sarck

Pierre de Leke

Plymount-   Le Tour
        Greve de Leke   Bonvyte   Le Conet
                                          Rosell haven
Groville   Castell de   Le Caperonne
Castle   leke   Le Couppa
                           Fremonte Badley
         S. Johns   Bell Inga
              Trinitie manor   Trinite   Rosell
         S. Marye   S. Martyne miner
     JA   RS   EY.   Vercleffe
Semproun   S. Trom ons   Le Nago   crest   S. Kathrens point
Poele S. Ovens ma=   S. Cathrons bay
S. Oven   nor   S. Laurence   Mount Orguil cast.
        S. Peters   S. Saviour   Grosvill   Newe Peere
                               S. Hillary
  S. Brelade   S. Dike   Samaris
         S. Albans   S. Albans Nostre   manor
               haven   Dame   S. Clement
erbore point   Elizabeth   the Rocks
               S. Albans
                Ilande   Hillarys Iland
                         S. Hillarys Asont S. Clemanns
  Voryne   S. Hillarys bed   The Poll
Brelade bay
     Payeronne
         Dubon point

Scotia regnum cum insulis adjacentibus

Both this and the two following maps were first published by Joan Blaeu in 1654, in the first atlas devoted to Scotland.

This completely new (in 1654) general map of Scotland owes its origin to the surveys of Robert Gordon (1580–1661) of Straloch in Aberdeenshire, acknowledged by Joan Blaeu himself as a 'Doyen of geographers'. Previously, mapmakers had had to rely on a map published by the great sixteenth-century mapmaker, Gerard Mercator, who had died in 1595, his map remaining as the standard outline for Scotland for some sixty years until the appearance of Gordon's map under the aegis of Blaeu.

The volume devoted to Scotland as published by Blaeu contains three general maps and some forty-six county maps, all engraved at the Blaeu establishment after the surveys and drawings of Robert Gordon, and those of a fellow Scot, Timothy Pont (c. 1560s–c. 1614?) who is believed to have carried out his surveys of the counties of Scotland at some time prior to 1601 before he became minister of Dunnet in Caithness. Very little is known of the life of Timothy Pont. His manuscripts came into the possession of Sir James Balfour, historian and antiquary, who purchased them from Pont's heirs sometime before 1629 with the intention of publishing them. Shortly after, in 1630, a correspondent of Willem and Joan Blaeu, Sir John Scot of Scotstarvet, informed the Blaeus of the existence of the manuscript maps. As early as 1626, Willem Blaeu had asked

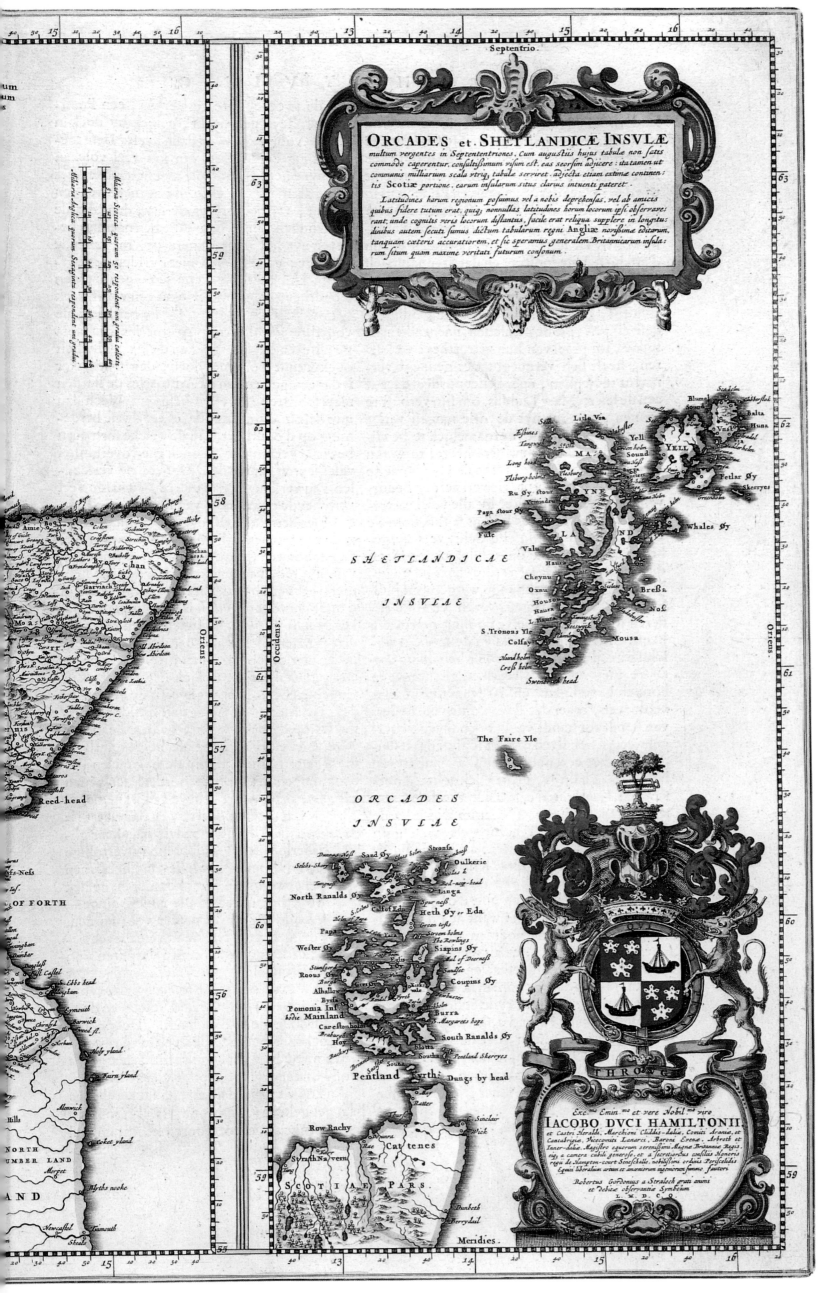

Scot to search for suitable maps of Scotland which could be published in any future atlas. It seems that Gordon was subsequently engaged to correct the manuscripts or bring them up to date in order that they could then be engraved and published in atlas form. Printing of the sheets appears to have been under way during 1649, but preparation and publication then seems to have been delayed because of the Civil War in England (Sir John Scot, a royalist, was removed from office as director of the Scottish Chancery) and also the Anglo-Dutch War of 1652–1654.

Of the published maps of Scotland, numbering forty-six in all, thirty-six are ascribed to Timothy Pont, the remainder either anonymous or attributable to Gordon. The text of the atlas was written by Robert Gordon, which he called 'Chorographical description', incorporating the work of Timothy Pont, as well as texts from antiquarians such as William Camden.

Of all the volumes of the Blaeu atlas, it is, therefore, this volume devoted to Scotland that is by far the best documented so far as its source materials are concerned, and it is also the only volume for which so much original manuscript cartographic material survives to this day. In fact, this can be said not only of the Blaeu atlas, but also of nearly all contemporary atlases published in Europe.

Skia vel Skiana. The Yle of Skie

This is Timothy Pont's map of Skye – the first separate map of the island – as engraved and published by Joan Blaeu in 1654. It should be noted that there no longer exists a manuscript of Pont's for this map as it appears to have been engraved and printed without further reference on the part of Blaeu to his correspondents in Scotland. It is quite probable that this and other manuscript materials perished in the fire at Blaeu's establishment in 1672.

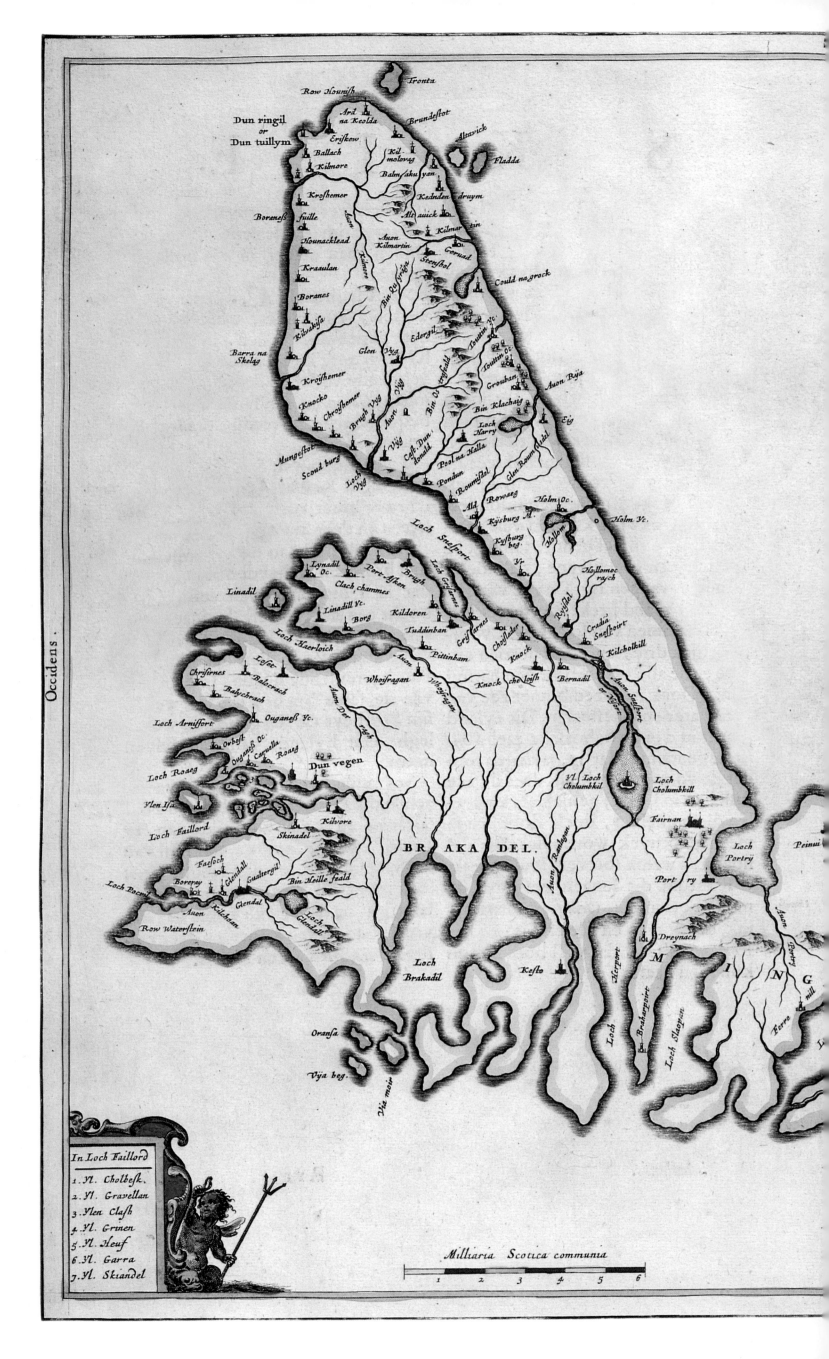

86

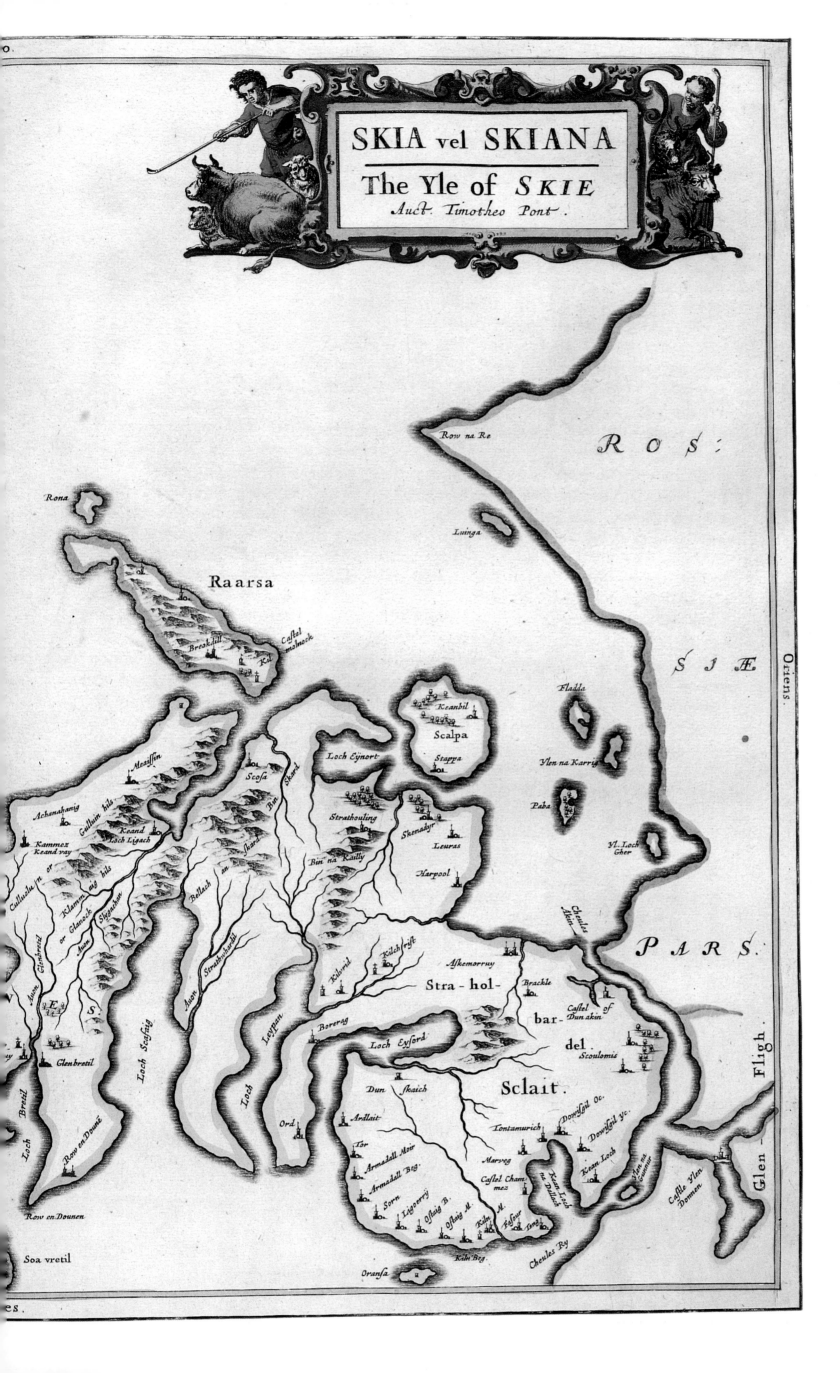

SKIA vel SKIANA
The Yle of *SKIE*
Auct. Timotheo Pont.

Row na Re

R O S :

Rona

Luinga

S I Æ

Raarsa

Oriens.

Fladla

Keanbil

Breakhill

Caftel molnock

Kil

Scalpa

Vlen na Karrig

Loch Eynort

Stappa

Paba

Meaffin

Scofa

Skerd

Bin

Achanahanig

Galluin hils

Strathouling

Skenadyr

Vl. Loch Gher

Kammez Keand may

Keand Loch Ligach

Bin na Railly

Leuras

Cullanlum or Klamm mig hils

Bellach an Shard

Aun

Harpool

Cheulas Akin

Sligachan

Strathnihardil

P A R S.

Aun Glenbretil

Kilchrift

Afkemorruy

Kilvril

Stra - hol -

Brackle

Caftel of Dun akin

E S.

Loch Seafnig

Aun

Leypain

Borerag

Loch Eyfford

bar -

del

Scoulomis

Glenbretil

Loch

Ord

Sclait.

Loch

Dun fkaich

Tontamurich

Dowifgil Oc.

Dowifgil Yc.

Ardlait

Row en Doune

Tor

Marveg

Kean Loch

Glen - Fligh.

Armadall Moir

Caftel Cham mez

Kean Loch na Dallach

Armadall Beg.

Vlen na Guamir

Row en Dounen

Sorn

Ligorry

Oftaig B.

Oftaig M.

Kile M.

Befour

Tong.

Caftle Vlen Donnen

Soa vretil

Kiln Beg

Cheulas Ry

Oranfa

es .

**Praefectura Renfroana
vulgo dicta Baronia.
The Baronie of Renfrow**

This fine and detailed map
is one of the Pont series for
which a manuscript still
exists, having been drafted
or corrected by Robert
Gordon from Pont's
sources, Blaeu's printed
version showing no fewer
than six-hundred-and-fifty-
six place names!

Marked on the map are
Glasgow, Govan, Renfrew
and Paisley as well as an
accurate depiction of the
river systems of the region.
This map shows another
feature of the Blaeu series
covering Scotland: the
blank cartouches and
escutcheons – not all of the
sheets having been given
dedications.

PRÆFECTURA
RENFROANA
Vulgo dicta
BARONIA

THE BARONIE OF
RENFROW

Timotheus Pont Auctor.

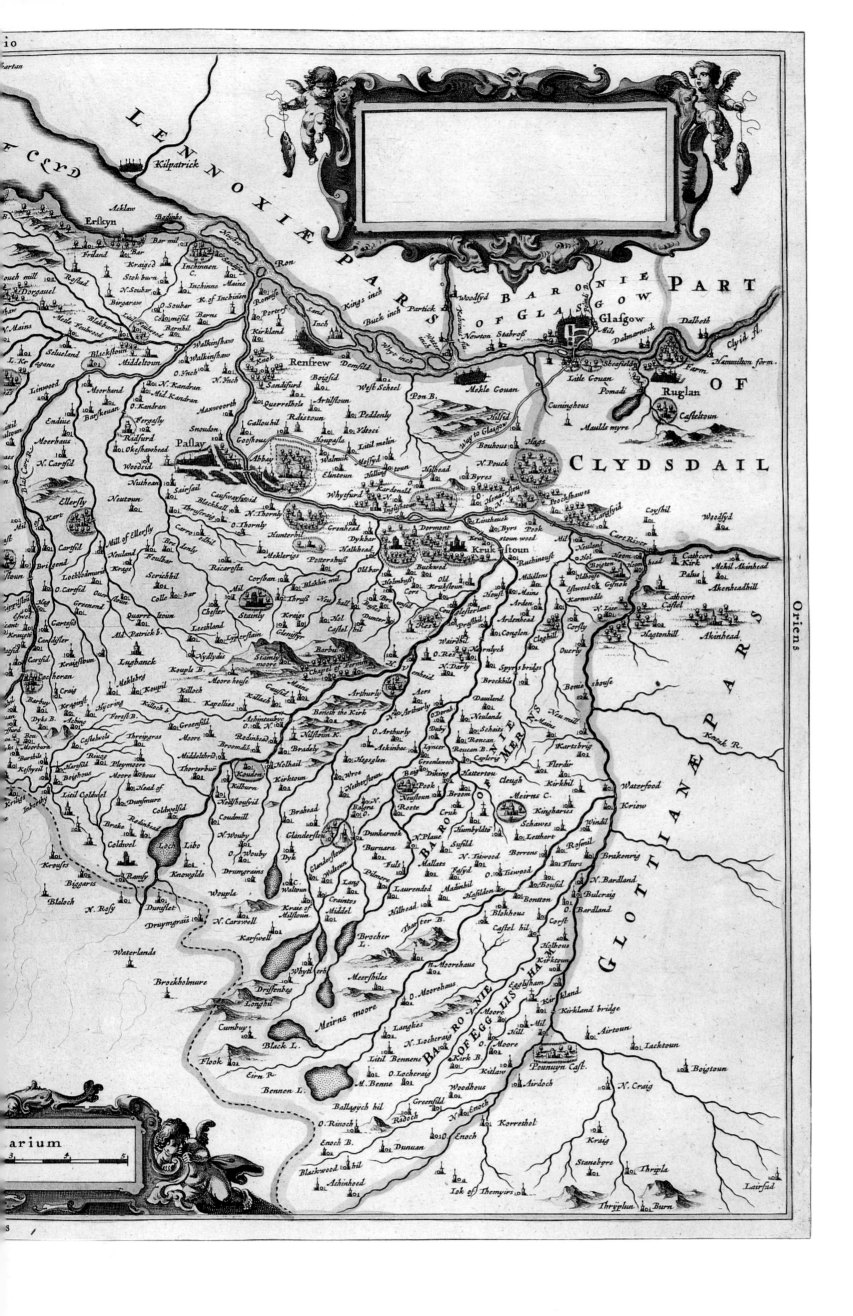

LENNOXIÆ PARS

F CLYD

BARONIE PART
OF GLASGOW

CLYDSDAIL

Kilpatrick

Erſkyn

Renfrew

Paſlay

Kruk stoun

Glasgow

Ruglan

Oriens

MERNS PARS

GLOTTIANÆ PARS

BARONIE OF EGGLISHAM

arium

89

Hibernia regnum vulgo Ireland

Willem Blaeu's highly decorative general map of Ireland is coloured to show in outline the ancient provinces of Connaught, Leinster, Munster and Ulster each of which, together with a map of Carlow, was given a separate map in a section at the end of the atlas volume devoted to Scotland.

The map, which Blaeu first issued in 1635 (twenty years prior to the publication of the Scotland and Ireland volume), was based on that published by John Speed in 1611 in his *Theatre of the Empire of Great Britaine*. In its turn, Speed's map was copied by Hondius and Blaeu's great rival Joannes Jansson. It was this latter version that Willem Blaeu used. His beautifully balanced design is complemented by the Royal arms and the relatively simple title cartouche at the left-hand side.

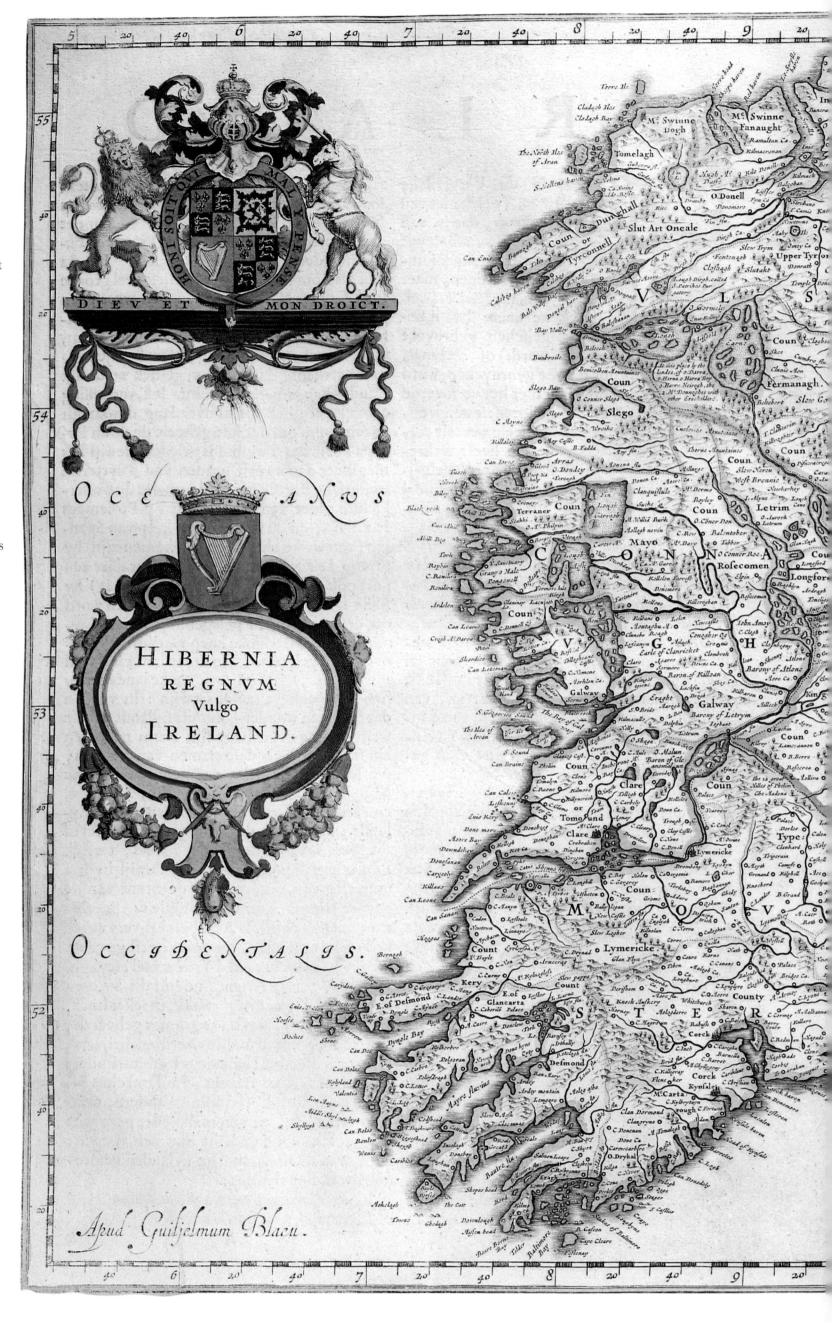

Ultonia; Hibernis Cui-guilly; Anglis Ulster

Joan Blaeu's handsome map of the province of Ulster (he produced separate maps for Connaught, Leinster and Munster as well) was issued in 1654.

One of the ancient provinces of Ireland, Ulster consists of nine counties, six of which, Antrim, Armagh, Down, Fermanagh, Londonderry and Tyrone, remain today in the United Kingdom. It was into this part of Ireland that settlers from outside the country were brought, mainly from Lowland Scotland, as 'planters'. This process began during the sixteenth century but continued until the middle of the seventeenth after Cromwell's conquest of Ireland in 1649–1650, the consequences of which remain unresolved to this day. Belfast is shown as a relatively insignificant town. Blaeu indicates several castles and forts as well as, by the banks of the Blackwater in County Armagh, *Owen Maugh the ancient seat of the Kinges of Ulster.*

Much of the information on this map comes from the regional map made by the English cartographer John Speed (1552–1629) for his British Isles atlas in 1611.

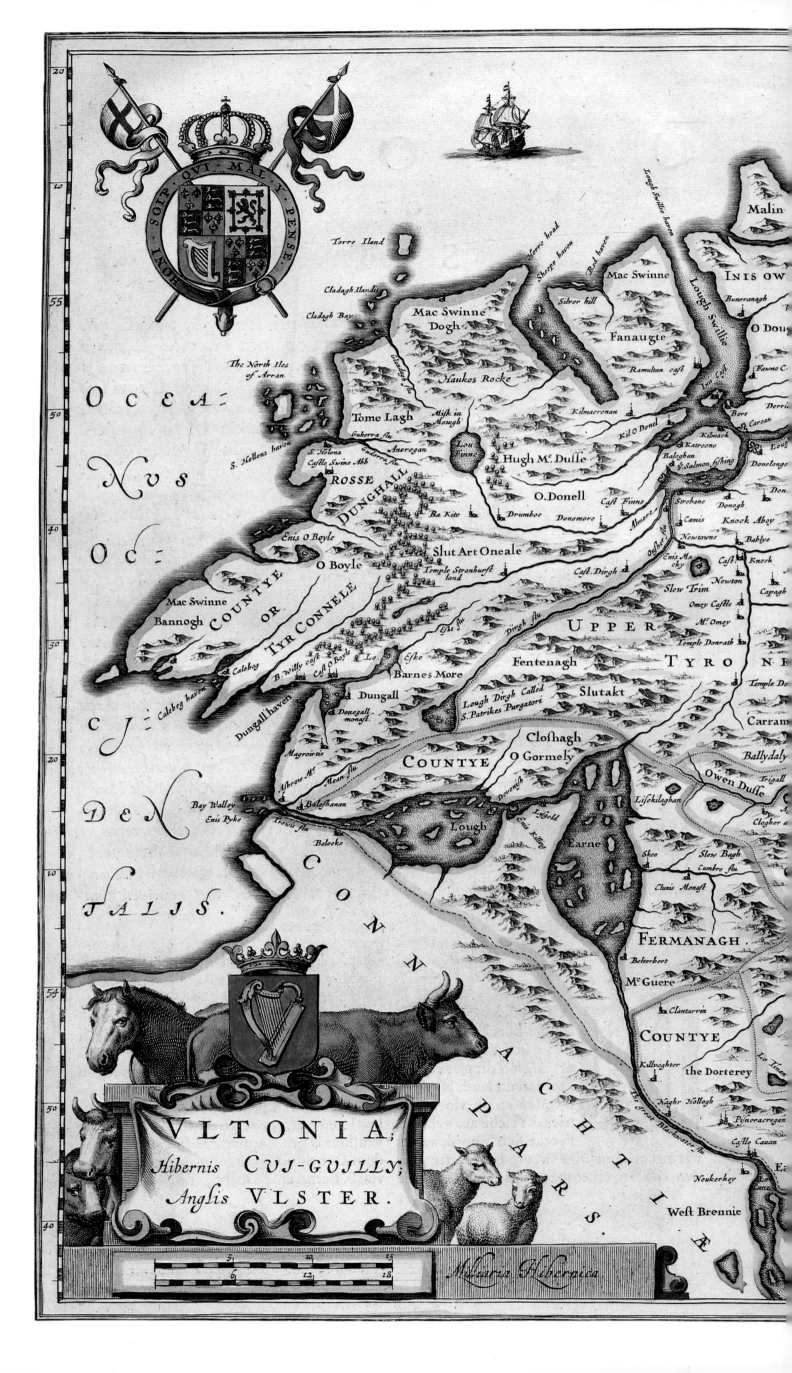

Gallia. Le Royaume de France

This magnificent general map was first published by the Blaeus in 1631, enjoying a long life as an atlas map into the 1660s. By the time the great atlas was published, the map was the first of a series of general and regional maps of France numbering more than sixty sheets spread over two volumes.

Blaeu shows a France that was the largest unified nation of Western Europe, stretching from the Pyrenees to the Pas de Calais and from Bretagne to Provence. But although unified in a political sense, France was still essentially regional in character, with a line of buffer territories, according to Blaeu's map at least, between it and the German Empire to the east.

Blaeu dedicated a copy of his atlas to Louis XIV in 1663 during a time of relative peace in the affairs of France. Although both civil and international wars had impeded progress and trade, the early years of the reign of Louis XIV from 1661 onwards gave France an opportunity to catch up with its rivals, the richness of French resources and a population of some twenty million playing a large part in these developments. No doubt the inclusion of a large number of maps of the kingdom of Louis enabled Blaeu to sell a significant number of copies of his atlas there. Nevertheless, Blaeu mapped a country of which Louis could write in his *Mémoires* that 'Tout était calme en tout lieu; ni mouvement ni apparence de mouvement dans le royaume qui pût m'interrompre et s'opposer à mes projets: la paix était établie avec mes voisins…'.

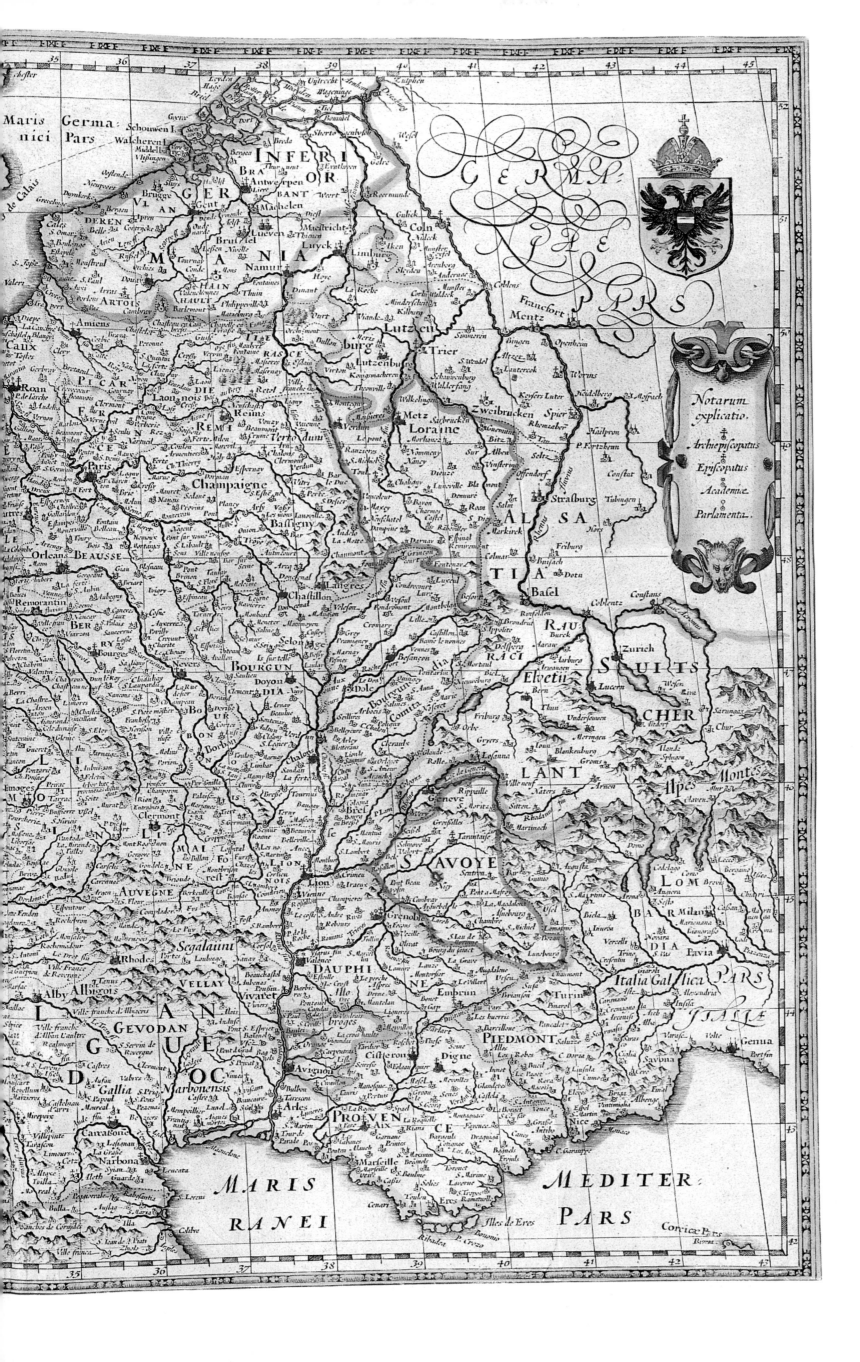

Ager Parisiensis vulgo l'Isle de France

This map of the immediate environs of Paris dates back in origin to the late sixteenth-century map by the cartographer François de la Guillotière of Berry. It was later used by Jean le Clerc in about 1620 and it was this version that Willem Blaeu adapted for his own atlas of 1634.

Many of the small towns surrounding Paris, shown here as a compact, walled city astride the Seine, remain familiar as the names of the several surburbs, or *faubourgs*, of modern Paris.

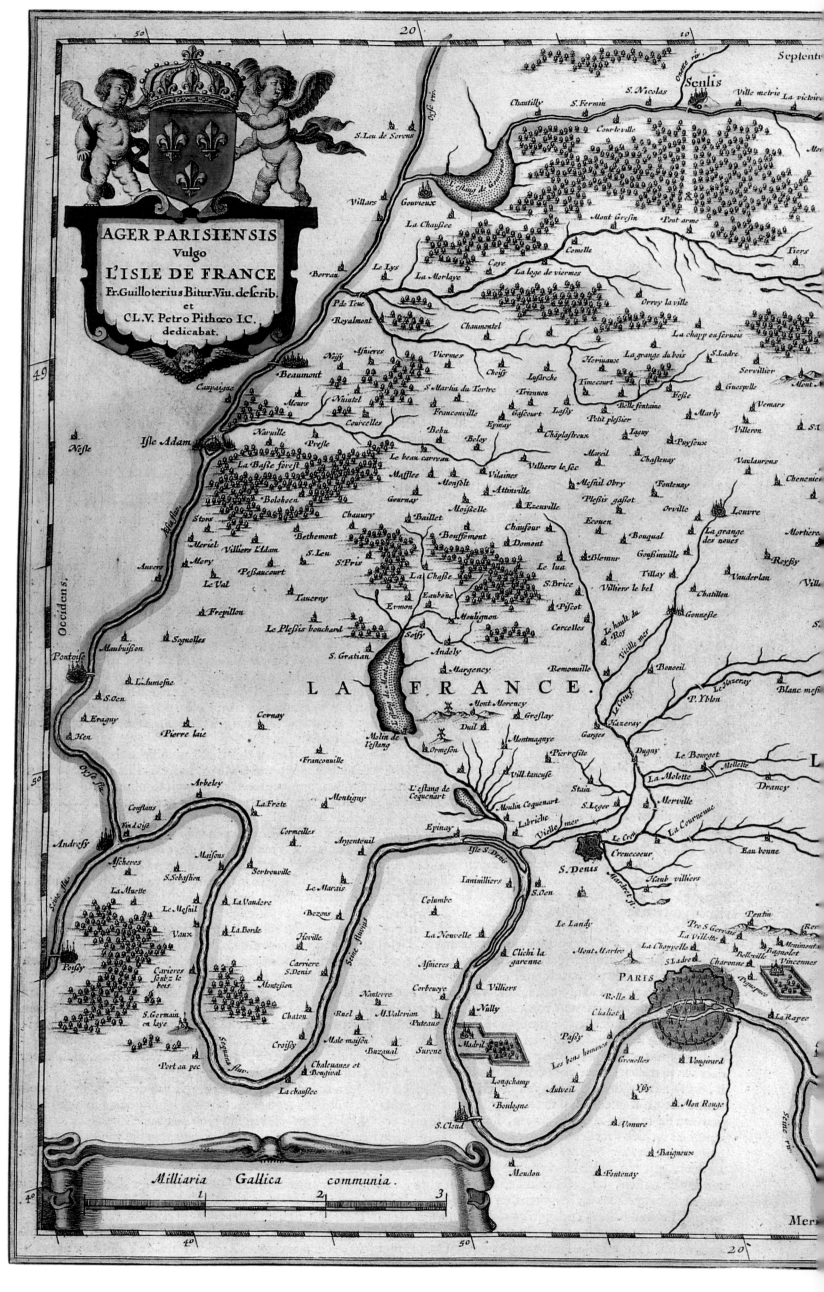

AGER PARISIENSIS
Vulgo
L'ISLE DE FRANCE
Fr. Guilloterius Bitur. Viu. deſcrib.
et
CL. V. Petro Pithœo I.C.
dedicabat.

LA FRANCE.

PARIS

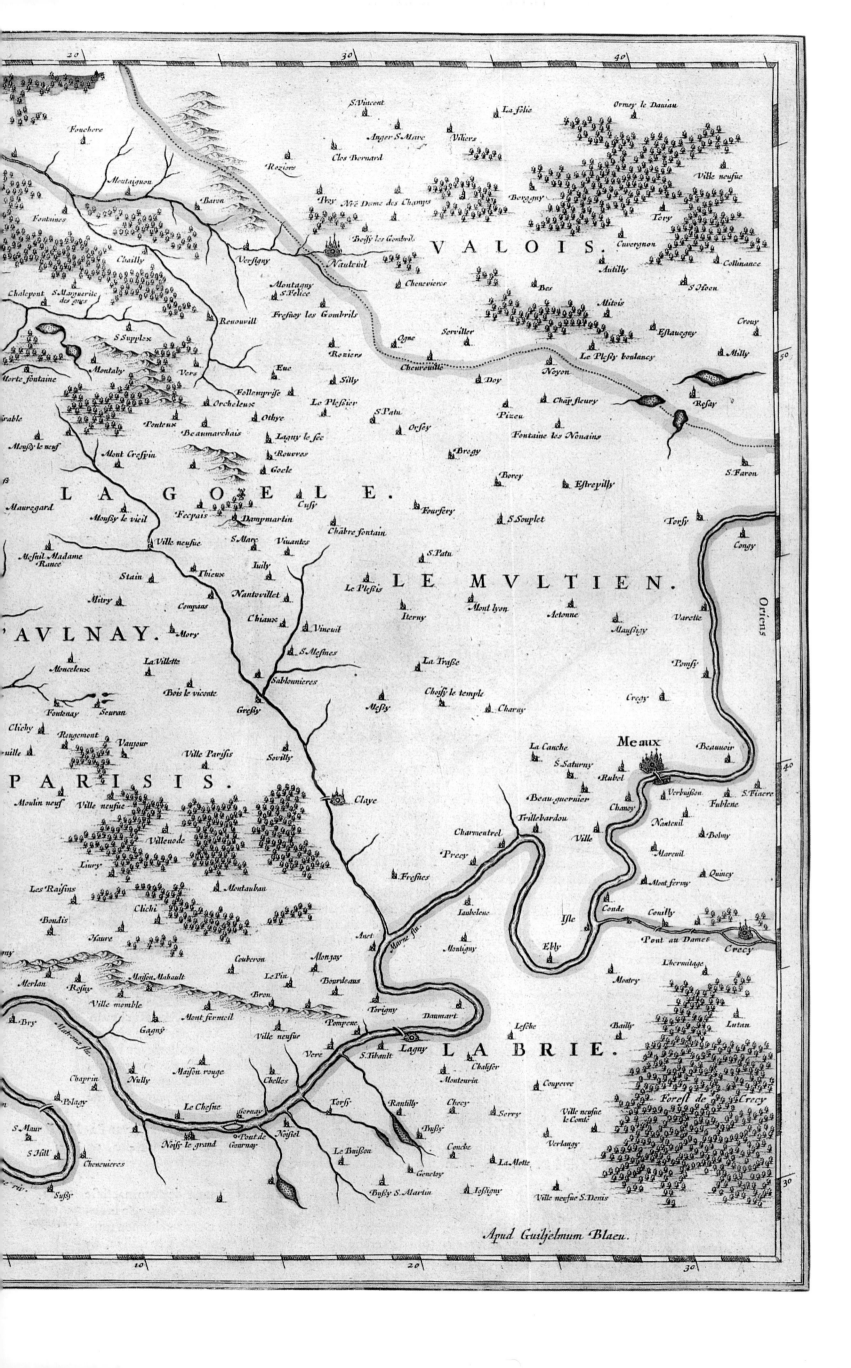

Le Pais de Brie

Willem Blaeu's map of the Brie region to the south-east of Paris, first published in the atlas of 1634, was based on a map by Jean le Clerc published sometime before 1620.

This part of the Paris basin produced much of the foodstuffs to feed the half million or so inhabitants of Paris at the time, in particular wheat and the famous cheese which takes its name from this region.

PARTIE DE LA

LE PAIS DE BRIE.

CHAMPAGNE

Chateauthierry · Meffy

Effonne · Parois

Beffy · Sauigny

Villers · Chertaife · Saconnel

Vanerou · Changy · Neuteial · Mont en: · bonnet · Beaulne

La ferte Souz Jouerre · S. Falde · Conde · Montigny · Pecigny

Euffy · Couigny · Luffenfy · Cherly · Cochery · Nogentel · Vabande

Marne · Trilport · Armentier · Villers · La Malle Maifon · Verbeny

Nanteuel · Monceaulx · Iouare les nonnains · Les Mulliers · Sitey · Pauem · Nogen lartot · Vifort · Remandice

Marueille · S. Iehan des Iumeaulx · Fais · La Grange Meouffee · Bailleaux · Buffiere · La Chapelle Soubz chery · Rozois gatebles · Leculle

Roife · Coulaume · S. Fiacre · Barbuffe · Signaus · Dou · Lille · Vieulx Maifons · Verdeu

Creffy · Fauffy · Ville marcuile · Serbonne · Pierre · Lera deneloure · Sablonierre · La Chapelle Verenge · Viemone · Fontenelle · Mondefin · Lepme du bois · Verdou

Mafar · Maifonfelle · Lavibe · Nologne · Vardelot · Mont miralle

Tigeft · Guerard · Villers · Coulommiers · Rebes · Les broiffes · Lacelle · Ceuus · Vernam

Demarlin · La Celle · Bornay · Montenglo · Meuren · Boify · S. Martin en beaulieu · Coleson · Montollinet · Meringes · Corbetout

Orneeux · Frennoher · Poumerfe · Chailly · S. Augustin · S. Simeon · Vierfcheu · Poumeffon

Pezarche · Torguin · Bizay · Beautel · La vanne · Villers les Mailles · Montigny · Marches · Rieux · Bergere

Le pleffy franffon · Vodois · Lais · S. Remy de la Vanne · S. Bertolme · La Chapelle Verenge · Chalidon · Yeziee · Madenay · Bouchy

Landois · Buffier · Les bordes · Malleuoux · La ferte gauche · Villeneufue · Morfigne · Sedane

Grange Ieaeaux · Courtuenay · La garge mouerri · Petrelct · La Lionne S. Coulombe · Meloray · Teefont · Chaudion · Lanoue · Efternay

Peffy · Ancorbiet · Villers Templon · Charterouge · Rouillon · Neuuy

Galin · Beaulieu · Les tris maifons · Fetnuict · Ludon · Vieux maifons · S. Coulombe · Belleau · Lshert

Chapelle liger · Iouy le chaflellet · Brislan · Maifonfelle · Bonfrey · S. Martien du Bouchet · Eftarde · Les effere le Vicente

Cromuoify · Le petit pais · Bezica · Baeu · Courben · Mars · Monglas · Sauify · Coureinaule · Les bois de la Conteffe

Clois fontaine · Villessemm · Chaufenay · Chancoille · Monceaux · S. Bon · S. Genois · La forftiere

Chateau beau · La Croix · Geudelet · Anaris · Flins · Villers · S. george · Bouchery · Neue · Bet

Rampillon · La Courolige · Couttemieux · Chenaife · Savigny · Repeeufe · Boffay · Villegnay · Ment Efaillon · Fontigni · Dina · Chaytamarne

Vanvilles · Vieux Champagne · Le pleffy aux tuirnelles · Mortery · Roully · S. george · Limet · S. Martin des · Pignou · Villenoce

Foulque · La maifon Rouge · Chalebenois · Villeneufue · Dacolt · Le pleffy poil de chien · S. Martin du chantron · Fonteney · La gueas au bois · Courriole

Senguel · La Chapelle S. fuplice · Landois · Prouins · Lemee · Le chale · Mont le Pelier

Feuify · S. Leup · Courtan · S. Brice · Richekour · Le pleffy soubz baruaille

Moup en montois · Lazinee · Lours · Seneille · Charlotte la petite · Soukouy · Le pleffy · Gaillard · Mont genoul

Dame marie · Intigny · Longueuille · Courriole · Villenoce

Deutilly · Samins · Charlamaifon · Vachy · Fantome au bois · Charlotte la grande · Le pleffy

Preailly · Segis · Lemollin Dourle · Gois · Hermee · Feuhiers · Refon · Courriman

Coureflles · Segis · Vifpell · Pallois · Couture · Enerly · Lecheffes · Blunet · Beaulieu · La Chapelle S. Nicolas · La feffola

Charltraie · S. Saucur · Les ormes · Flambeing · Noien · Aefte · Merlot · Pons Sur Seinne

Le pleffy · Bellouet · Monfeaut · Aomy · Quegay · Fleury · Afmily · La Mote · Bernier · Courman

Grauon · Baxoche · Bray · Villiers · Villeneffe · Corferoy · Nogen · Marnay

Oriens

CHAMPAGNE

50 · 40 · 30 · 20 · 10 · 48

Guilielmus Blaeu excudit.

99

Willem Blaeu's fine map of Lac Léman or Lake Geneva, first issued in 1634, credits authorship to the Genève mapmaker, Jacques Goulart (1580–1622).

An important Hansa town with a fair for traders from northern and southern Europe during the Medieval period, Genève also gave rise to the new wave of Protestantism which swept through Europe during the sixteenth century. Jean Calvin (1509–1564), a Frenchman, spread his ideas from Genève from 1541, the movement which became known as Calvinism gaining a rapid hold in France, Germany and the Low Countries within a few years.

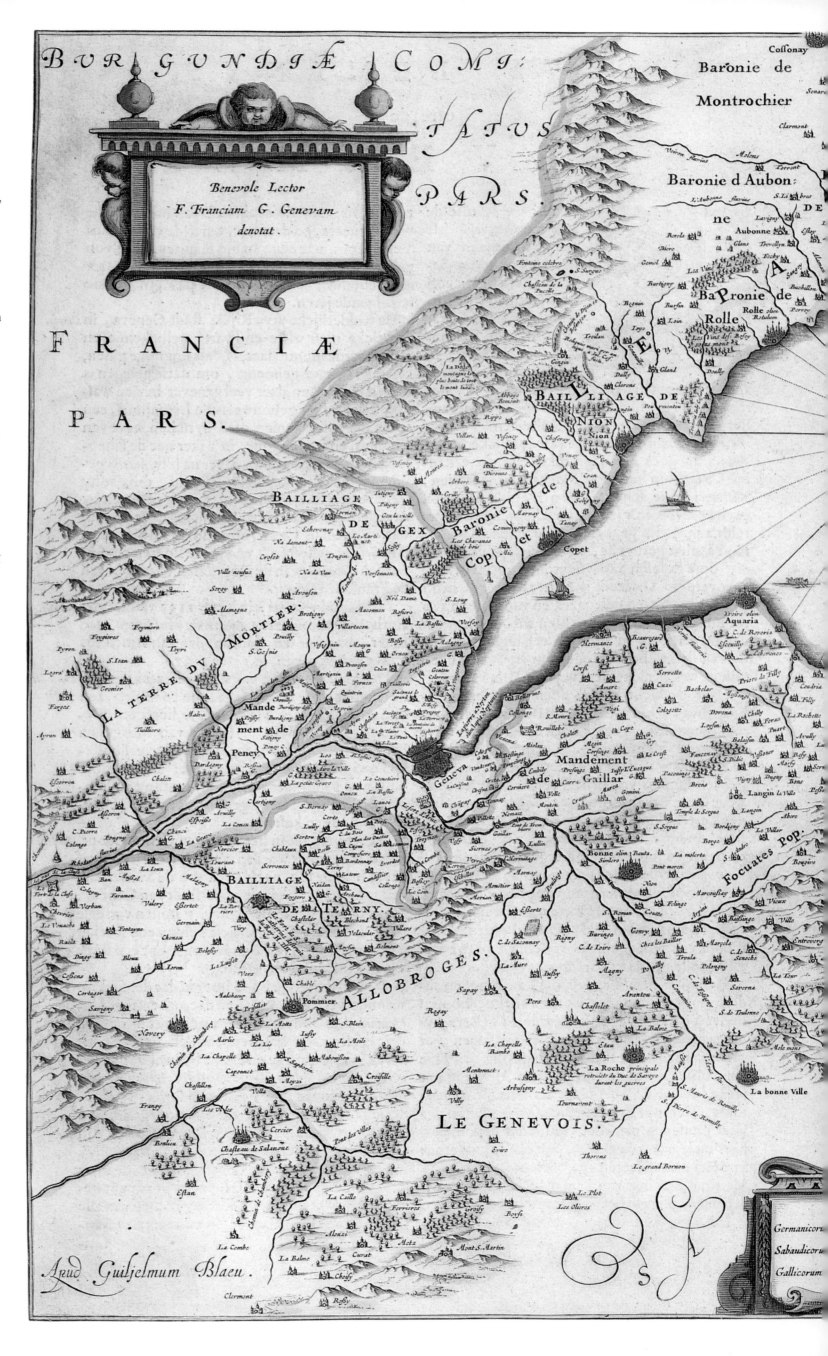

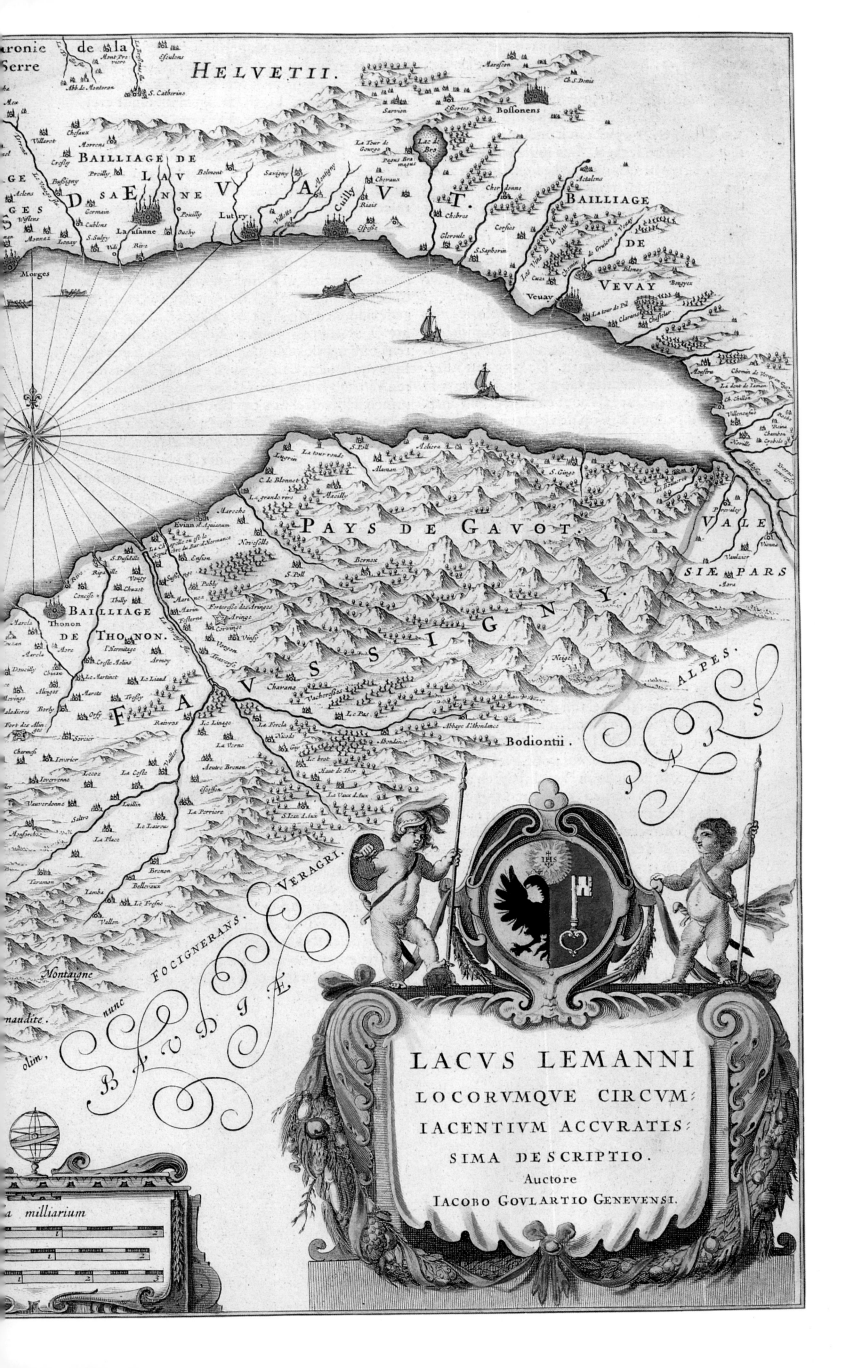

HELVETII.

BAILLIAGE DE
LAV D SAE NNE VA V T.

BAILLIAGE DE VEVAY

PAYS DE GAVOT.

VALE SIÆ PARS

BAILLIAGE
DE THONON.

FAVSSIGNY.

ALPES.

PAYS

VERAGRI.

Bodiontii.

FOCIGNERANS.

nunc

olim,

BAVDIE.

a milliarium

LACVS LEMANNI
LOCORVMQVE CIRCVM:
IACENTIVM ACCVRATIS:
SIMA DESCRIPTIO.
Auctore
IACOBO GOVLARTIO GENEVENSI.

This map, signed by Willem Blaeu, was first included in his atlases in 1634, but it dates back to a much earlier series of maps published by the French mapmaker Jean le Clerc before 1620.

Normandie was home to skilled navigators, particularly those from Le Havre at the mouth of the Seine, following the establishment of the port there in 1517. Dieppe, on the north-eastern coast, was at one time the seat of a renowned school of chartmakers which has become known as the 'Dieppe school', as well as being noted for its herring fisheries.

During the lifetime of Blaeu's map, Normandie was also very badly affected by outbreaks of plague. In 1651, at Rouen for example, there are records of some 17,000 victims of an outbreak there alone, with, it has been said, up to eight hundred victims being cared for at a time in the town's hospital.

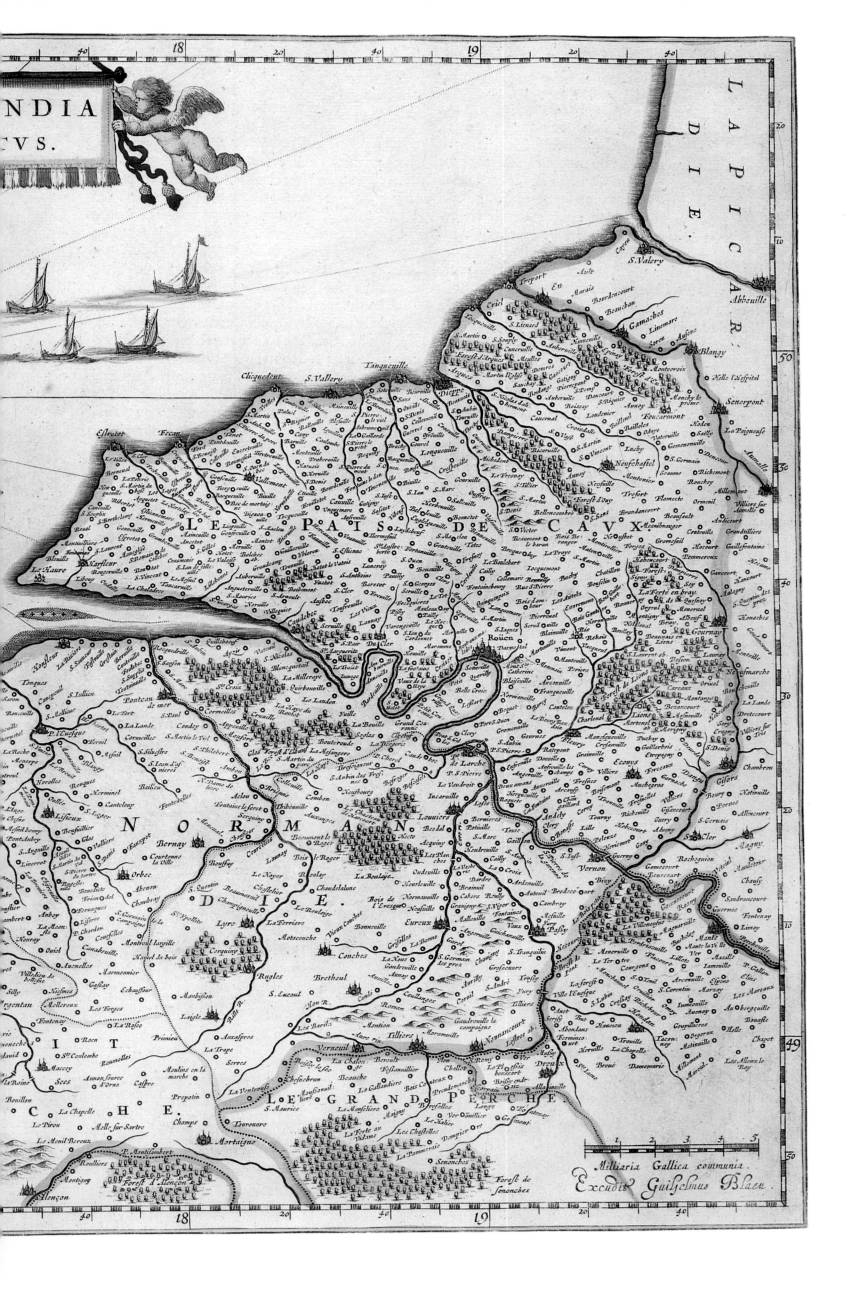

Gouvernement de La Guienne & Gascogne

The general form of this relatively new map of south-western France, which includes the Bordeaux region, owes much to the map of the same title published by Nicolas Sanson in 1651. Joan Blaeu first published his own map in the atlas of 1662.

In the Bordelais region, viticulture (symbolized in the decoration of the title panel at the lower right-hand corner) was the mainstay of the local economy, particularly the production of the celebrated clarets. Even in the 1640s, some 60,000 barrels of wine were being shipped annually through Bordeaux, Bayonne, Bourg and other towns to markets in the Low Countries and in England.

Nova Italiae delineatio

Blaeu's atlas use of this splendid general map of Italy dates from 1631. The detail shown is derived from the map in the atlas *Italia* published by the astronomer and mapmaker Giovanni Antonio Magini (*d.* 1617, his work being published posthumously).

Blaeu's map at first glance appears to show an Italy united within the geographical extent as we know the country today. But in seventeenth-century Europe, this was very far from the truth, for half of the peninsula was ruled by the Spanish line of the Habsburgs, the remainder composed of small states, even city states. Although several were rich and prosperous, they proved quite incapable of co-operating for long against outside threats. The political scene was complicated by the presence of over a hundred small and independent units, one of which still survives in the form of the Republic of San Marino.

NOVA ITALIÆ DELINEATIO

SCALA MILIARIVM

Miliaria Italica communia
Miliaria Germanica communia

Dominio Veneto nell' Italia

The northern Italian dominions of the Serene Republic, the northernmost part of an empire that once stretched into the eastern Mediterranean by way of the footholds along the Dalmation coast and southern Greece, and the island of Crete.

The city of Venezia itself can be made out in miniature plan form in the lagoon at the head of the Adriatic.

By the time this map was published (it had first appeared in 1635), Venezia had lost most of her Mediterranean possessions to the Turkish Empire, and it would not be many more years before Crete would face the same fate, leaving Venezia in possession of her Adriatic territories and but little else besides.

The large crest at the upper left-hand corner shows the Lion of St Mark, symbol of Venezia, while those cities subordinate to the Republic are named on a ribbon entwined about the title.

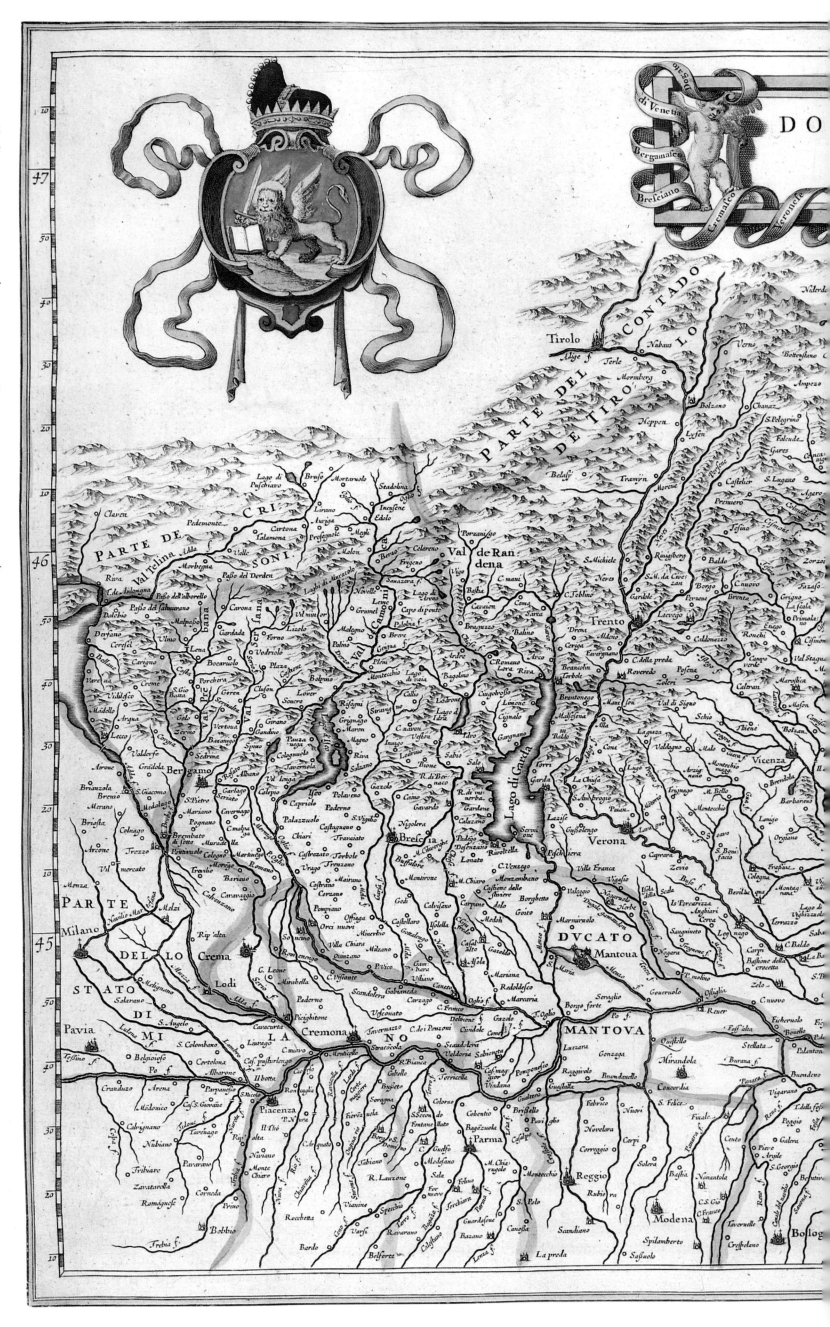

NOVA ITALIÆ DELINEATIO

Corsica Insula

A small number of maps in the Blaeu atlas were printed as insets within the text matter. Corsica is one such example.

Throughout its history the island has changed hands many times: Saracen in 850, Pisan in 1077 and Genuan in 1300, in whose dominion it remained until annexation by France in 1768, for example.

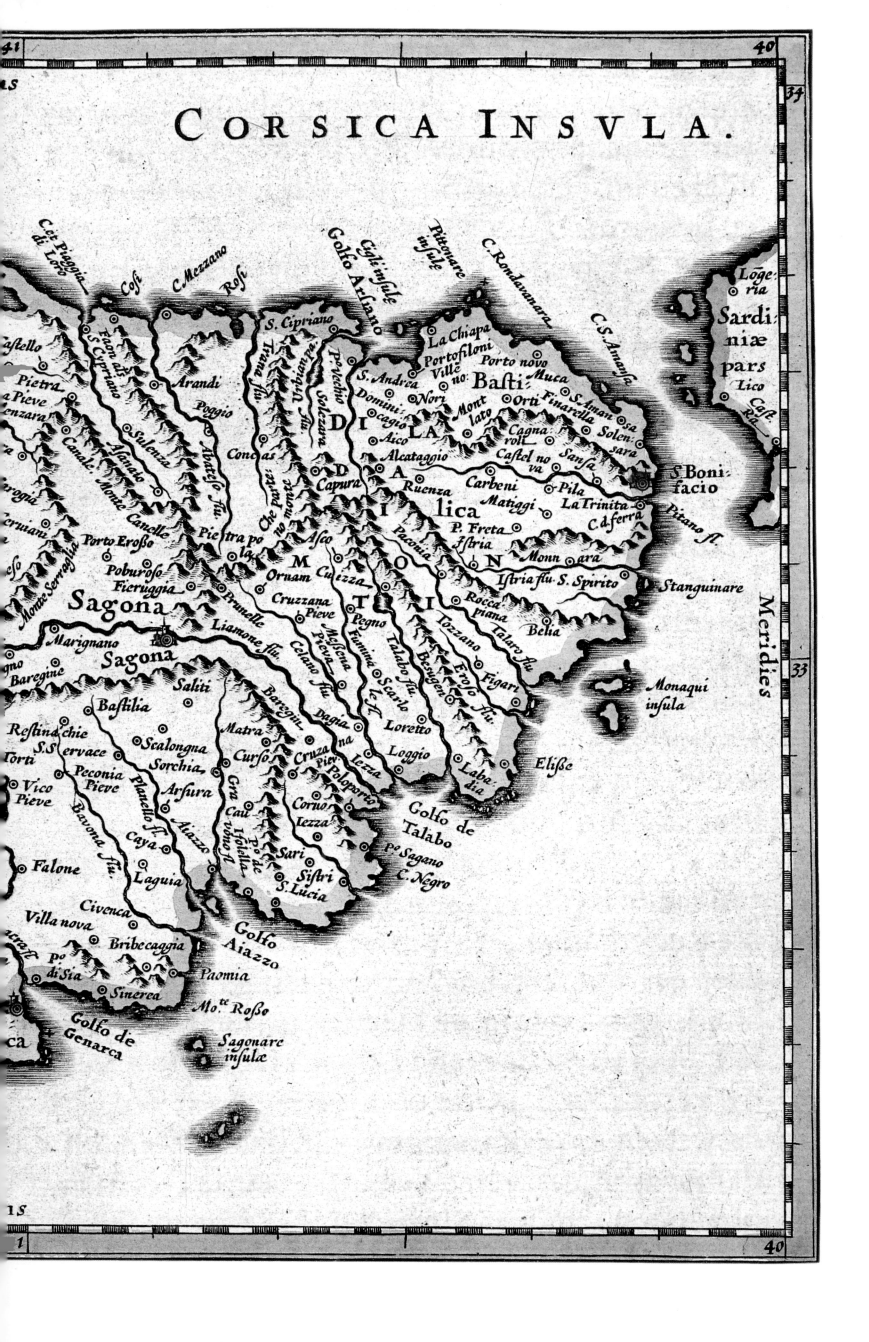

CORSICA INSVLA.

Dominio Veneto nell' Italia

The northern Italian dominions of the Serene Republic, the northernmost part of an empire that once stretched into the eastern Mediterranean by way of the footholds along the Dalmation coast and southern Greece, and the island of Crete.

The city of Venezia itself can be made out in miniature plan form in the lagoon at the head of the Adriatic.

By the time this map was published (it had first appeared in 1635), Venezia had lost most of her Mediterranean possessions to the Turkish Empire, and it would not be many more years before Crete would face the same fate, leaving Venezia in possession of her Adriatic territories and but little else besides.

The large crest at the upper left-hand corner shows the Lion of St Mark, symbol of Venezia, while those cities subordinate to the Republic are named on a ribbon entwined about the title.

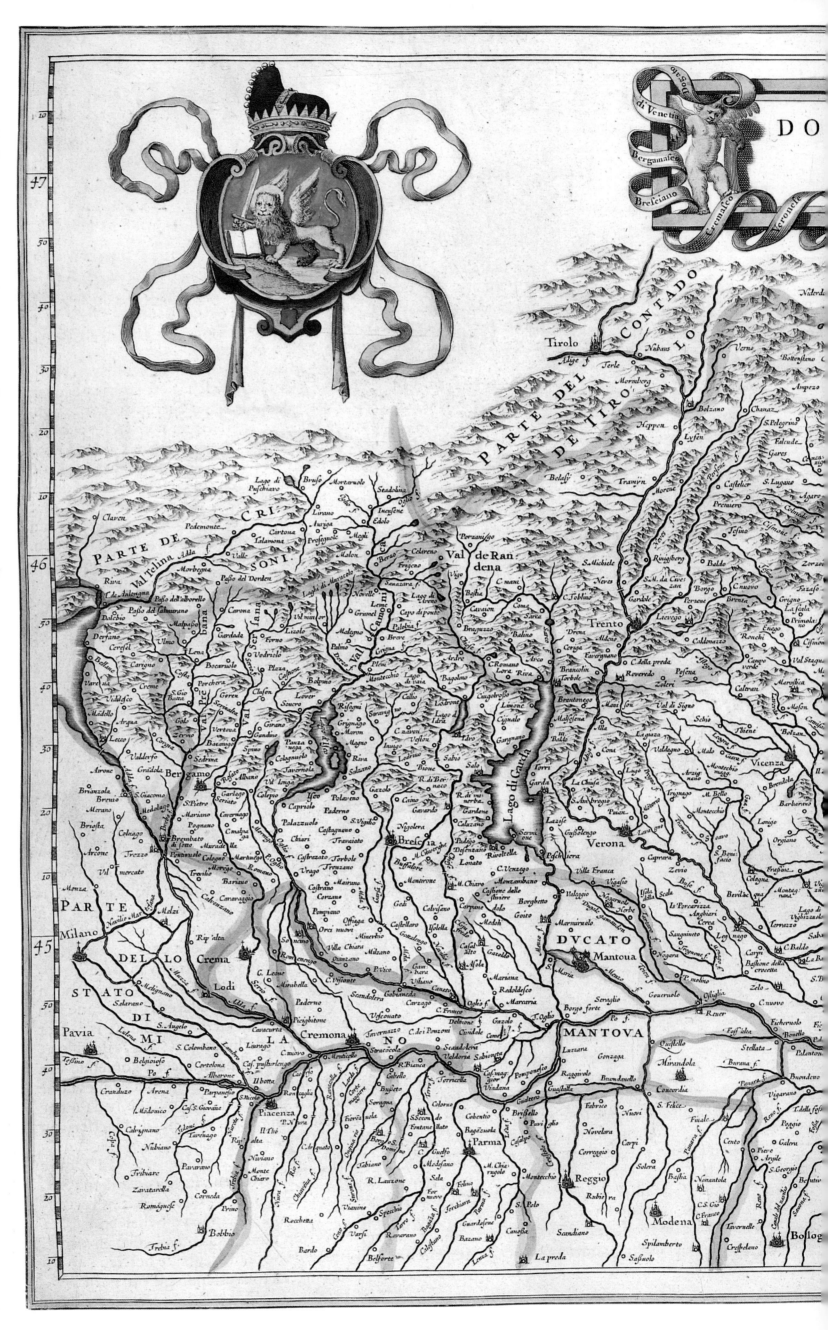

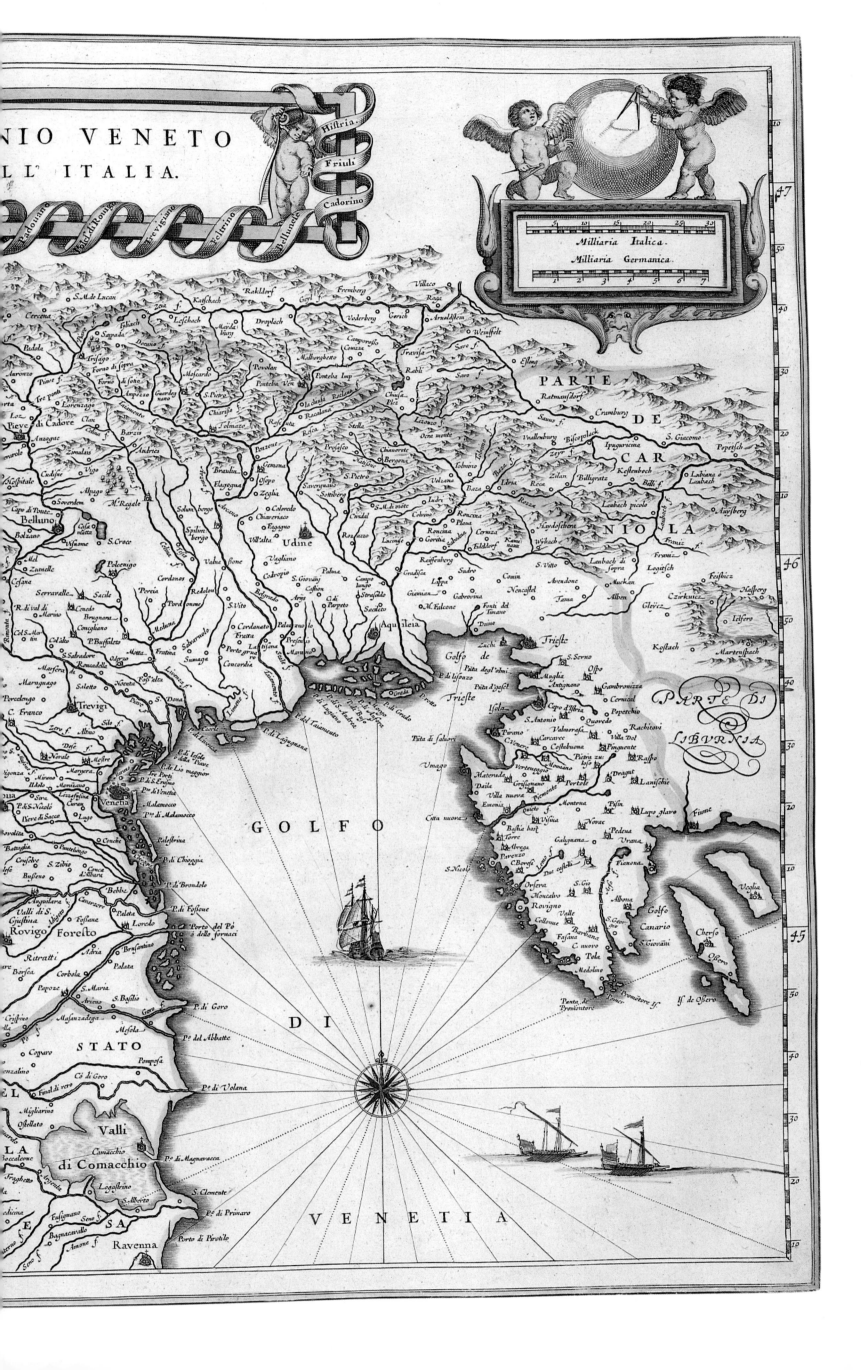

NIO VENETO
LL' ITALIA.

Histria
Friuli
Cadorino

Milliaria Italica.
Milliaria Germanica.

PARTE DE CAR NIOLA

PARTE DI LIBVRNIA

GOLFO

DI

VENETIA

Udine

Aquileia

Trieste

Belluno

Trevigi

Venetia

Rovigo   Foresto

STATO

Valli di Comacchio

Ravenna

Veglia

Chersi

Ossero

Stato della Chiesa con la Toscana

The Papal States and the Grand Duchy of Tuscany in central Italy, a map of which Blaeu included in his atlases from 1640 onwards.

The Papal States had been established during the papacy of Innocent III (1198–1216) as a buffer zone between the Holy Roman Empire to the north and Rome to the south, and for most of its existence until the later part of the nineteenth century, existed as one of a hundred or so separate political units in Italy alone. The presence of Spain is apparent in this region in the form of the small patch of territory on the mainland opposite Elba, the Stato dei Presidi, the Spanish Habsburg naval base and garrison.

The title cartouche shows the seated figure of the Mother Church wearing the Papal Crown flanked by the figures of St Peter and St Paul.

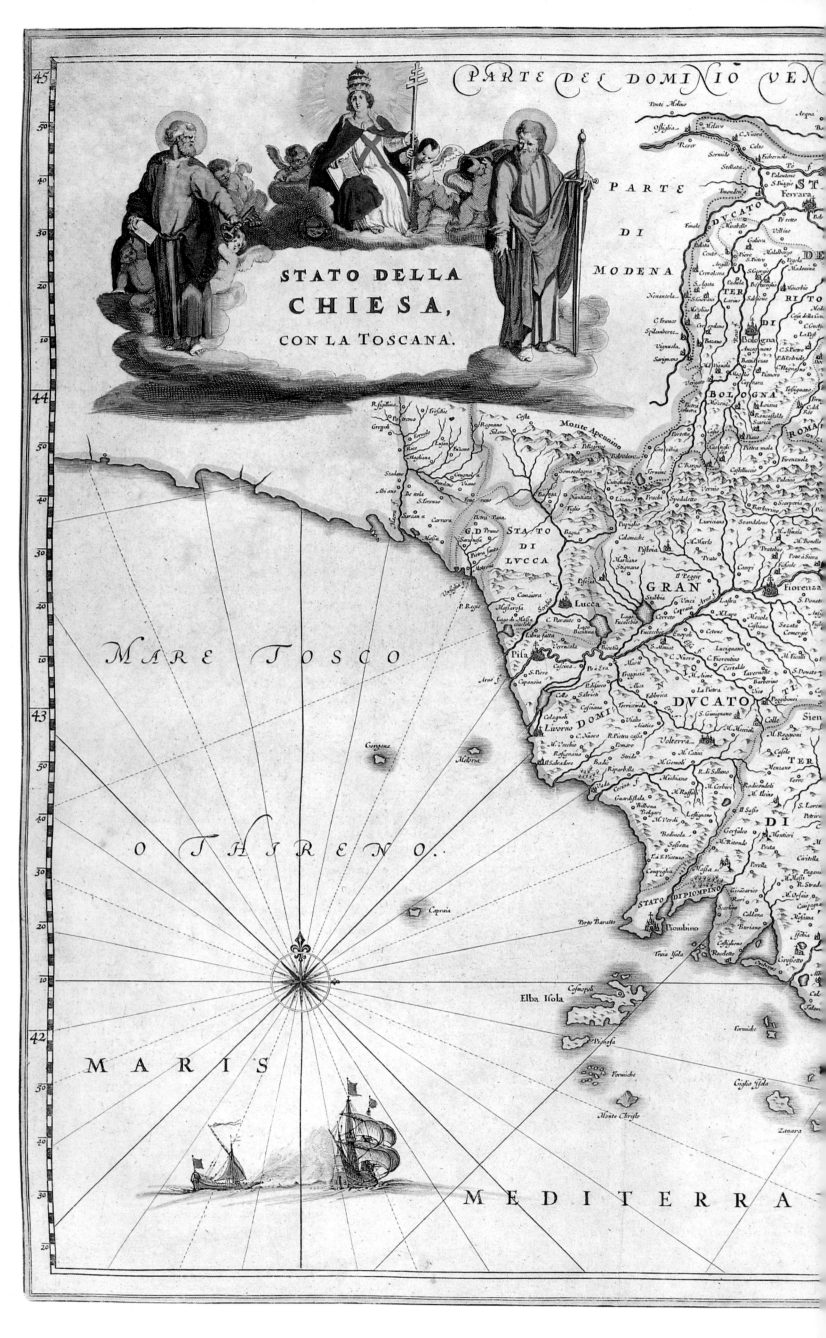

GOLFO DS

VENETIA

FER
RA

Polefino
di Ariano

Valli di
Comacchio

Rauenna

CHIE   SA

S.P.Q.R.
Rimine

DVCATO

Vrbino   DI

STATO

Pefaro

Ancona

DELLA   CHIESA

MARCA

DI

ANCO

NA

Fermo

Spoleto

CANA

SIENA

Orvieto

PATRI

CHI

Viterbo

TRI

MO

BI

SA

Narni

Terni

NIO

Rieti

PARTE

DEL

Monte Apenino

Lago di
Celano

REGNO

DI

NAPOLI

CASTRO
DI
Corneto

S.PIETRO

STATO DI

CAM

PA   Roma

Frascati

Velletri

DI

ROMA
Terracina

Gaeta

PAGNA

I   PARS

45

50

40

30

20

10

44

50

40

30

20

10

43

50

40

30

20

10

42

50

40

30

20

10

20

30

40

50

Milliaria
Italica.

Guilielmus Blaeu
excudit.

113

Dominio Fiorentino

This regional map of the territory around Firenze [Florence] bears the combined imprint of Joan and Cornelis Blaeu, having first appeared in 1640 during the short-lived partnership of the two brothers.

Still a relatively prosperous region of Italy in the seventeenth century, with Firenze itself as one of the most populous cities in the country, the region was by this time in decline. Firenze had derived most of its wealth throughout the sixteenth century from the product of high quality woollen cloths. But while production had remained more or less constant, the city was facing increasing competition from imports of cheaper cloths from England and the Low Countries, whose products were already dominating Mediterranean markets by the time Blaeu's map appeared.

The most important towns, Lucca and Pisa as well as Firenze, are clearly shown in miniature plan form, the scale of the map also allowing the city walls to be depicted with some accuracy.

114

Regno di Napoli

This map of the southern
portion of Italy was first
included in the Blaeu atlas
in 1640. The Kingdom of
Naples was at the same
time a part of the Spanish
dominions of the Habsburg
Empire in Europe. Note the
Spanish arms at the upper
right-hand corner. In
addition, the design is
further embellished by the
colourful provincial arms
shown in the side borders.

As with most of the
regional maps of Italy in his
atlas, Blaeu used as his
source an atlas map
published in 1620 by the
Italian mapmaker Giovanni
Antonio Magini, whose
work, *Italia*, had been
published posthumously at
Bologna.

Sicilia regnum

Willem Blaeu issued this map of Sicily in 1635. The island had been under the rule of the Spanish line of the Habsburgs since 1479 and the island, together with the neighbouring Spanish-ruled parts of southern Italy, were important suppliers of wheat from the fertile lands on the volcanic soils around Etna. That fertility is symbolized in the figure of Ceres at the lower left, seen holding sheaves of corn.

The Royal arms of Spain are included in the upper left-hand corner.

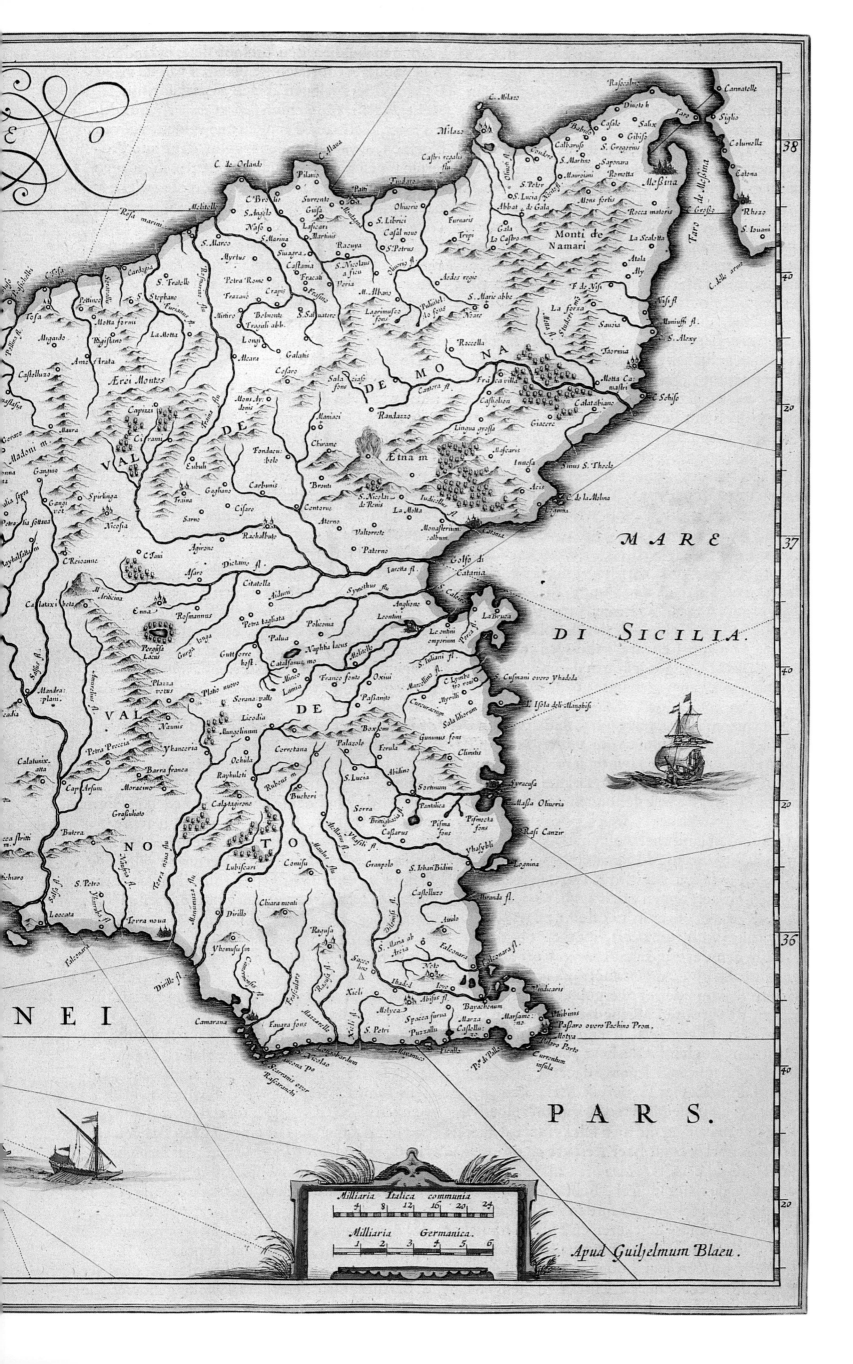

Graecia

This general map of
Greece, which covers nearly
all of the area of modern
Greece, is one of the
relatively few maps in the
Blaeu atlas series to bear
the combined imprint of
Joan and his brother
Cornelis who died in 1644
after a brief partnership of
about six years.

The seated figure above
the title cartouche at the
lower left attests to the fact
that Greece was at the time
a part of the European
Turkish Empire. The map
itself was the standard atlas
map of Greece in the
seventeenth century. It first
appeared in 1640.

Cyclades Insulae in Mari Aegaeo, hodie Archipelago

This detailed map shows the southern part of the Aegean archipelago: the Kikládhes [Cyclades] in the western half near Evvoia, and part of the Dhodhekánisos [Dodecanese] to the east.

Joan Blaeu included the map of the same title by the German classicist and historian Johann Wilhelm Laurenberg (1590–1658) as his source. Laurenberg wrote an influential history of Ancient Greece, his *Graecia antiqua*, which was published posthumously in Amsterdam. Most of the islands shown here, such as Sámos, Khíos, and Náxos, were in Turkish hands, having been captured during the long reign of Suleiman I the Magnificent.

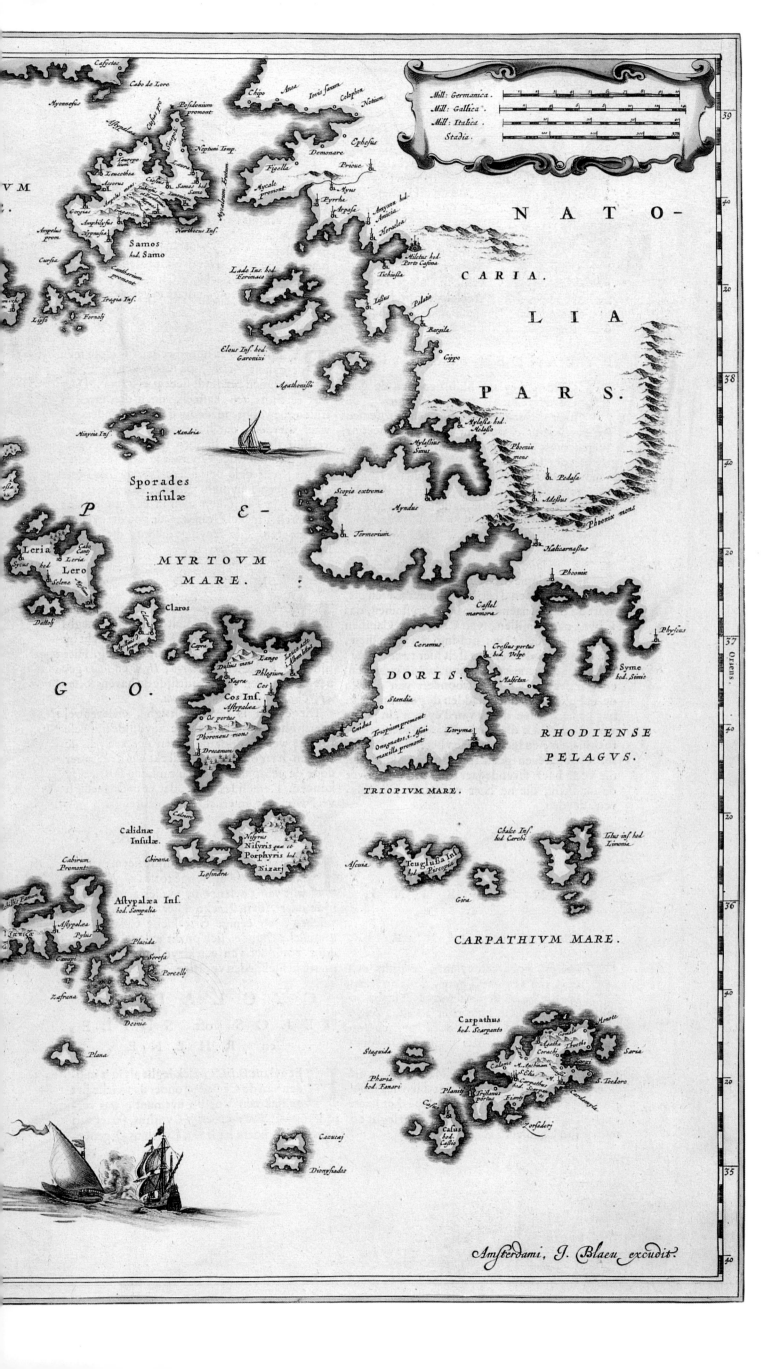

NATO-

CARIA.

LIA

PARS.

Casyetos
Cabo de Loro
Myonnesus
Chipo *Anta* *Iovis fanum* *Colophon* *Notium*
Posidonium promont.
Neptuni Temp.
Ephesus
Figella *Demonare* *Priane*
Mycale promont. *Samos hod. Samo* *Xyus*
Pyrrha
Arposa
Samos hod. Samo
Narbecus Inf.
Amynona hod. Anticia
Heracleo
Miletus hod. Porto Casma
Lado Inf. hod. Forimaco *Tichiussa*
Iassus *Palatio*
Borgila
Eleus Inf. hod. Garonisi *Gippo*
Agathonissi

Mylassa hod. Molasso

Ninycia Inf. *Mandria*
Mylassias Sinus
Phoenix mons
Pedasa
Sporades insulae *Scopia extrema* *Adassus*
Myndus *Phoenix mons*
Termerium
Halicarnassus

Leria hod. Lero *Cabo Canti Leria*
Sicus *Selene*
Phoenix
Castal marmore
MYRTOVM MARE.
Dattos
Claros
Ceramus
Crossus portus hod. Volpo
Capra
Dolius mons *Lango* *Letus Acte Album Litus*
Malfetan
Syme hod. Simie
Physcus
Phlegium *Cos*
Segra *Cos Inf.* *Astypalea*
Or. portus *DORIS.*
Stendia
Phoroneus mons *Cnidus* *Triopium promont.*
Drecanum *Onugnathos, i. Asini maxilla promont.* *Loryma*

G O . *RHODIENSE PELAGVS.*

TRIOPIVM MARE.

Caloieri
Calidnæ Insulæ. *Chirana*
Nisyrus quae et Porphyris hod. Nizari *Ascura* *Teuglussa Inf. hod. Piscopia* *Chalce Inf. hod. Cerchi* *Telus inf hod Limonia*
Cabirum Promont. *Lefendro* *Gira*
Achilles fanum
Astypalæa Inf. hod. Sampalia
Astypalæa
Janvica *Pylaa*
Placida
Canupi *Serofa*
Porcelli

Zafrana *CARPATHIVM MARE.*
Deonia

Plana

Carpathus hod. Scarpanto *Amorte*
Staguida *Agatha Coracho* *Thoetho* *Saria*
Pharia hod. Fanari *Calamo* *M. Echio M. Trachias hod. Carpathus hod. Scarpe* *Cazucaj*
Planiy *Tristanus portus* *Fiamto* *S. Toedoro*
Dionysiades *Casus* *Zorfadori*
Casos hod. Casso

Mill: Germanica.
Mill: Gallica.
Mill: Italica.
Stadia.

39

40

20

38

40

20

37

40

20

36

40

20

35

40

Oriens.

Amsterdami, J. Blaeu excudit.

Regnorum Hispaniae nova descriptio

Willem Blaeu's general map of the Iberian peninsula is one of the oldest maps compiled for his atlas series, having first appeared in 1631.

The title is specific in naming the map as including the Hispanic Kingdoms: Spain and Portugal were unified for a period of sixty years between 1580 and 1640, as demonstrated by the highly elaborate arms shown at the upper right-hand corner.

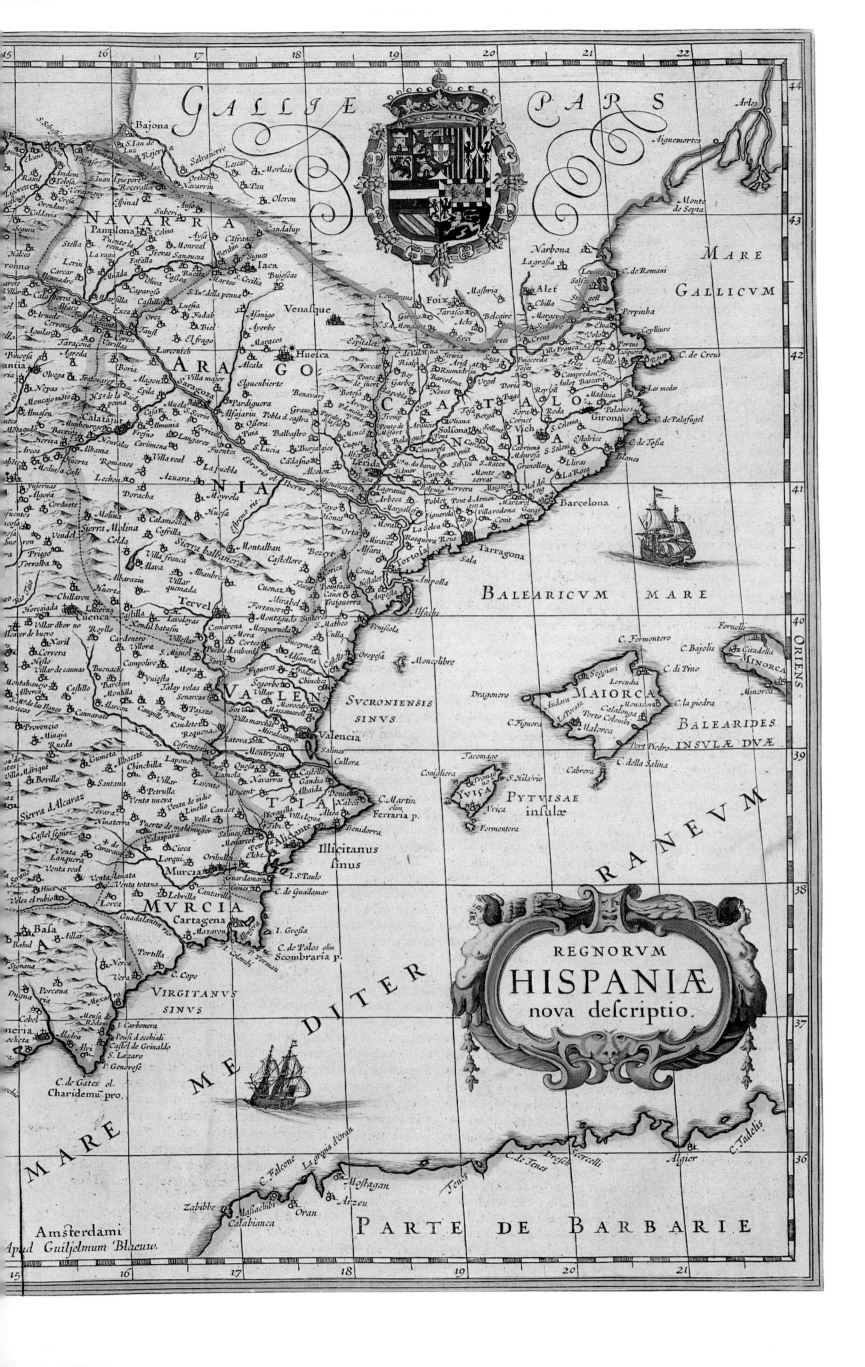

Catalonia

Willem Blaeu's detailed map of this north-eastern province of Cataluña (or Catalunya) dates from 1635, having been based on maps made by a Portuguese cartographer in the service of the Kings of Spain, João Baptista Lavanha.

Whereas the neighbouring province of Valencia immediately to the south was important during the years contemporary with the publication of Blaeu's map for its sugar crop, Cataluña had a long-standing reputation for its viticulture, particularly around the towns of Tarragona, Mataró and other coastal towns, which had produced wines since classical times.

During the Middle Ages, after a long period of stagnation, Cataluña experienced a revival of its fortunes in its trade with the rest of Spain and the Mediterranean, partly as a result of trade brought about by pilgrims *en route* to and from the shrine at Santiago de Compostela in north-western Spain.

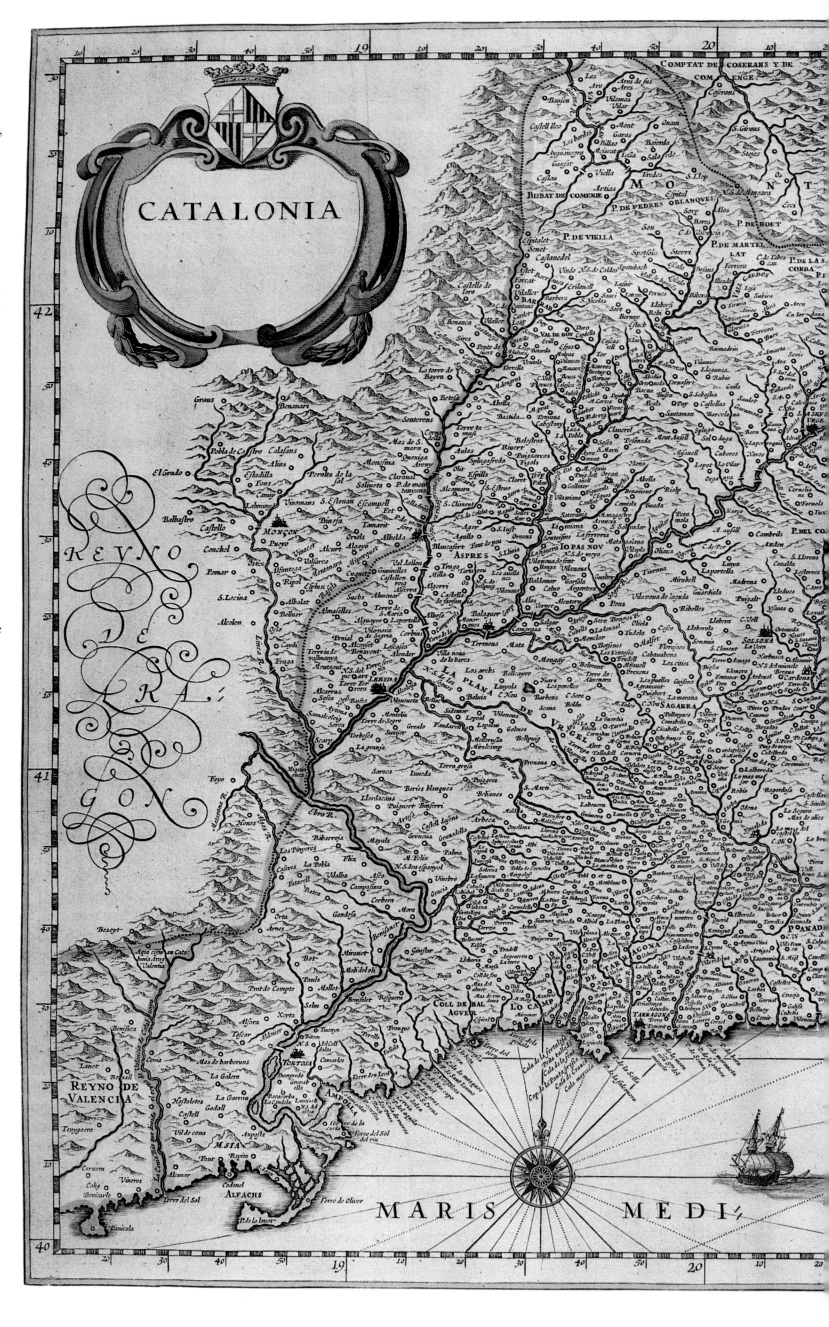

PARTE DE FRANCIA

MARE

C. DE ROMANI

GALLICVM

PYRENEI

SALANCA

ESPI

DE FOIX

CERDANA

AMPVRO

PENI M.

C. DE CREVS

C. DE BIARA

LES MEDES

LA SELVA

C. DE BAGVR

C. DE PALAFVGELL

VALL PARO

C. DE TOSSA
LVNARIVM PROM

VALLES

P. DE PINEDA

P. DE CALELLA

BARCELONA

S. DE CARRAF

PARS

TERRANEI

Guiljelmus Blaeu excud. Amsterdami.

Scala milliarium.

Hispanicorum.

Gallicorum.

The province of Valencia
on the Mediterranean
eastern coast of Spain.
Oriented west to the top of
the plate, Willem Blaeu's
map of 1635, compiled
from Spanish sources, shows
the region around the city
of Valencia itself as a
densely populated area, the
prosperous *huertas* (or
gardens) region.

Throughout the sixteenth
and seventeenth centuries,
sugar was still a great
luxury in Europe, but until
the plantations of South
and Central America
became fully established as
significant producers of the
crop later in the
seventeenth century, Spain
was one of the few
European sources. The crop
had its greatest success in
the *huerta* of Gandía, to the
south of Valencia.

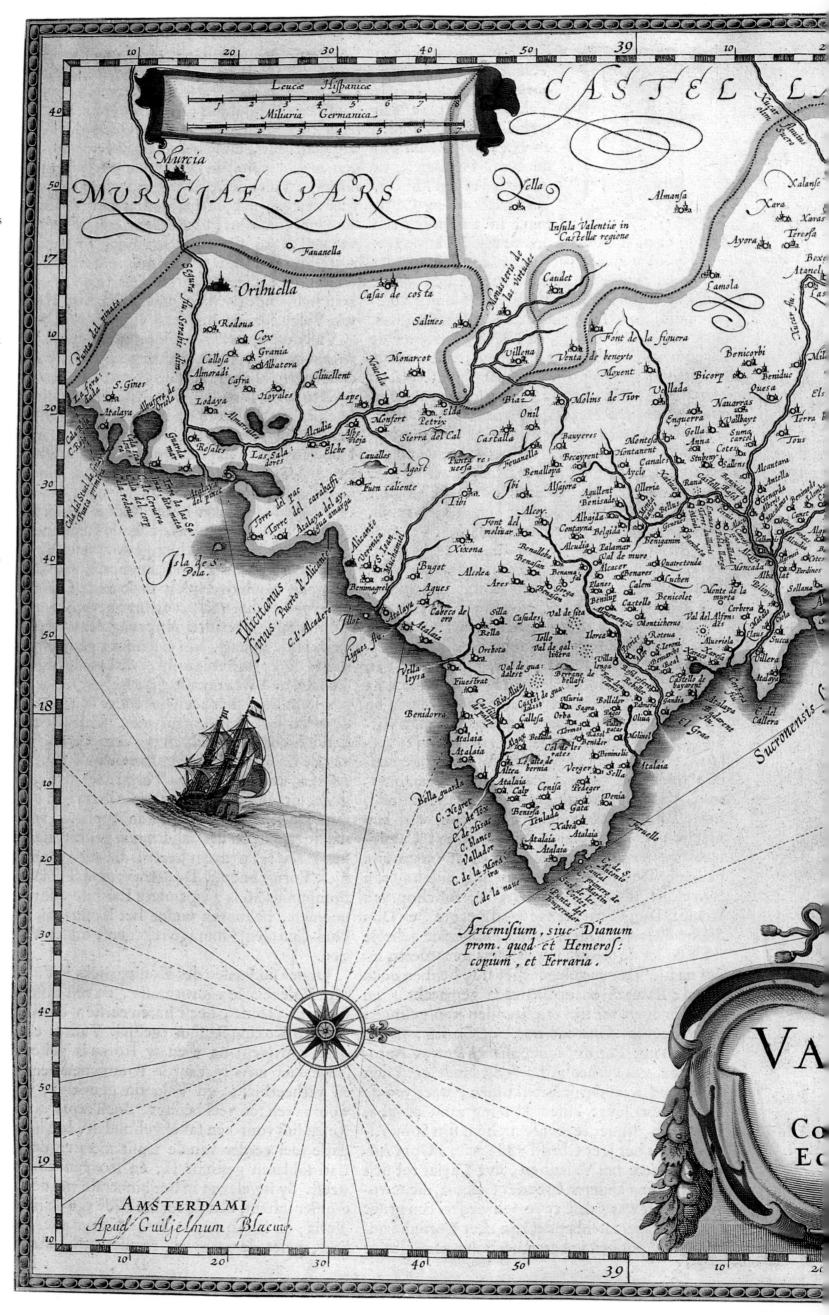

Arragonia regnum

The map shows the combined imprint of Willem and Joan Blaeu, but authorship is credited to the Portuguese cartographer, João Baptista Lavanha (1582–1624), who made several maps of the provinces of Spain and Portugal between 1610 and 1620, many of which were used as a source for Blaeu's namesake atlas maps. The Portuguese origin of the map is betrayed in some of the place name spellings, notably that of Zaragoza (given here as *Çaragoça*) placed near the centre.

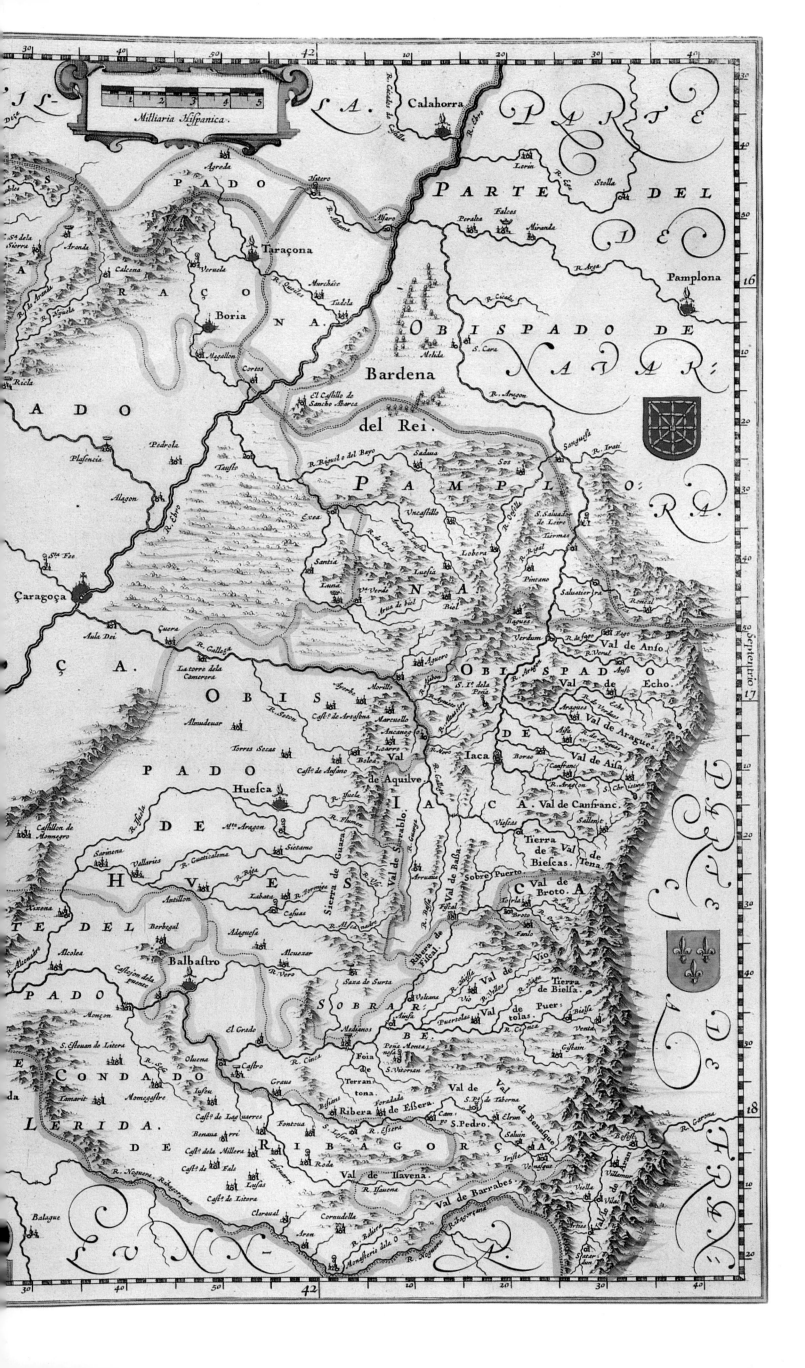

Milliaria Hispanica.

ILL—

Diz

S.ª de la
Sierra
S

A

RACO

PADO

Agreda

Moncas

Aranda

Calcena

R. de Aranda

Vijuela

Veruela

Taraçona

Boria

Magallon

Cortes

Murchàe

Tudela

Calahorra

R. Ebro

R. Ciudad de Castilla

PARTE

PARTE DEL

Lerin

Stella

R. Ega

Peralta

Falces

Miranda

R. Arga

R. Cidac

OBISPADO DE

NAVAR:

Pamplona

PADO

Ricla

Plasencia

Pedrola

Alagon

Sta Fee

Çaragoça

Aula Dei

Çuera

La torre de la
Camerera

R. Galleg

Tauste

R. Ebro

Eyea

R. Queiles

Magallon

El Castillo de
Sancho Abarca

R. Riguel o del Bayo

Sadua

S. Cara

Melida

Bardena

del Rei.

R. Aragon

PAMPLO

Sos

S. Saluador
de Leire

Tiermas

R. Irati

R. Onsella

R. Regal

Santia

Luna

Vncastillo

Vd Verde

Zona de Huesca

R. de Orés

Luesia

Arua de biel

Biel

Lobera

Pintano

Salustierra

Roncal

N

A

Sanguesa

Aguero

Iverk

Morillo

Cast.º de Artasona

R. Seton

Almudeuar

Torres Secas

R. Isuela

Casas

OBIS

PA

DO

HUES

DE

Castillon de
Monnegro

Sarinena

Vallaries

Antillon

Xixena

Berbegal

Alcolea

Castejon de la
puente

S. esteuan de Litera

Monçon

Oluena

Castro

Grado

Balbastro

R. Alcanadre

Tamarit

Iuseu

Graus

Benauarri

Cast.º de Laguarres

Cast.º de la Millera

Cast.º de Fals

Lusas

Cast.º de Litera

Claraual

Balague

R. Noguera Ribagorçana

Cornudella

Aren

R. Ballera

Monasterio dela O

R. Noguera

Caft.º de Anfano

Caft.º de Anfamo

Loarre

Bolea

Val

de Aquilve

Huesca

Mt.ª Aragon

Sietamo

R. Flumen

Labata

Alaguesa

R. Guatizalema

R. Rita

R. Algemies

R. Alcanadre

Sana de Surta

Saza de Surta

R. Vero

Alcuezar

SOBRAR

Medianos

Peña Monta
nesa

Foia
de
Terran
tona

S. Vitorian

Bisians

Poradala

Ribera de Essera

R. Cinca

R. Essera

S. Iglesia

S. Pedro

Roda

Val de Ilavena

R. Isauena

S. Ilera

R. Noro

S. I.ª de la
Peña

Loarre

Ancanego

Marcuello

R. Gallego

IA

Iaca

Borao

Canfranc

Cambre

C

A

Val de Ansso

Val de Echo.

Araguas

R. de Echo

Asso

R. de Aragues

Val de Aragues.

Val de Aila

Val de Canfranc.

Viescas

Sallent

Tierra de Val de
Biescas

Val de
Tena.

Sobre Puerto

Val de
Broto. A

Torla

Broto

Fanlo

VIO

Val de
Vio

R. Vio

R. Ballo

R. Fiscal

Ribera de Fiscal

C

Ainsa

BE

Volcana

Puertolas

Val

de
tolas.

Puer

R. Cinca

Gistain

Val de

S. Pe de Taberna

Cam

F.º S. Pedro

Elrum

Saluin

A

Vielha

R. Garona

Val de Barrabes

Tierra
de Biella.

Biella

Venta

de Benasgue

R. Garona

Bosost

Velnasque

Artes

Villemur

Villas

S. Juan
de Isaba

R. de Sato

Verdum

R. Veral

Baquea

Fago

Anso

CONDADO

DE

RIBAGORÇA

LERIDA.

TE DEL

PADO

E

da

S

P

I

R

E

N

E

This map covers Navarra in northern Spain and includes part of the Basque region of the north coast as well as the western Pyrenees frontier region with France. Formerly a separate kingdom, Navarra was incorporated into the Spanish kingdom in 1512–1515; its arms appear in the upper left-hand corner.

The map itself was first published in a Blaeu atlas in 1635.

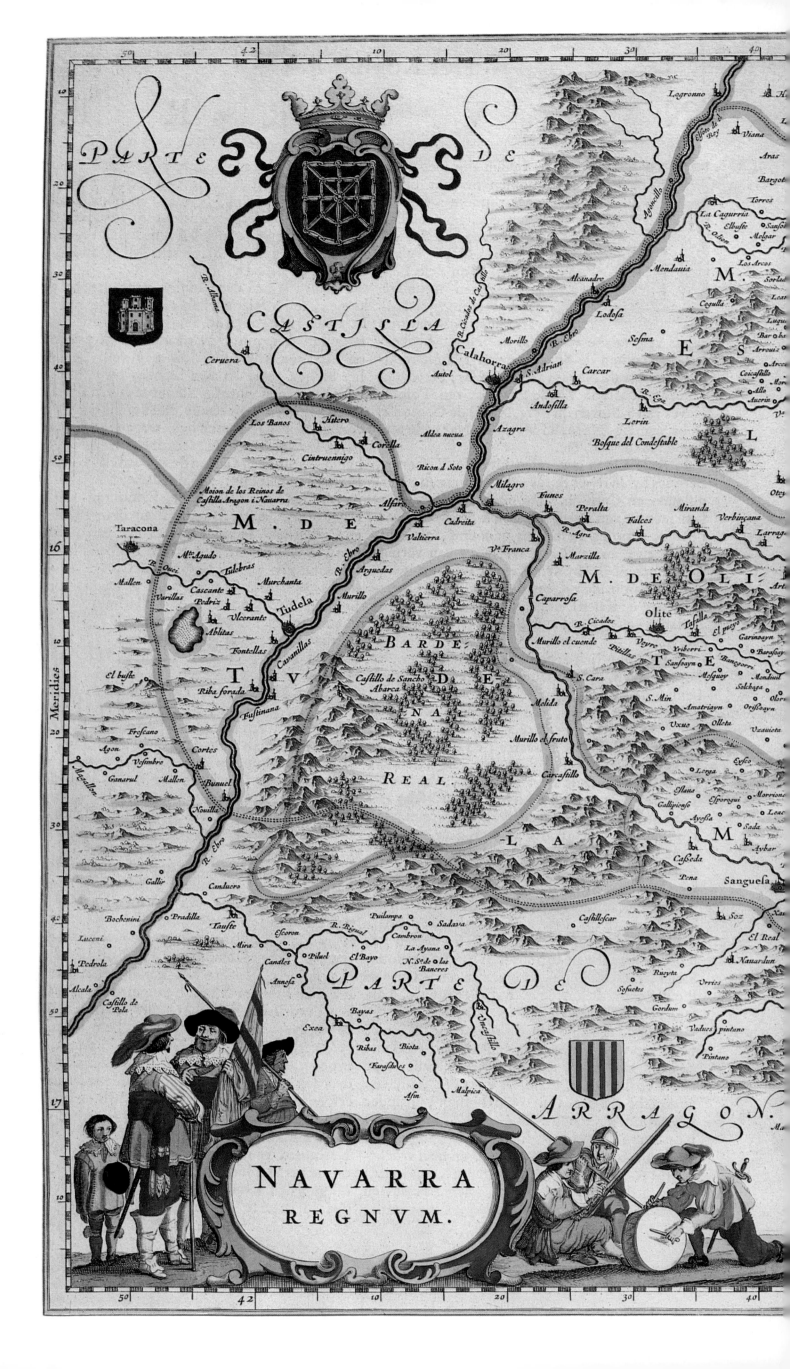

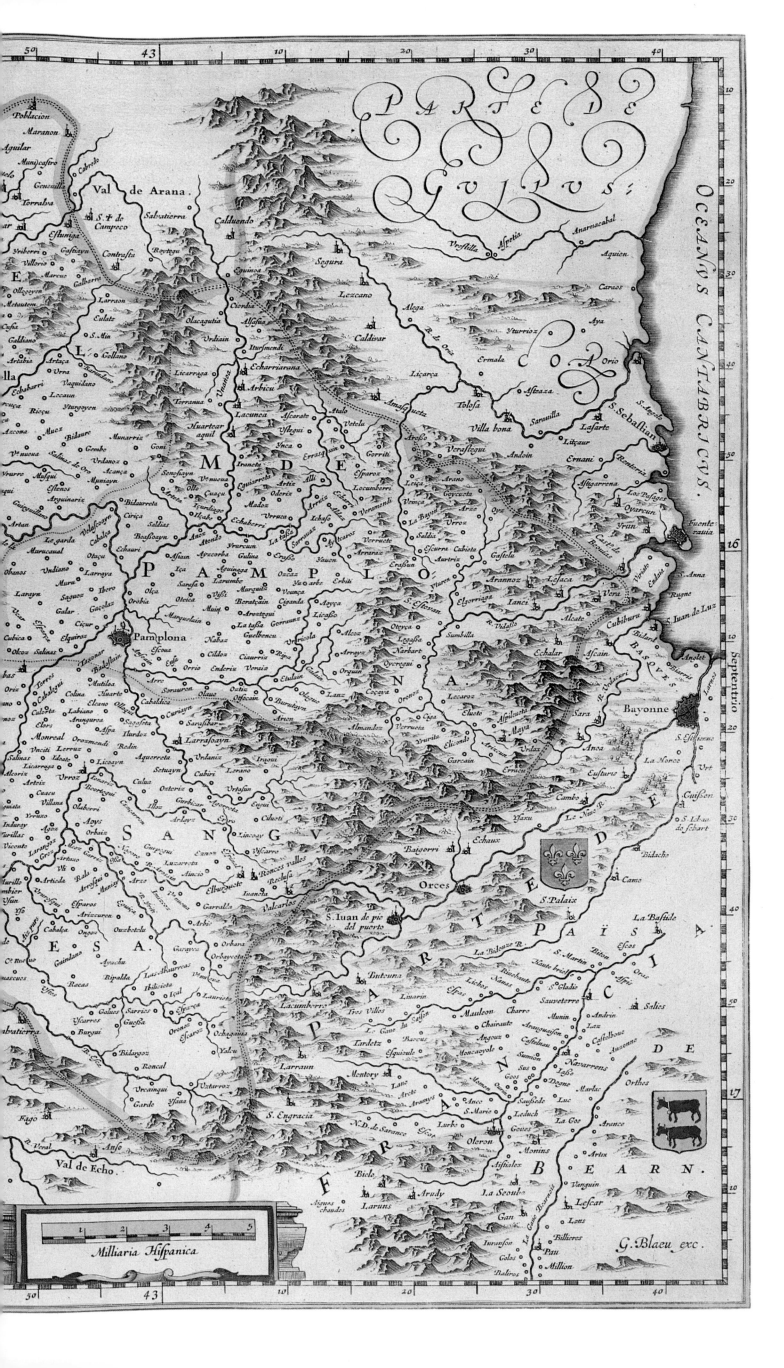

PARTE DE GVLPVS

OCEANVS CANTABRICVS

Septentrio

Poblacion
Maranon
Aguilar
Municaftro
Geneuilla
Cabredo
Torralba
Eftuniga
Val de Arana.
S. ✝ de Campeco
Salvatierra
Calduendo

Vriberri
Gaftiayn
Contrafta
Royttgu
Equinoa
Segura
Lezcano
Vreftilla
Afpetia
Anarnacabal
Aquien
Caraos

Olloqueuen
Metautem
Cafa
Galbarro
Larraon
Cioda
Alfafua
Ciorda
Caldivar
Aloga
Yturrioz
Aya
Ermala
A. Orio
Aftraza

Galdiano
Arbeiza
Artaça
S. Min
Gollano
Olacagutia
Vrdiain
Iturfmendi
Liçarça
A Orio
Tolofa
Villa bona
Sarauilla
S. Sebaftian
S. Agita
Lafarte

Echabarri
Ricçu
Vaquidano
Licarriaga
Echarriarana
Arbicu
Lacunea
Afcarate
Atalo
Votelu
Amafmuetu
Veraftegui
Andoin
Ernani
Renteria
Lizaur
Aftigarrena
Oyarcun
Yrun
Fuenterauia
Caftelde Bourles

Azcona
Muez
Bidaura
Munarriz
Goni
Huartear aqui
Iraneta
Inca
Erraguin
Gorriti
Efparoz
Locumberri
Veramendi
Efcurra
Cubieta
Aurtriu
Gaftelu
Arannoz
Lefaca
Vera
S. Anna
Cadaix
Rugne

Sanguefa
Pamplona
Sanguefa

FRANCIA
PARTE DE PAÏS

BEARN.

DE Navarrens
Orthes

Milliaria Hifpanica

G. Blaeu exc.

133

Scenographia Fabricae
S. Laurentii in Escuriali

This panorama of the
Escorial is one of a series of
seven architectural plates
which Blaeu added to the
atlas in 1662. It is possible
that Blaeu included these
plates both as a token of his
sympathies with Roman
Catholicism (at the time he
was actively preparing a
series of townbooks devoted
to Italy and the States of
the Church) and as a
possible inducement to sales
of the atlas in Spain. An
edition of his atlas with the
text printed in Spanish
existed in part, but this
project was never to be
completed.

The monastery-palace of
the Escorial, built in
1563–1582, fifty or so
kilometres from Madrid,
was the most important
product of the Renaissance
in Spain. It was
commissioned by Philip II
to house the mausoleum of
his father, Charles V, in a
manner designed to
symbolize Spanish imperial
power and Spanish
Catholic piety. The plans
were drawn up by the
architect Juan Bautista de
Toledo who had assisted
Michelangelo at St Peter's
in Rome from 1546 to
1548. The colouring of the
building in Blaeu's
panorama rather
emphasizes the spiritual
austerity of the structure
built of the local grey
granite.

It was here that Philip II,
half king, half monk, ruler
of one of the greatest
empires in history, died in
1598.

SCENOGRAPHIA FABRICÆ

Portugallia et Algarbia quae olim Lusitania

This map bears the combined imprint of Willem and Joan Blaeu. As a source, they credited the Portuguese mapmaker Fernão Álvares Seco who made the first modern map of Portugal in 1560, this Blaeu version first appearing in 1635, towards the end of a period which, since 1580, had seen Portugal incorporated into the Spanish kingdom.

The Moorish figures flanking the title cartouche recall an earlier period in the history of Portugal when Algarve and Portugal to the south of the Tejo were under Muslim dominion. In contrast, the several sailing ships hint at the maritime power of Portugal providing a lifeline to an empire that included a large part of South America, the settlements in Africa and the possessions in Asia and the East Indies.

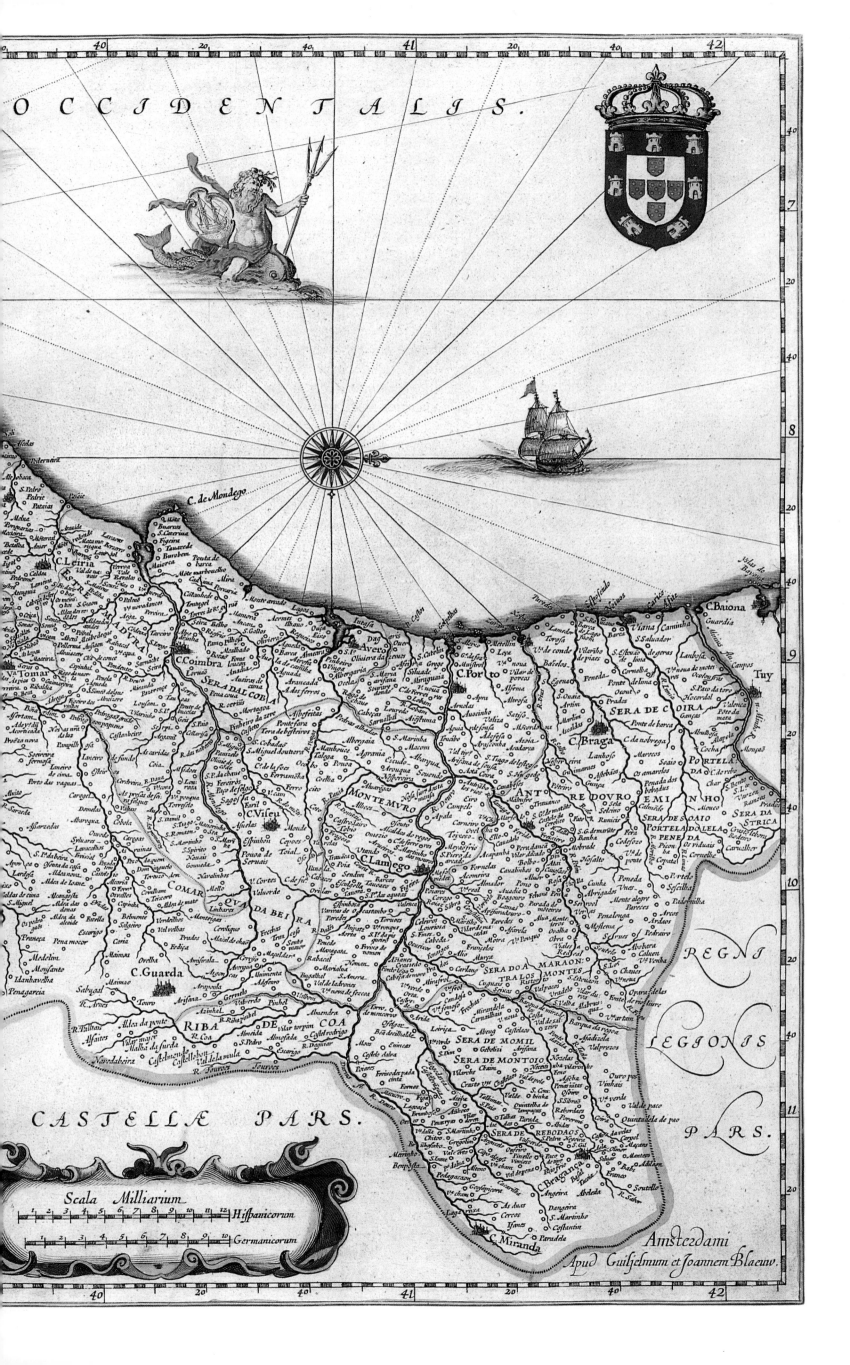

Andaluzia continens Sevillam et Cordubam

This is Willem Blaeu's regional map of the southern provinces of Spain, first published in 1634.

Here are shown the cities of Córdoba, Sevilla, Cádiz as well as Gibraltar and, on the southern coast of the neighbouring province of Granada, towns such as Málaga, Marbella, and Estepona, nowadays best known to millions of tourists from northern Europe.

In the seventeenth century both Cádiz and Sevilla, aside from their particular importance in the trade with the Spanish empire in the Americas, were of increasing importance in the trade with the rest of Europe. The Dutch in particular used Cádiz as a kind of entrepôt, carrying products from the New World to northern Europe as well as the fruits and wines of southern Spain.

The title is lettered on a lionskin stretched between two columns which may be interpreted as a seventeenth-century view of the Pillars of Hercules of Classical Antiquity.

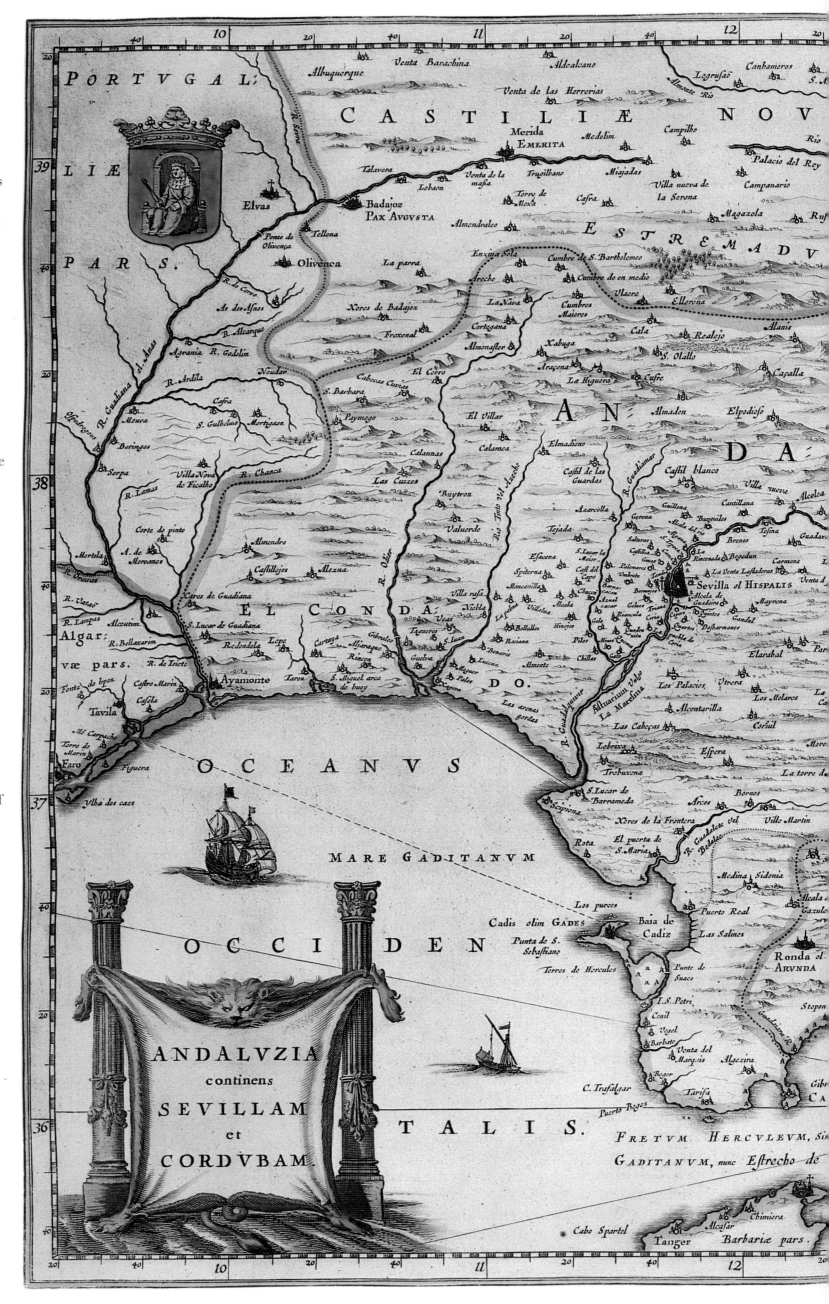

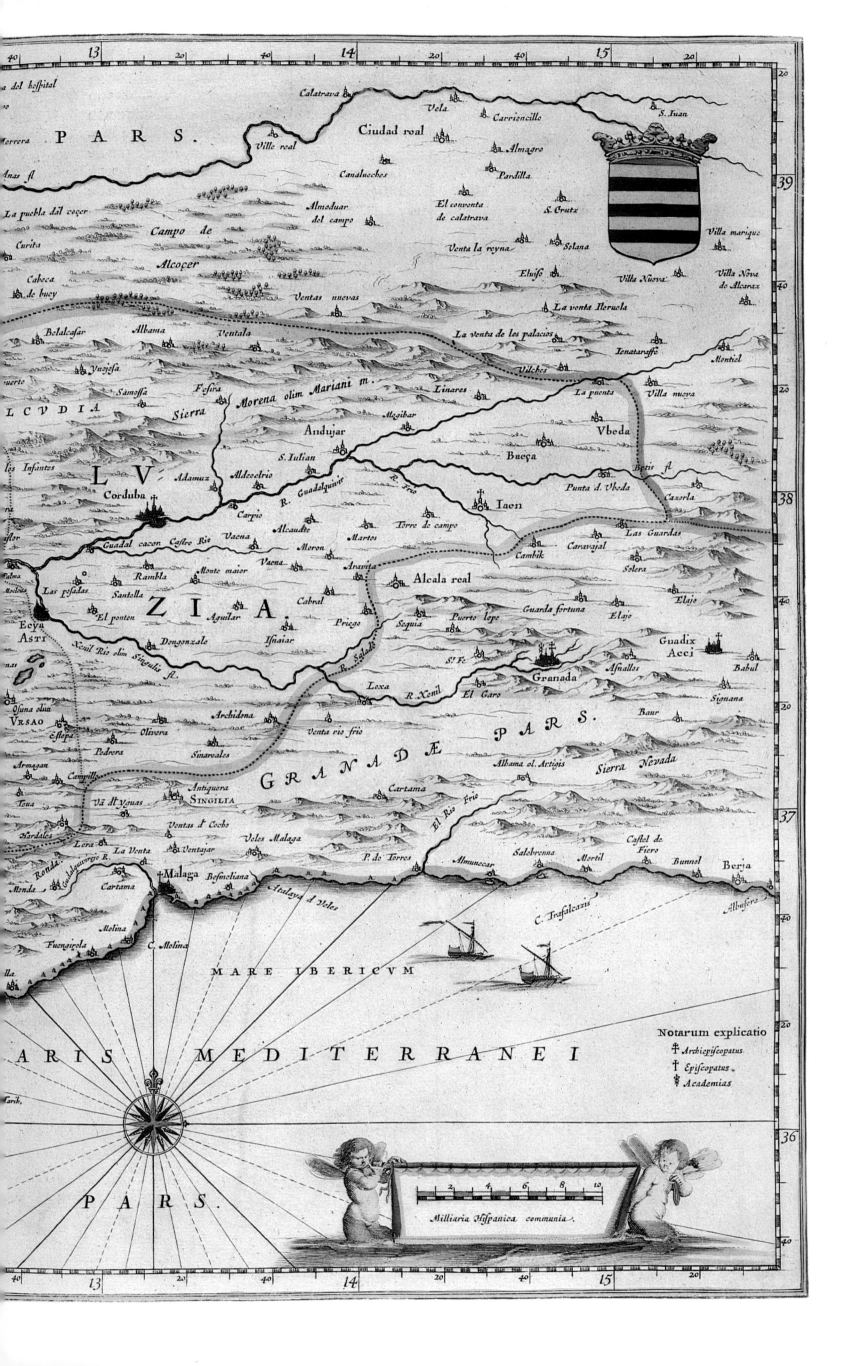

Africae nova descriptio

In common with Willem Blaeu's other maps of the continents, this beautiful and highly decorative map of Africa dates back to the relatively early period of his activity as a map publisher, to about 1617, when it first appeared as a separately published map. It remained a feature of the Blaeu atlases from 1630 to the 1660s.

Long a favourite of the collector, it is adorned and crowded with all the detail and charm that epitomizes the seventeenth-century map: the side-border vignettes of costumed figures, like early fashion plates, the frieze of nine town views forming the top border (Tangiers, Ceuta, Algiers, Tunis, Alexandria, Cairo, Moçambique, São Jorge de Elmina and Gran Canaria), as well as the pictures of animals filling the emptier spaces near the centre of the continent. Perhaps it was maps such as this that prompted Jonathan Swift's gentle satire,

> 'So Geographers in *Afric*-
>   maps,
> With Savage-Pictures fill
>   their Gaps;
> And o'er unhabitable
>   Downs
> Place Elephants for want
>   of Towns.'
(From *On Poetry,
        A Rapsody*, 1733).

All these features offer a visual feast for the twentieth-century eye. But although the general outline of the continent had been mapped with surprising accuracy within a few years of the Portuguese discovery of the Cape of Good Hope in 1488, large parts of the interior remained, to all intents and purposes, unknown until the middle of the nineteenth century.

Blaeu had, therefore, to rely on hearsay as to what

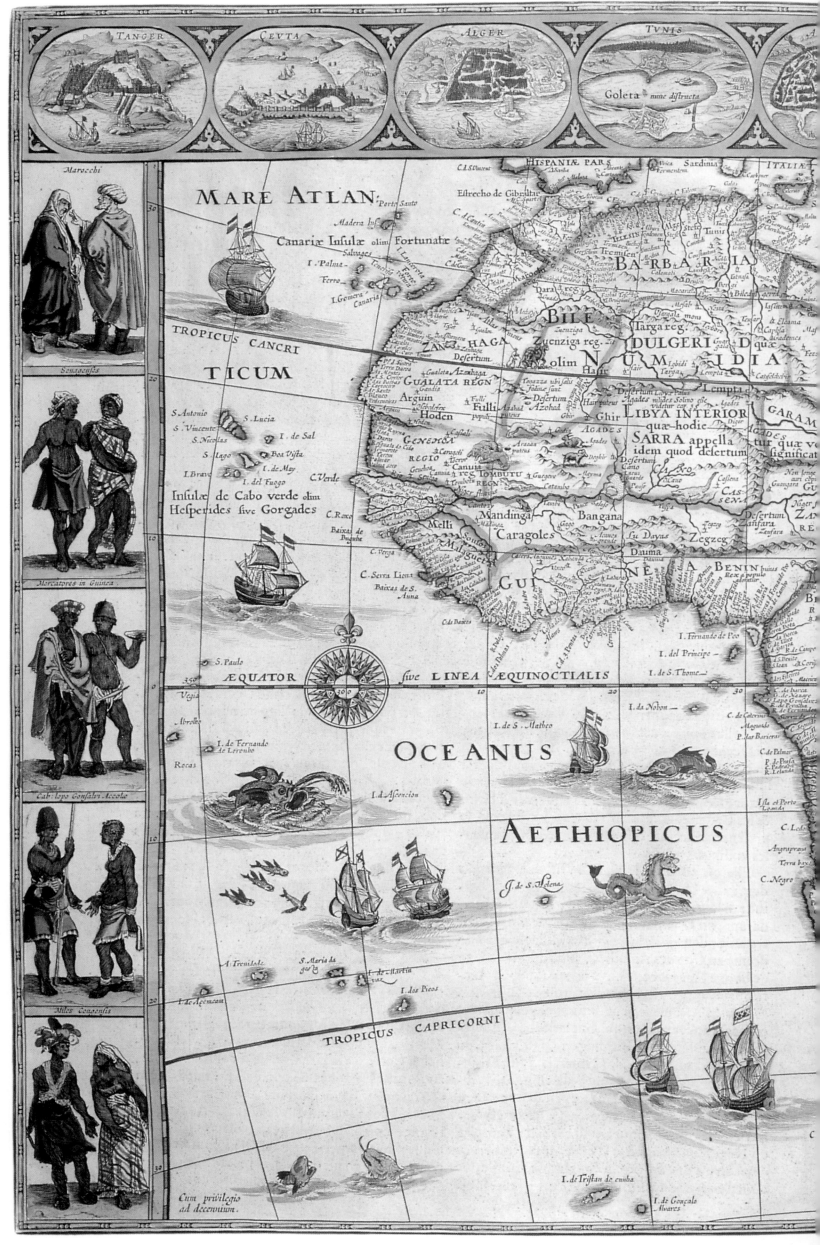

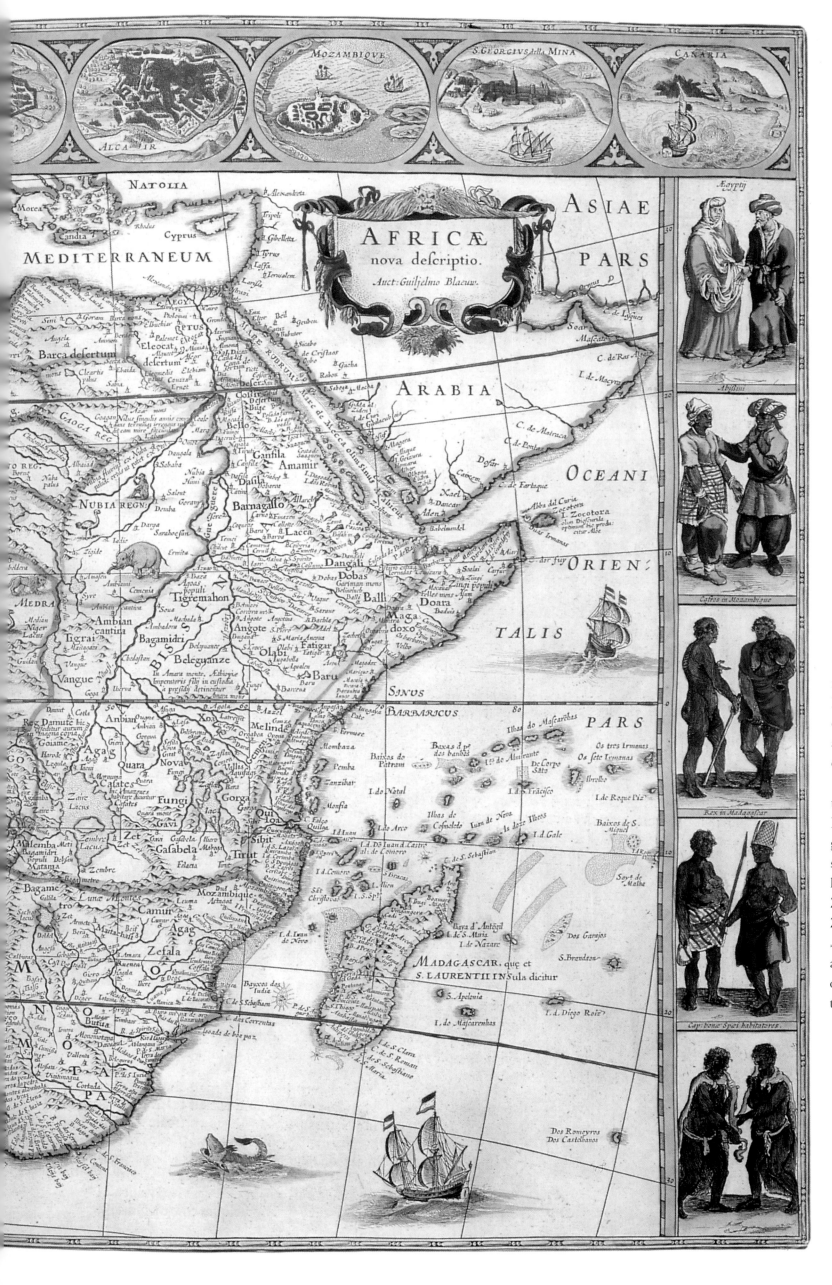

lay beyond the coastal regions of Africa. One source of information was the account left by the Moorish traveller and geographer 'al-Hasan ibn-Muhammad al-Wazzan (better known as Leo Africanus after his conversion to Christianity by Pope Leo X). Leo's *History and Description of Africa* was first published in Italy in 1550. Leo travelled in West Africa and the Sudan, in Gao, Hausaland, Bornu, Timbuktu and Niani. He also saw the Niger, declaring that it flowed westward, confirming the views of another Arab writer, 'al-Idrisi, who four hundred years earlier had stated thus, but had never seen the river for himself.

Other confusions and errors arose after the publication of Leo's history, largely as a result of misinterpretation and misreading of the work on the part of later writers and mapmakers who were in the habit of repeating and confounding existing errors, and often adding new errors of their own.

Blaeu shows the course of the Nile according to Ptolemy, the second-century geographer, flowing from a source placed in the two large, sub-Equatorial lakes Zaïre and Zaflan; the Zambeze river (or *R. de Spirito Sa[n]to*) rises from another spurious lake, called *Sachaf lacus*, placed to the south of Zaïre.

141

Melite Insula, vulgo Malta

Joan Blaeu included this map of Malta, Gozo and Comino, here oriented west to the top of the plate, in the atlas of 1662.

The heavily fortified natural harbour of Valetta is shown in some detail as constructed since the arrival of the Knights of St John in 1530. Ever since the middle years of the sixteenth century, Malta has been a popular cartographic subject, particularly in the years after 1565 when the Knights successfully defeated the fleet of Suleiman the Magnificent which had been sent to lay siege to Malta. Over forty years previously, in 1522, Suleiman had forced the Knights to leave their stronghold in the eastern Mediterranean on the island of Rhodes almost within sight of the Turkish coast. But this time, the Turkish forces themselves withdrew in September 1565, leaving the Order unassailed in their island fortress.

Blaeu's map shows the engagement of a fleet of Turkish vessels off Valetta. Tribute to the Order is paid in the form of the two figures on either side of the title at the lower right: a member of the Order facing the Turk. This is complimented by the vignette in the upper left-hand corner, showing the seated figures of Christ and a representation of a Grand Master.

Overall, this late map is almost plain in aspect by comparison with many of the maps in the Blaeu output; such plainness is, however, more than compensated by the rich, almost translucent colouring of this example.

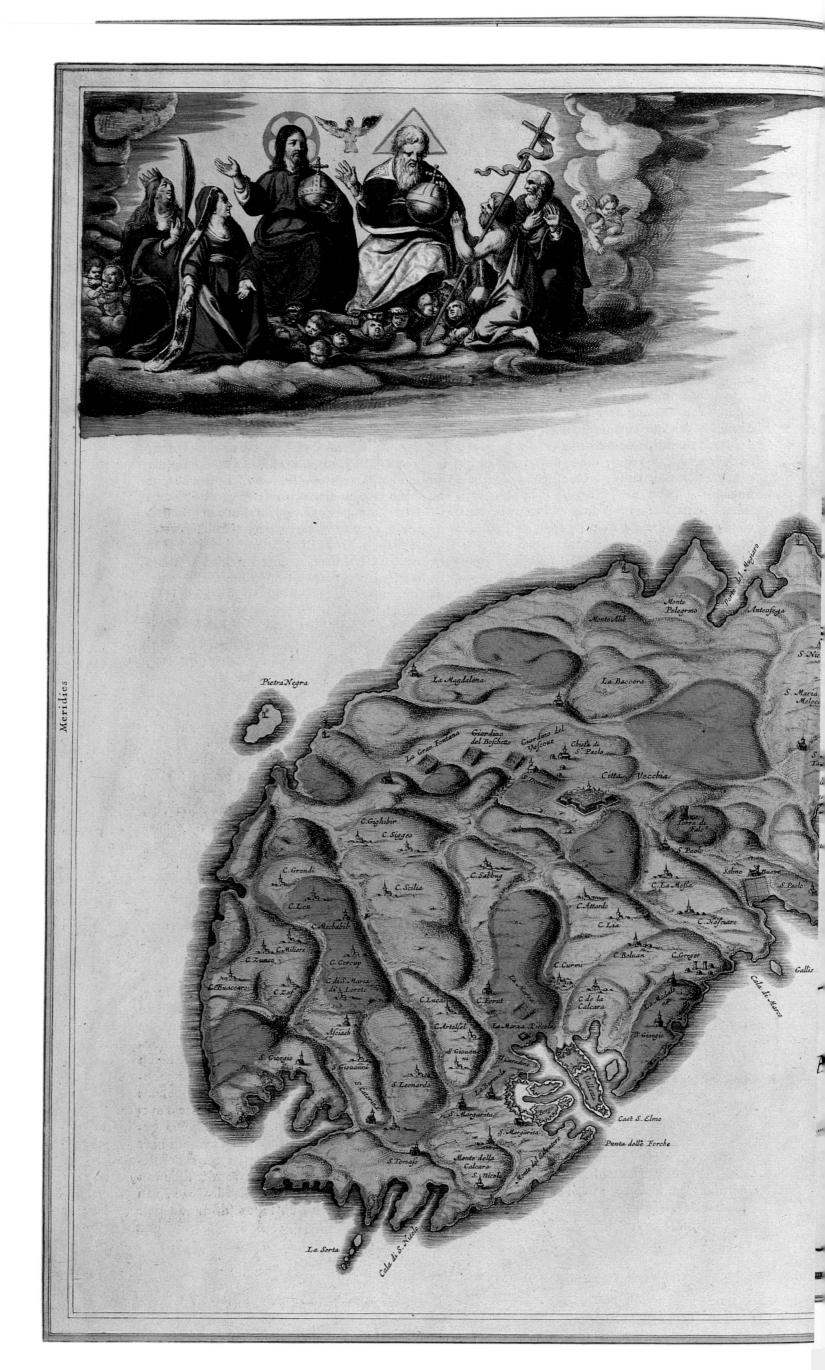

ens

GOZA

INSVLA.

Mugiaro

La Douvers

Scilendo

Cumino

Vecchie

La Caras

Porto
delle
Saline Vecchie

Rodum Cammar

Salamun

MELITE INSVLA,
Vulgo
MALTA.

Fezzae et Marocchi Regna Africae celeberrima

This map, which covers the area of modern Morocco, credits the Flemish mapmaker Abraham Ortelius as author. Willem Blaeu used a map dating from 1570 as a source for his map which he first issued in 1635.

Although this part of the North African coast resisted incorporation into the Turkish Empire, the Spanish succeeded in establishing a hold here between 1580 and 1640, at Ceuta, Tangiers, Arzila and elsewhere. For a time Tangiers was held by the English, from 1662 to 1684. Despite the raids on European vessels by pirates, often called Barbary pirates, considerable trade in such commodities as sugar, tobacco, gold and a fine leather, which came to be known as 'morocco', was carried on with France and England through their factors established here.

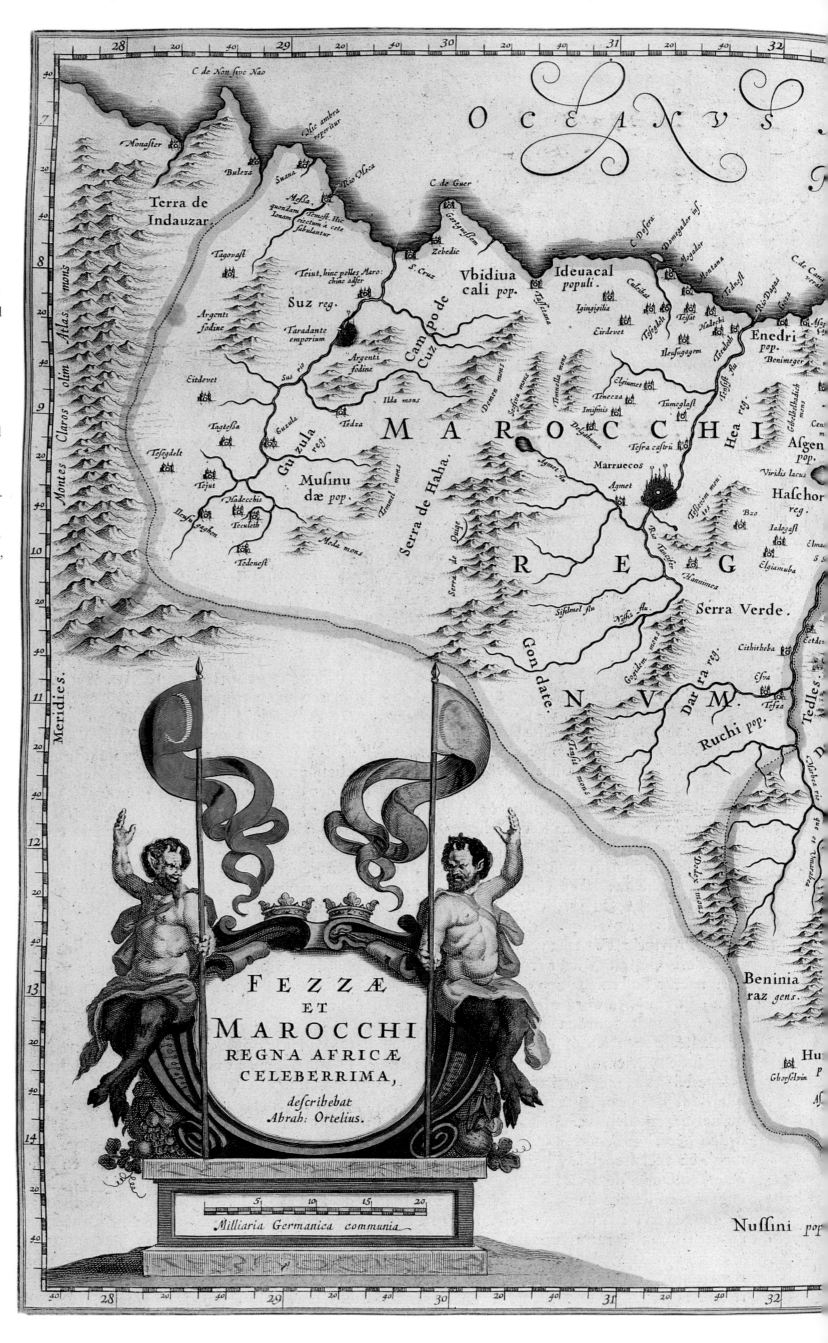

S A N T I C V S, QVI HODIE
R DEL NORT.

HISPANIÆ Septentrio.

P A R S.

Golfo de las yeguaz,
id est equarum.

C. S. Vincente

C. Blanco

Masagan

Elmedin

zamor

Subeit

Beniz

Anafe

Temesna
regio.

Zenetæ pop. qui
nunc Xauyi.

Rebat

Haunochal
lu

Rio Marbea

Rio Alcanxra

I. Fedale

Sale

Almancor

Rio Rebata

Rio Cebu

Mamora mechia

Sobaigne

Mamora

Rio Lecuz

Rio Tagadarte

Horari
pop.

Fanzara

Iesse Iseli

Larache

Cadiz

Rio Guadalquivir

Rio de Tarifylar

Gombeli.

Algara
regio

Elhalis
pop.

Basra

Alcacer

Arzila

Homa

Tanger

C. Espartel

Zennonus
mons

Podeaza
gar.

Arox

Ezagen

Narangia

Chehih
mons

Teteguis

Estrecho de Gibraltar.

Gibraltar

Benicheßen
mons

Tutuan

Gemera

Ha
bat reg. Alcacer

Almina

Ceuta

Elcha lati
pop.

Seusasena

Ponte de Tar
ga

Errifitis.

Salguisa

Fez

Mergo

Agla

Rio Vega

Velez

Pennon de
Velez

MARIS

Taufor

Baniteud

Guazeual

Nova

Garet.

MEDITERRANEI

Corate

Tamicaman

PARS.

Chauz.

Teza

Campos de
Anget.

Tarfogarello

147

Guinea

Dedicated to the celebrated Dr Nicolaes Tulp, anatomist and physician of Amsterdam, Willem Blaeu's map of the Guinea coast of West Africa made its first appearance in 1635, enjoying a long life of some thirty years as the standard European picture of the Ivory Coast, Gold Coast and Benin. It was also a general view of the source of one of the most regrettable results of European contact with West Africa, namely slaves for the developing plantations of the West Indies.

The coasts of Guinea were frequented by both Portuguese and English adventurers since at least the early years of the sixteenth century and, in the seventeenth, were the scene of considerable commercial rivalry between the Dutch, English, French, Danish and other nations. None of the European nations penetrated very far inland from their several coastal forts such as São Jorge de Elmina or Fort Nassau on the Gold Coast, and one result of this was that the true nature of the Niger remained undetermined until the nineteenth century.

European mapmakers had no authentic information of the source of this great river (see map 65 for Blaeu's depiction), neither on the direction in which it ran nor on the seas into which it flowed. The Moorish traveller known as Leo Africanus wrote a description of Africa which was published at Venice in 1550; he had indeed seen the Niger, but recorded that the river flowed westward.

That error led to cartographers showing the Niger as a broadly straight river flowing east to west to

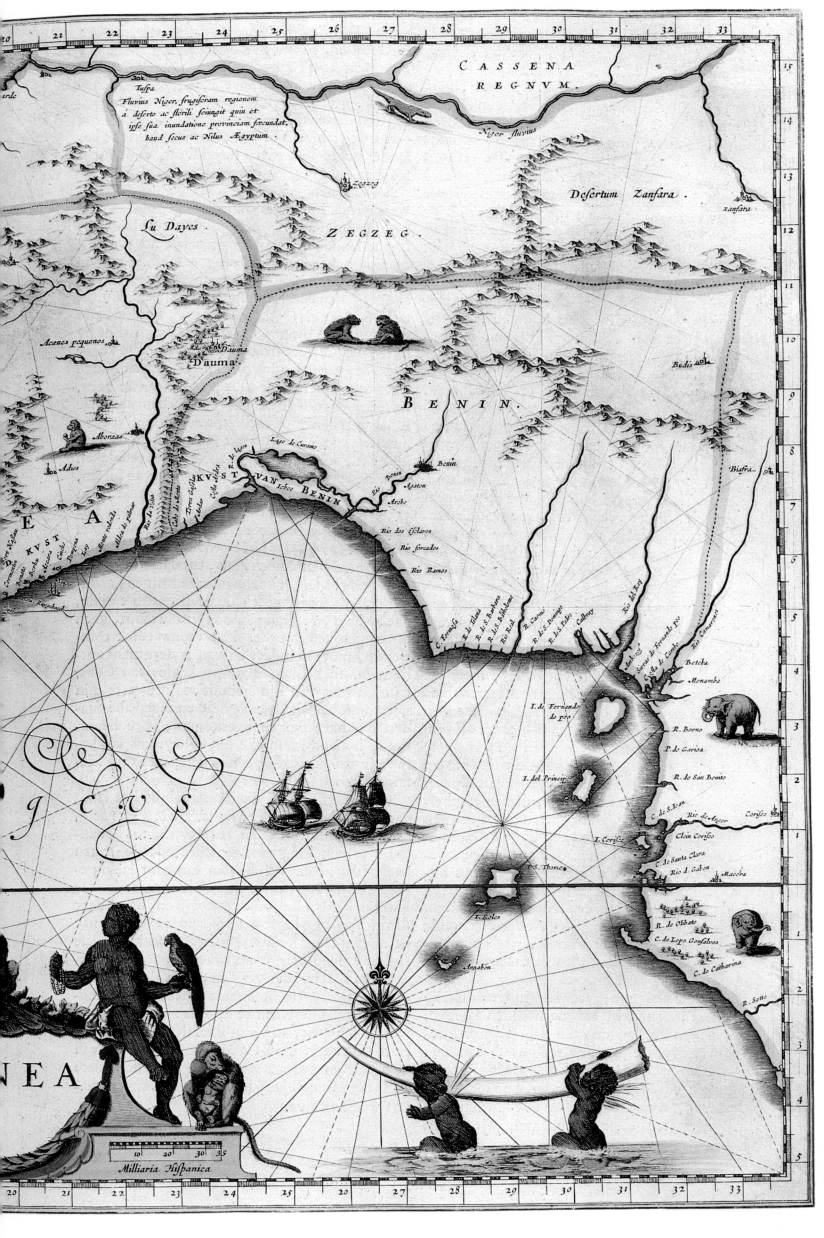

the north of the Guinea coastal region, connecting with the Senegal and Gambia rivers. Note also that Blaeu fills some of the emptier spaces of his map with pictures of lions, elephants, and baboons.

Negroes and apes decorate the title cartouche, and a hint of the flourishing ivory trade is included at the lower right.

Regna Congo et Angola

This map of the lower reaches of the great Zaïre river made its first appearance in the atlas of 1662.

It was very likely prompted by a desire to provide an up-to-date picture of recent explorations into this part of Africa during the years 1645 to 1660, which turned out to be the last exploratory expeditions in the region until the middle of the nineteenth century. A major tributary of the Zaïre River, the Cuango, is shown in some detail with numerous names given in Dutch, rather than Portuguese, reflecting the discoveries of the Dutch explorer Jan van Herder in about 1660.

Few towns are shown, aside from the Portuguese settlements at Luanda (founded in 1576) and Benguela (established in 1617), both late foundations after the initial Portuguese landings in 1484.

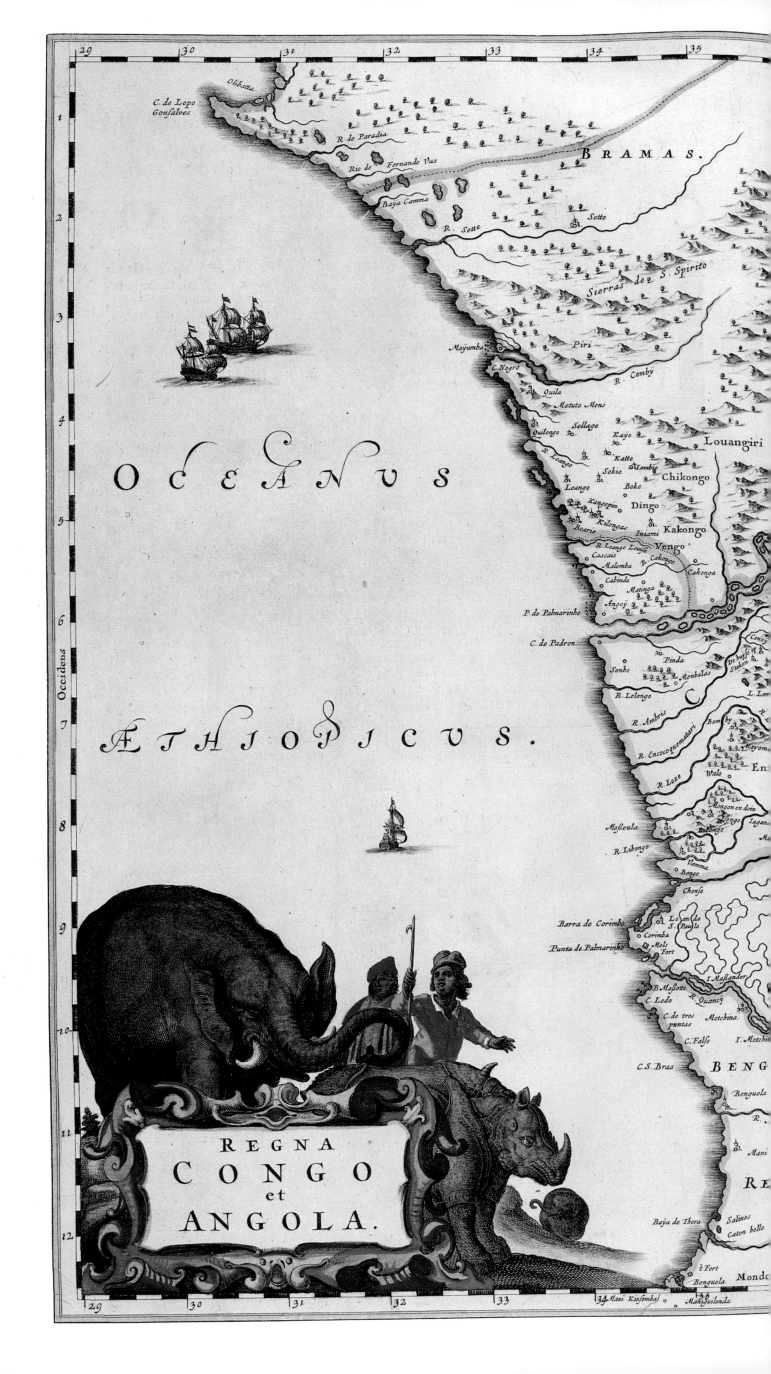

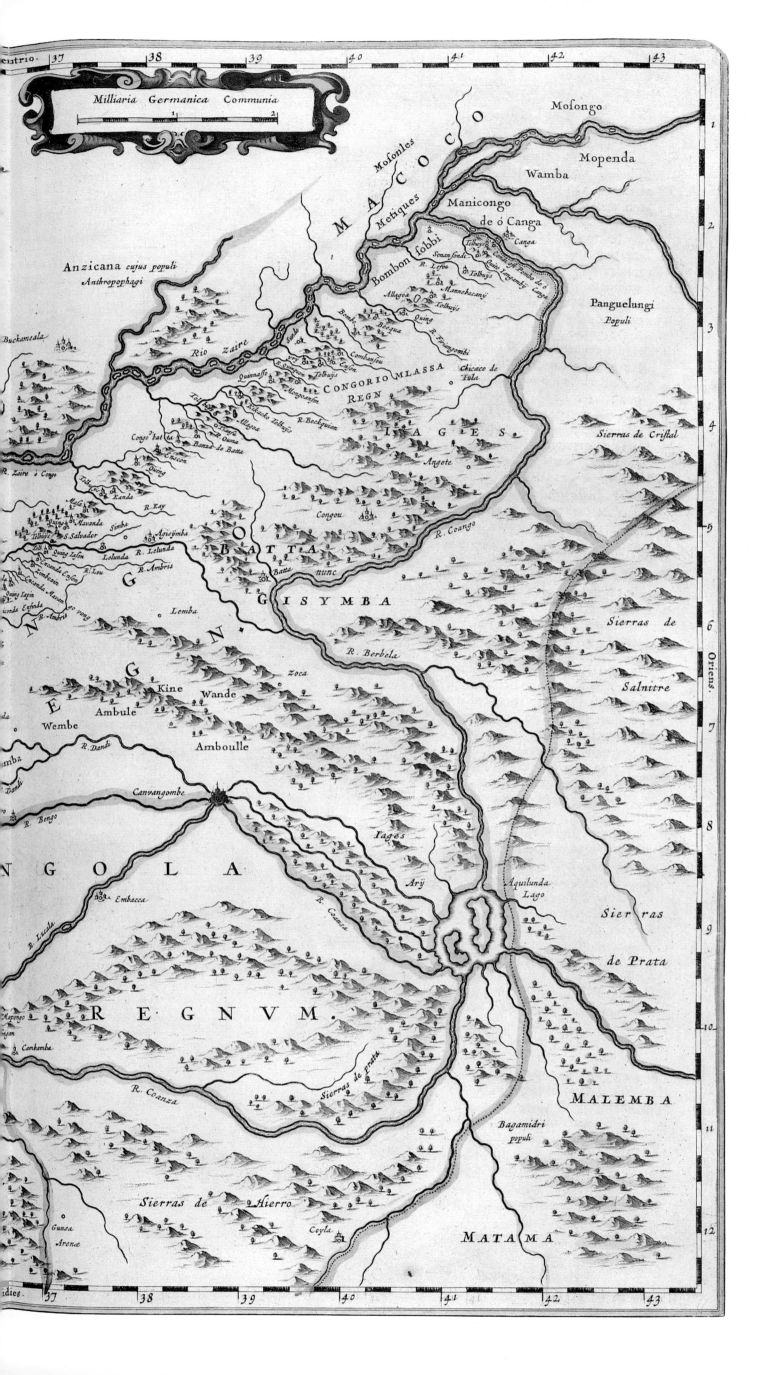

Milliaria Germanica Communia

1   2

MACOCO

Mosongo

Mosonles   Mopenda

Metiques   Wamba

Anzicana cujus populi   Manicongo
Anthropophagi   de ó Canga

Bombon sobbi   Canga
Senansondi   Tolbuijs   Cuites ofi Pumbo da
Buckamcala   R. Lefou   Tolbuijs   Quibó Pengambij Canga
Rio zaire   Allagoa   Mannebacanij   Panguelungi
Bombo   Beequa   Quing   Populi
Quinnasso   Combansou   R. Ferimgombi
R. Zaire à Congo   Tolbuijs   Tolbuijs   Chicace de
Mongoansin   Allagoa   CONGORIO MLASSA   Vulu
Tolbuijs   O. Pumbo   Ouma   REGN
Congo' bat ta   Banza da Batta
Checon   IAGES
Qusing   Sierras de Cristal
Mase
Masa   Mavanda   Simba   Angote
Gunsa   R. Kay
Tolbuijs   S. Salvador   Agisymba   Congou
Quing Iason   Lelunda   R. Lelunda   R. Coango
Cacanda Ensber   R. Leu
R. Ambris   BATTA
Quing Iapin   Batta
Enfunda   nunc
R. Ambris   Lemba   GISYMBA   Sierras de
zoca   R. Berbela
Kine   Wande   Salnitre
Ambule
Wembe   Amboulle
R. Dandi
Canvangombe   Iages
R. Bengo   Arij   Aquilunda
Embacca   R. Coanza   Lago   Sierras
NGOLA   de Prata
Mopingo   REGNVM.
Cambamba
R. Coanza   Sierras de prata   MALEMBA
Bagamidri
populi
Sierras de Hierro
Gunsa
Arenæ   Coyla   MATAMA

Aethiopia Superior vel Interior; vulgo Abissinorum sive Presbiteri Ioannis Imperium

Much of the romance of old maps can be demonstrated by a look at this splendid map of eastern and central Africa: legendary kingdoms, fabled rivers, and illustrations of animals to fill otherwise empty spaces.

For the most part Blaeu's map, which first appeared in 1635, is based on a map of the Kingdom of Prester John made by the Fleming Abraham Ortelius in 1573. Medieval legend had located the Christian kingdom of Prester John in central Asia. However, when European contact with the Moghul Empire disproved the legend, the kingdom was relocated in the unexplored interior of north-eastern Africa, giving the legend a new lease of life, as it were, and a new respectability. A close look at the centre of the map, above *Amara mons*, reveals a note in Latin to the effect that here the sons of Prester John are held in confinement, a custom recorded by a Portuguese embassy to Abyssinia in 1520–1527.

By the time this map appeared, the legend, which traces the lineage of Prester John back to the time of Solomon, was nearly five hundred years old.

The east coast of Africa is shown in some detail, reflecting both Portuguese and Arab trading interest in the area. Mogadishu, Mombasa, Quiloa [Kilwa] and Moçambique are shown as major towns. The west coast from Benin to Angola appears, with the Zaïre River named as *Zaïre fluvius*, and some coastal detail taken from

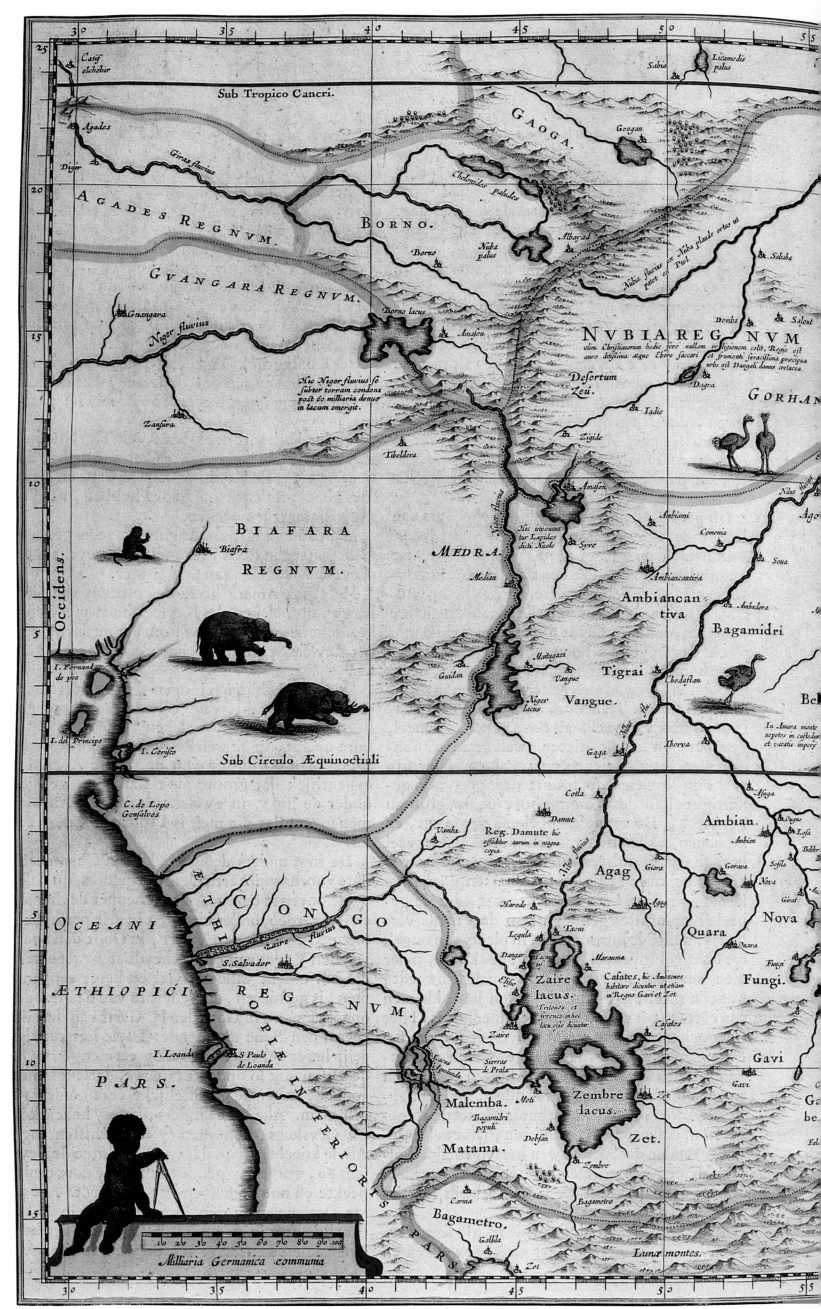

Portuguese descriptions of the region.

Shown below the Equator are two large lakes or inland seas according to the descriptions of the second-century geographer Ptolemy. These were held to be the source of the Nile. These lakes were called *Zaïre* (to the west) and *Zaflan* (to the east), and beyond them Africa remained unknown to the Ancients. In the north-west, the Niger issues from a lake called *Niger lacus*, flows north and then continues west via a subterranean course and another lake to the Atlantic.

Then, just to the south-west of the Niger, in *Biafara Regnum*, Blaeu illustrated what Swift would later satirize as 'elephants for want of towns…'.

Insula S. Laurentii vulgo Madagascar

Very few seventeenth-century atlases contained a detailed separate map of Madagascar, the Blaeu atlas being no exception until 1662 when this fine map appeared.

Prior to the European discovery of Madagascar by Diogo Dias in 1501, the island had long been known to the Arab traders of the east coast of Africa as the Island of the Moon, and Chinese traders are known to have visited this part of the Indian Ocean in the late twelfth century. The Portuguese, who called Madagascar after St Laurence on whose day (2 February) they landed there in 1506, established a small coastal settlement in the south-east at Matatane and occupied part of the west coast at the beginning of the seventeenth century.

Most of the toponymy, however, is French, reflecting their interest in this island since 1640 as 'la France Orientale'. A French settlement at *Fort Dauphin*, near the south-eastern tip of the island, flourished between 1643–1672. The small island off the south-east coast (marked as *S. Apollonia Gallis Isle Bourbon*) had been French since 1649, when Étienne de Flacourt landed there. The island later became known as Réunion.

It was the map made in 1658 by de Flacourt on which Joan Blaeu based this splendid atlas map.

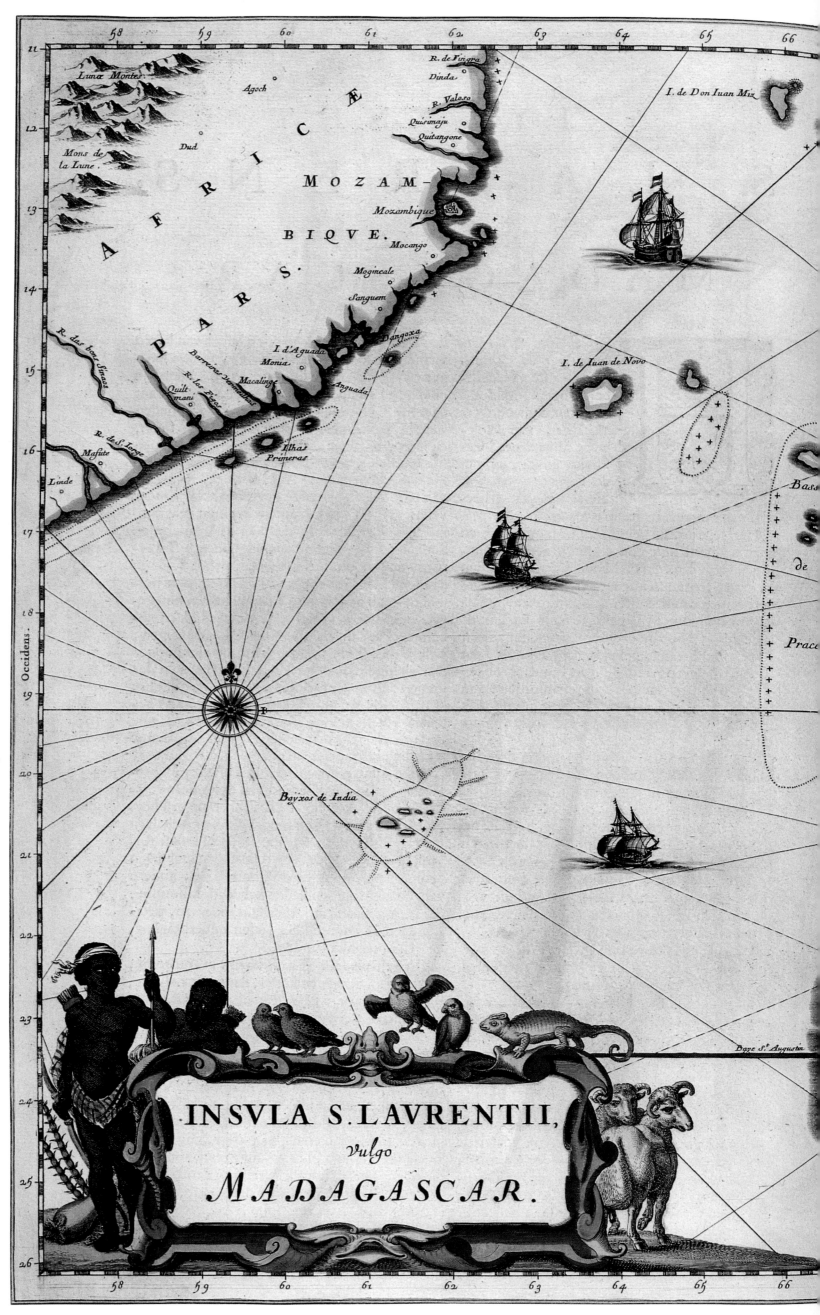

I. de Don Iuan de Castro
al. de Comoro

S. Braças

de Comoro

I. Aliola

I. du S.t Esprit

C. S.t
Sebastien

C. Natal

Pays

Incogneu

Vohemaro

Baye de Vohemaro

Cap. di N.ra Dona
de Cugna.

Diego Soarez

Terre de
S.t
André.

Baye d'Antongil

Maningare R.

Mandegourou R.

Noßi Hibrahim.
ou
Isle S.te Marie.

Angalemboule

Terre
de
Pracel

Mansiatre R.

Longue Poincte

Sahaueh

Port aux Prunes

Maroharats R.

Inonrhon R.

Terra
la
Rançomund.

Pays riche
en bestial

M. de Bohissemens

Ambahé R.

Pacanile R.

Andrasahé R.

Manghourou R.

Lamanouffi Riu. et Cap.

Mununbabun R.

Mananzari ou
Antanares

Pays
nommes
res

Ontaisotrouha

Mananghare R.

Ontasaca

Sandry

Vatomanahom

Mantacaua R.

Moronbe R.

Farahon R.

Itaponle R.

F. des François

Matatana R.

Mananghare R.
au 7. bouches

Massianach R.

Andraghintha R.

Randrauinanxha R.

Auiboule

Vinaughauarats
bouches de manatengha R.

S. Apollonia
Gallis
Isle Bourbon

Onghlahe R.

Pays
de
Alan
Andres Hombe

Fan-
ga
tere

Vallee
Anchibuch

Same R.

Fautac

Manasiaf R.

S. Luce

Itapere

S. Claire

Font Dauphin

C. Ranohate

Ance aux Galions

Estang d'Anjong

Mananbato R.

Manonabat R.

Manandru R.

Tropicus   Capricorni.

Americae nova tabula

The New World. Originally issued by Joan's father, Willem, as early as 1617, this general map of the Americas was one of the longest-lived plates in the atlas, having been used as an atlas map since 1630.

Here is the general seventeenth-century European view of the Western Hemisphere: the delineation of the coast and the nomenclature of the Pacific as well as of the Atlantic coasts are basically Spanish in origin and follow the maps of the Fleming Abraham Ortelius and his countryman Cornelis Wytfliet. To these, Willem Blaeu inserted, on the east coast, the English names given by the Roanoke colonists in Virginia and by Martin Frobisher, John Davis and Henry Hudson in the far north. In Florida and along the St Lawrence, Blaeu added the names given by the French settlers, almost the only memorials of their ill-fated venture in Florida during the latter part of the sixteenth century.

When Blaeu first made his map in the early years of the seventeenth century, Europeans still had no real knowledge of the nature of the Mississippi system. From the expedition journals of Hernando de Soto (1539–1543), they had inferred an extensive range of mountains trending east-west to the north of the coast of the Gulf of Mexico in *la Florida*, apparently precluding a great river system. The Great Lakes were, as yet, unknown, although by the time Blaeu issued this map in its atlas form in the 1630s, Samuel de Champlain's travels in the Huron region together with his hearsay accounts from

Coral Indians were becoming well known through his 1632 map of the region. Evidently, this appears to have been unknown to Blaeu at the time, but surprisingly, he never incorporated the information on later printings of the map. The same applies to Manhattan and Long Island as well, despite the fact that only a short distance from Amsterdam, the Leiden academic Johannes de Laet had published the first edition of his monumental work on the Americas which provided source materials for any number of maps of the Americas throughout the remainder of the century and beyond.

In common with the other general continental maps in the atlas, Blaeu has provided perspective plans or views of settlements in the Americas, including Havana, St Domingo, Cartagena, Mexico, Cusco, Potosi, I. la Mocha in Chili, Rio Ianeiro and Olinda in Pharnambucco, as well as the vignette illustrations of native figures taken from the accounts of John White (Virginia) or Hans Staden (Brazil) and others.

Whereas Joan Blaeu was content to reprint the old general map of the Americas to serve as the introductory plate to the Americas volume of his atlas, the regional maps were sometimes based on much more recent sources.

For his map of eastern Canada and Labrador, Joan Blaeu appears to have used Samuel de Champlain's great map of 1632, the most extensive and accurate portrayal of New France then available.

This version of part of Champlain's map was first published by Blaeu in 1662 and shows Nova Scotia, Newfoundland, the St Lawrence Gulf, Labrador and the Davis and Hudson Straits as well as the southern tip of Greenland. Note the title cartouche at the upper right-hand corner, the design of which indicates the continuing importance of the Grand Banks fisheries.

This late introduction into the Blaeu atlas is also a good example of the subtly different, later style of Blaeu's maps: somewhat less ornamental perhaps, but more geographically accurate.

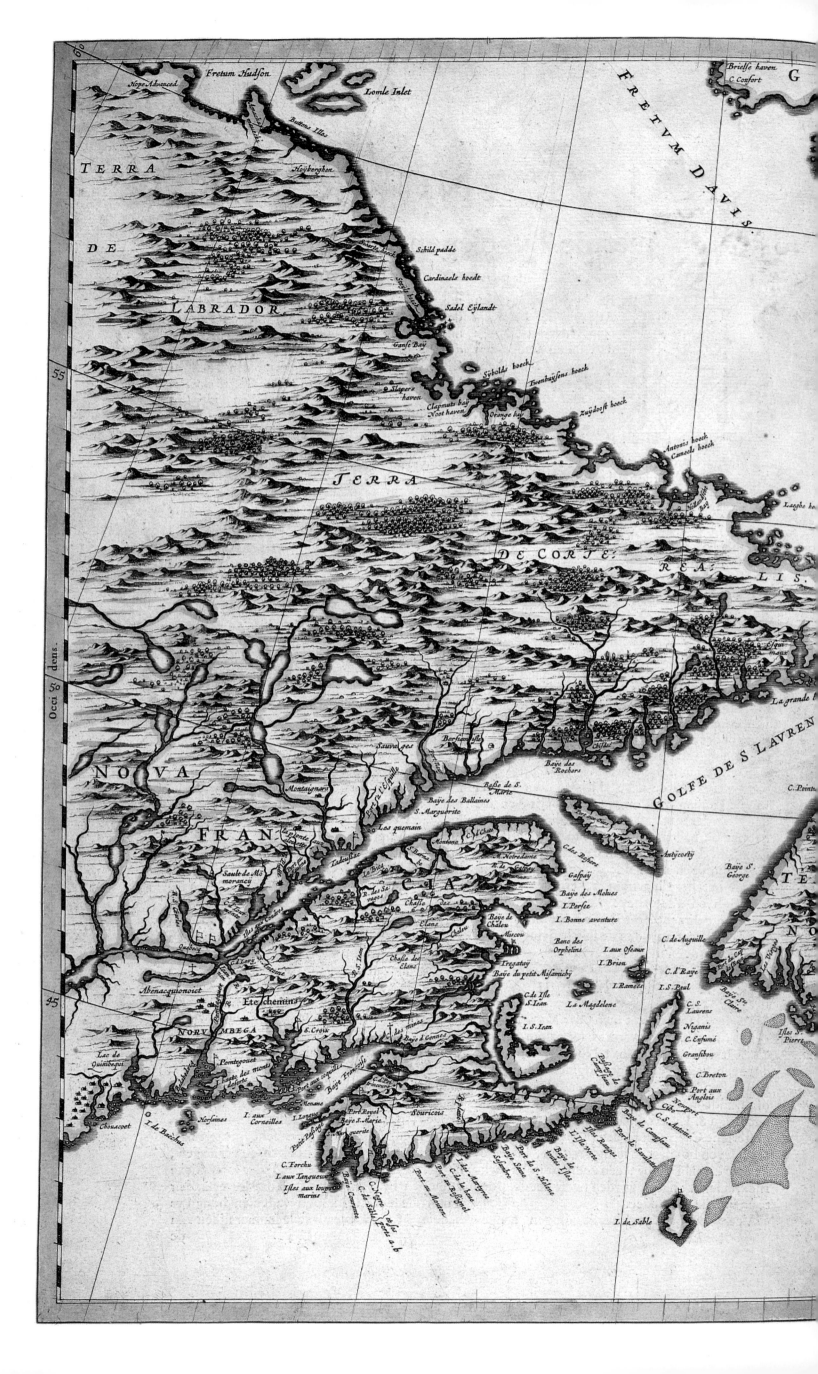

N LAN-
IA.

C. Goede hoope

Withe Cape

C. Discord

C. Farewel

EXTREMA AMERICÆ
Versus Boream, ubi
TERRA NOVA
NOVA FRANCIA, Adjacentiaq.

Croix Blanche

Belle Isle

I. Fichot

C. de Grat

Groye

Bello Isle

Isle aux Apovois

Las Isles

a Chaveux

Baye Blanche

I. das Aves

C. S. Iean

I. des Fougues

Pra Lafe

I. de Moy

C. de Bona vista

Baye

N. Claire

I. de Bacalaos

Portugals

Dos patur

Trinite

Baye de Conception

C. S. Fresaye

C. S. Francisco

I. S. Iean

Frinouse

C. de Esphera

I. d'Espoirs

Abre de Brigas

Agua Fuerte

Rennosa

C. de Raze

55

5o
ens.

Ori.

45

Amsteledami Io: Blaeu Exc.

Insulae Americanae in oceano septentrionali, cum Terris adiacentibus

This very handsome general map of the entire Caribbean region was another long-lived map in the Blaeu atlas. First issued in 1634, it covers the area between Virginia in the north and the mouth of the Orinoco River on the northern coast of South America.

All the familiar island names are here: the Bahamas group, Cuba, Hispaniola and Jamaica, as well as the smaller islands in the Leeward Island group and the great Spanish trading ports of Cartagena and La Habana, all recalling the days of the Spanish Main and the English buccaneer fleets.

In the frame of the title cartouche at the upper left-hand corner, Blaeu has incorporated illustrations of marine and other fauna found here, such as turtles, iguanas, alligators and large bats.

This is one of the maps that Willem Blaeu based on the regional maps of the Americas produced by Johannes de Laet of Leiden. This is particularly evident in the outline of the North American south-east region with the outline of Florida, for example, more like that with which we are familiar today in contrast to the older, wedge-shaped outline as shown on the general map of the Americas (see map 67).

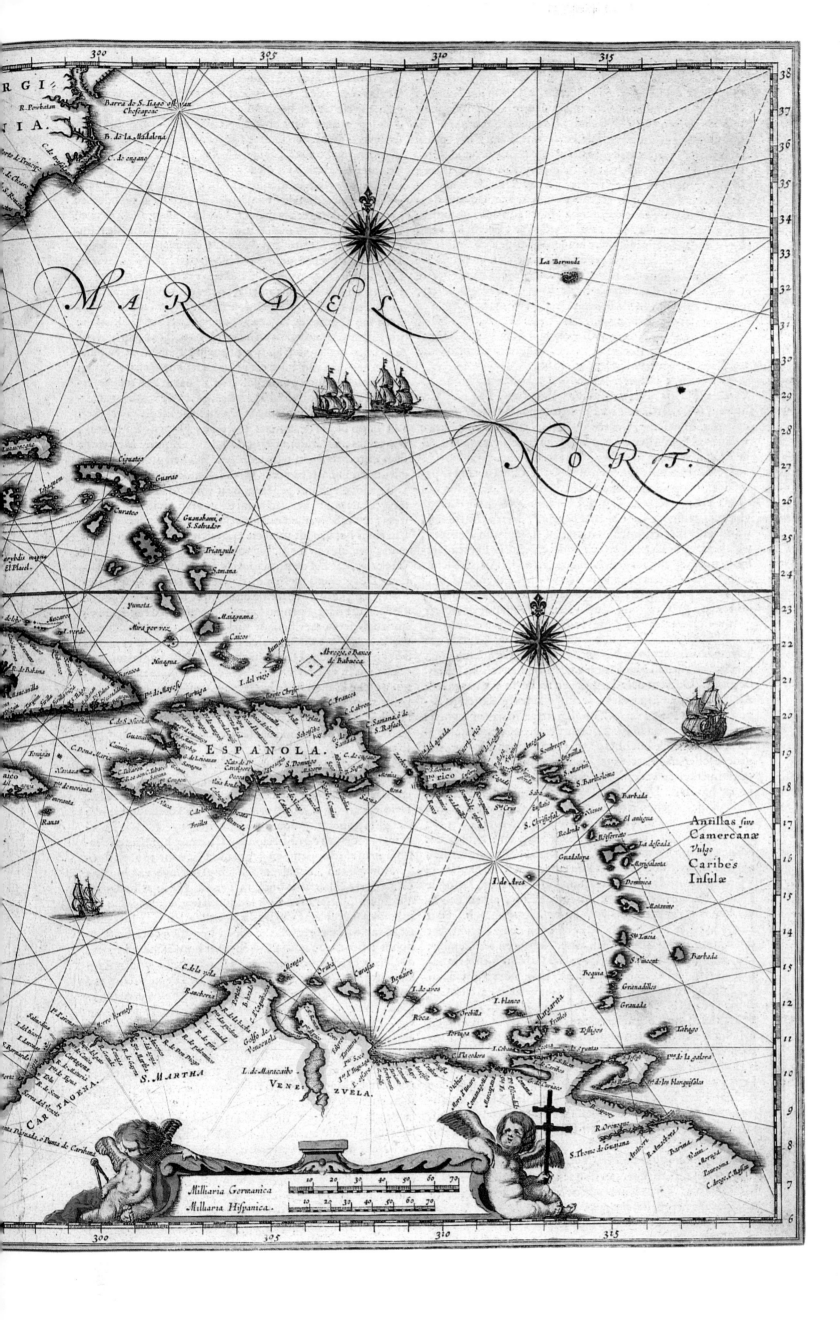

MAR DEL

NORT

La Bermuda

ESPANOLA.

S. Domingo

porto rico

Antillas sive
Camercanæ
vulgo
Caribes
Insulæ

Barbada

El antigua

La deseada

Guadalupa

Dominica

Matanino

St Lucia

Barbada

S. Vincent

Bequia

Granadillos

Granada

Tabago

I. blanco

Margarita

Frailes

Testigos

I. de Aves

C. de la vela

Curasao

Bonaire

I. de aves

Orchilla

Roca

Portuga

Golfo de
Venezuela

L. de Maracaibo

VENEZVELA

S. MARTHA

CARTAGENA

S. Thome de Guaiana

R. Orenoque

Milliaria Germanica
Milliaria Hispanica

10   20   30   40   50   60   70

10   20   30   40   50   60   70

Canibales insulae

This is another of the 'new' maps which Joan Blaeu produced for the 1662 atlas. Oriented west to the top of the plate, it shows the sweep of the Leeward and Windward Islands between Puerto Rico at the upper right and Trinidad at the lower left.

This 'new' map also appears much plainer than the earlier, more decorative maps in the Blaeu atlas, and even has the appearance of being unfinished, especially as the title of the map is without any embellishment in the form of the traditional sea-monsters or sailing ships. Instead, the map has the appearance of a practical navigational chart with its intersecting network of rhumb-lines (also known as loxodromes) or lines of constant true course making non-right angles with meridians.

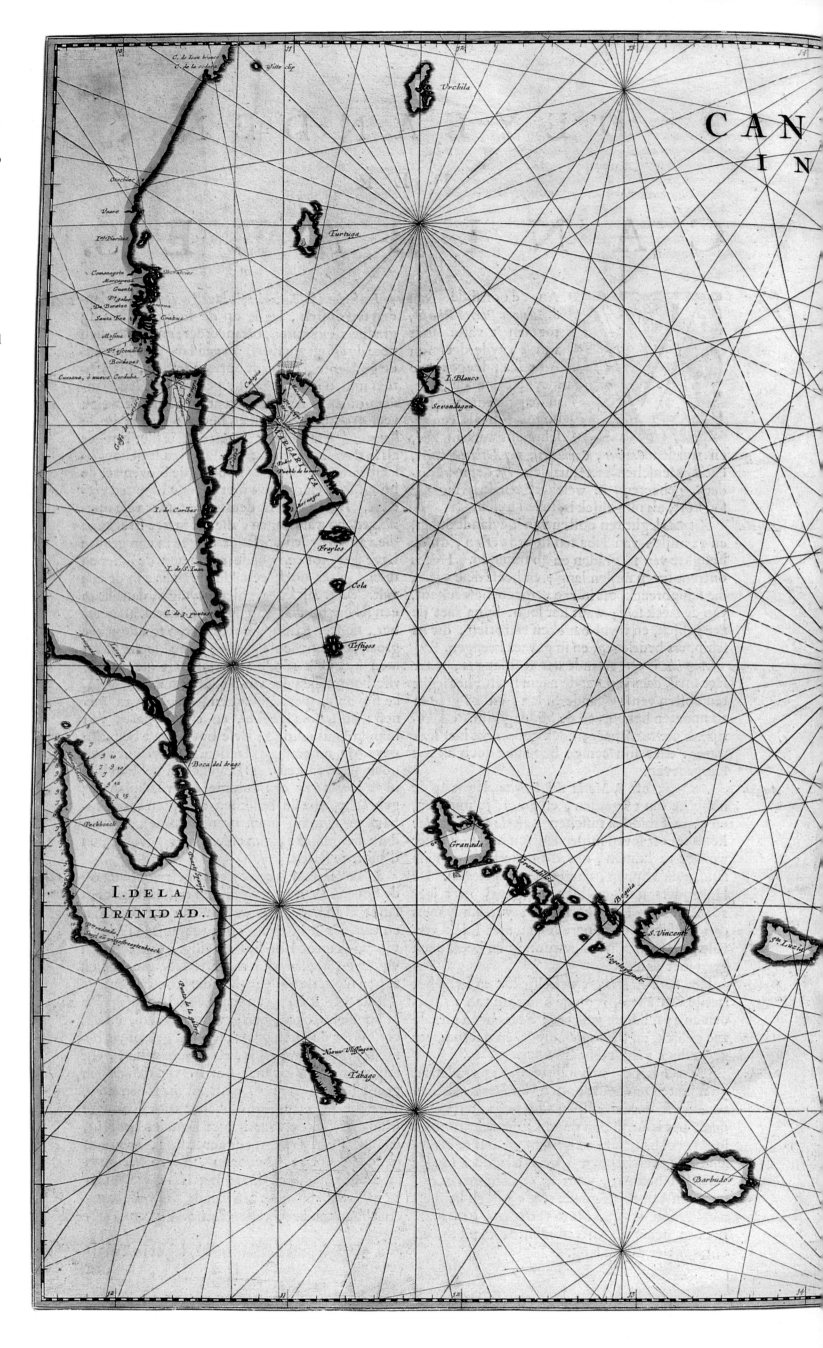

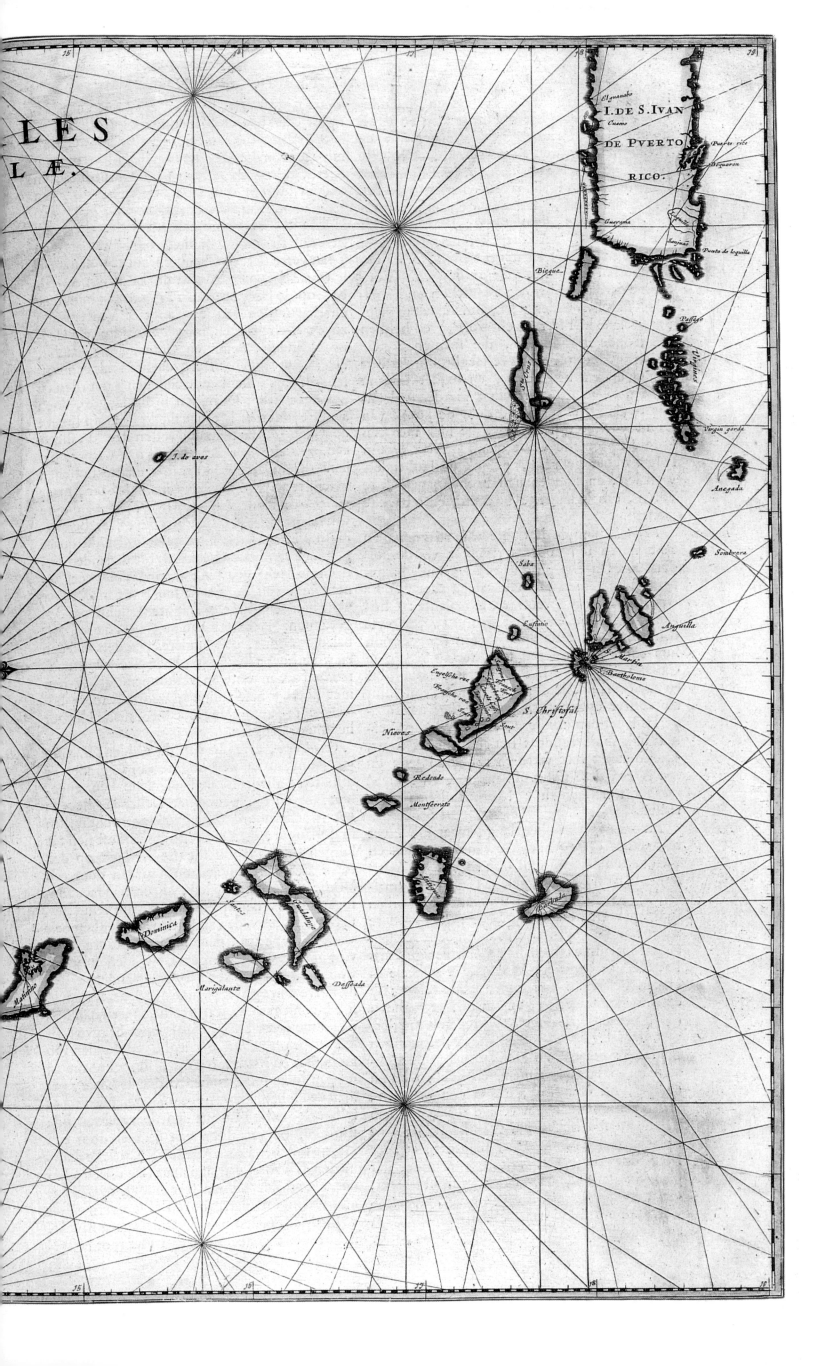

Nova Belgica et Anglia Nova

Oriented west to the top of the plate, this beautiful map of New England and the New Netherlands is one of the earliest detailed maps to include that part of North America colonized by the Dutch, and is the first printed map showing Indian canoes and several North American fauna such as turkeys, beavers, polecats and otters.

First produced by Willem Blaeu in 1635, it exercised considerable influence for many years. The geographical details were derived mostly from a manuscript map of the region drawn in 1614 by the Dutch explorer Adriaen Blockx (now in the Algemeen Rijksarchief at 's-Gravenhage), and from a map in Johannes de Laet's *Nieuwe Wereldt* of 1630.

Blockx, a fur trader as well as an explorer, first arrived in North America in 1611 and set out on a coasting voyage in 1614. His ship, *Onrust*, was the first boat built on Manhattan Island. He sailed through the *Hellegat* [East River] into *De Groote bay* [Long Island Sound] exploring the shores and noting the locations of the various tribes of Indians, such as the *Manhattans*, *Morhicans*, *Pequatoos* and others. Note also the illustrations of palisaded Indian villages, dug-out canoes and the male and female figures decorating the title cartouche.

Adriaen Blockx himself is commemorated by *Adriaen Blockx Eylandt*, nowadays known as Block Island, off the Rhode Island shore.

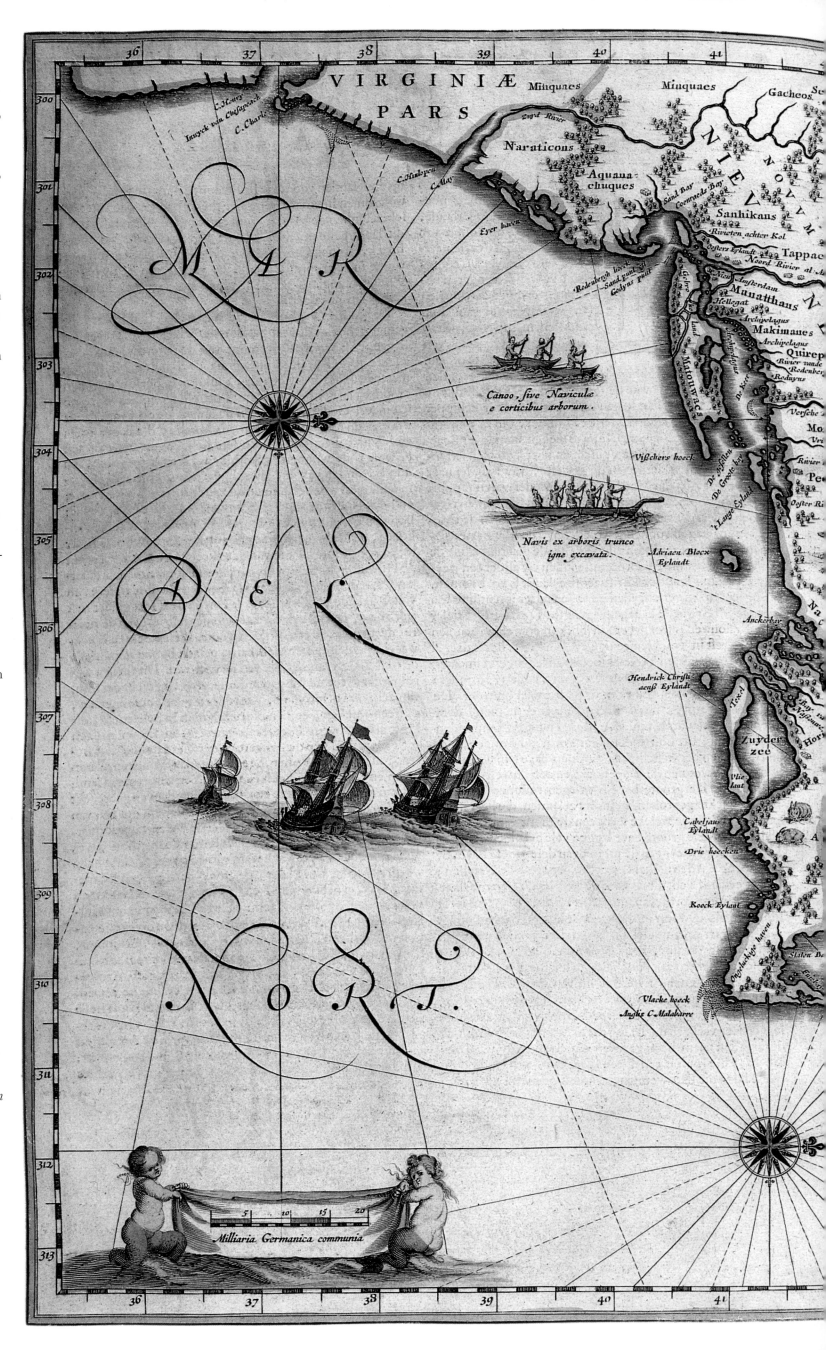

Modus muniendi apud Mahikanenses.

NOVA
BELGICA
ET
ANGLIA
NOVA

NOVÆ

FRANCIÆ PARS

Mappa Aestivarum Insularum, alias Barmudas dictarum

Like all seventeenth-century maps of Bermuda, Willem Blaeu's map is based ultimately on the survey made by John Norwood of the Bermuda Company in 1618 in the form as published by the English mapmaker, John Speed, in 1627. Blaeu's version first appeared a little later, in 1630.

Although discovered in 1515 by the Spaniard Juan de Bermúdez, after whom the island was supposedly named, it was the shipwreck of a party of Virginia colonists in 1610 led by Sir George Somers that gave Bermuda its first known inhabitants. Blaeu's Latin title reflects this fact, for *Aestivarum Insularum* means Summer (or Somers) Islands. The experience of Somers and his men inspired William Shakespeare, who dispatched Ariel to 'fetch dew from the still-vext Bermoothes' and populated the islands with the cast of *The Tempest*.

The place names and the list of Proprietors given below the map itself all recall the original members of the Bermuda Company, the latter being listed as eight tribes (or parishes): the Marquis of Hamilton, Sir Thomas Smith, the Earls of Devonshire, Pembroke, Warwick and Southampton, William Paget, Sir Edward Sandys and others including Sir Thomas Russell, Shakespeare's friend and executor.

In 1610, the Virginia Company, in *A True Declaration of the Estate of the Colonie in Virginia*, said of Bermuda: 'These Islands of the Bermudos, have evere beene accounted as an inchaunted pile of rockes,

and a desert inhabitation for Divels; but all the Fairies of the rockes were but flocks of birds, and all the Divels that haunted the woods, were but heards of Swine'.

In the upper left-hand and right-hand corners of the map appear the adjacent coasts of the North American colonies of Virginia and New England with, just below the large and ornate centrally placed title cartouche, a tiny outline of Bermuda itself, intended to show its correct proportion and position in the North Atlantic against the mainland. The cartouche incorporates the seated figure of Neptune, the Royal arms, fish and several kinds of navigational instruments in use at the time. The lower corners show the seals of the colony of Virginia and of Bermuda.

Nova Virginiae tabula

Although this map of the Chesapeake Bay region bears the name of Willem Blaeu, it comes from one of the plates Willem purchased from the plate stock of the Amsterdam publisher Jodocus Hondius the younger in 1629. Blaeu then issued the map in his *Atlantis Appendix* in 1630, and in most editions of the firm's atlases thereafter.

The map is a version of the one made in 1612 by the Englishman, Captain John Smith. His map was the first to depict with reasonable accuracy Chesapeake Bay with its tributaries and became the accepted prototype map for most subsequent maps of the colony published either in England or in continental Europe during the remainder of the seventeenth century. Captain Smith's map acted as a promotional piece for that vast area of North America called Virginia and it exerted a great influence on the history of English colonization in America.

John Smith (1579–1631) was the foremost English settler in Virginia. His many adventures included being captured several times, defeating an Indian chief in hand-to-hand combat as well as the celebrated incident in which Pocahontas saved him from being killed by Powhatan, who is himself the subject of the portrait engraved at the upper left-hand corner of Blaeu's map.

While the geographical detail of the map shows information accurate at the time of Smith's travels, earlier descriptions of Virginia are recalled. When Smith's map appeared in 1612, the engraver turned to an engraving by the German Theodor de Bry

based on the drawings made by John White in the 1580s for the portrait of Powhatan, and the figure of an Indian in war paint at the right to represent the Susquehanna chief. All of these elements were combined by the Amsterdam engraver Dirk Grijp for the Dutch version of Smith's map as issued by the Hondius firm in 1618. Thus, when Blaeu purchased the plate it was already a decade old and it was issued unchanged except for his imprint and a few very small retouches until the 1660s. The Blaeu derivative was the most popular version of Captain Smith's map published during the seventeenth century.

Virginiae partis australis, et Floridae, partis orientalis, interjacentiumq. regionum nova descriptio

This map of the Southeast, extending from the southern part of Virginia to northern Florida, appeared in the Blaeu atlases from 1638 onwards.

It was based on a map of the region published in 1606 by Hondius after surveys by the Englishman John White in 1590 and the Frenchman Jacques Le Moyne de Morgues in 1564–1565, with the respective areas of English and French colonization indicated by the Royal arms of the two nations in Virginia and in Florida.

The map shows a region at the southern end of the Appalachians where gold and silver were obtained: *Apalatcy montes in quibus aes aurum et argentum invenitur,* referring to the sixteenth-century accounts of panning for these metals in the rivers of the region by the Indians.

Although the map is based on an older model, Blaeu attempted to incorporate some more recent geographical information, such as a settlement established in 1621 by Irish planters led by one Daniel Gookin, at Newport News in the north on the shores of Chesapeake Bay, and also Jamestown farther upstream on the James River (marked on the map as *Powhatan flu.*). The general outline of the Carolina coast on this map is another improvement on the earlier map, being shown here with two large cuspid bays which are now called Onslow Bay and Long Bay.

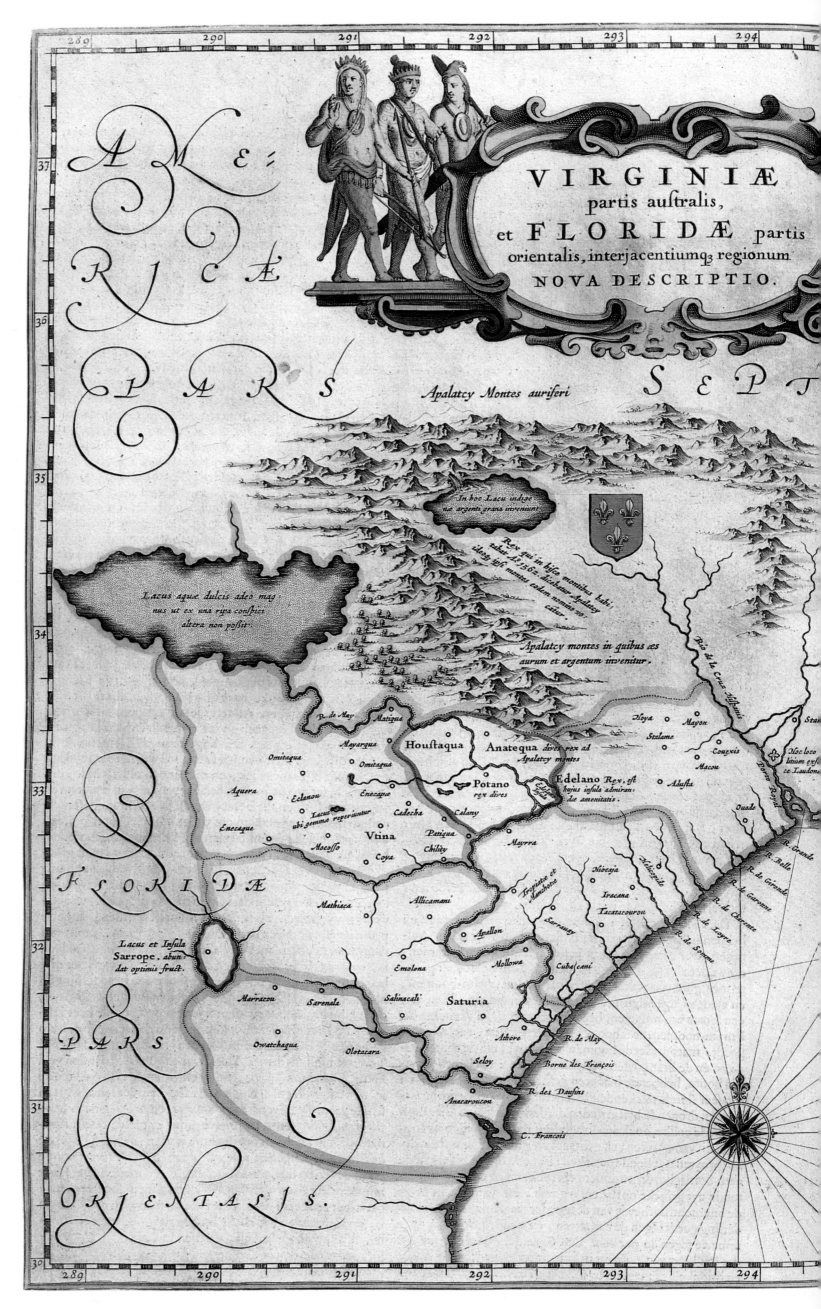

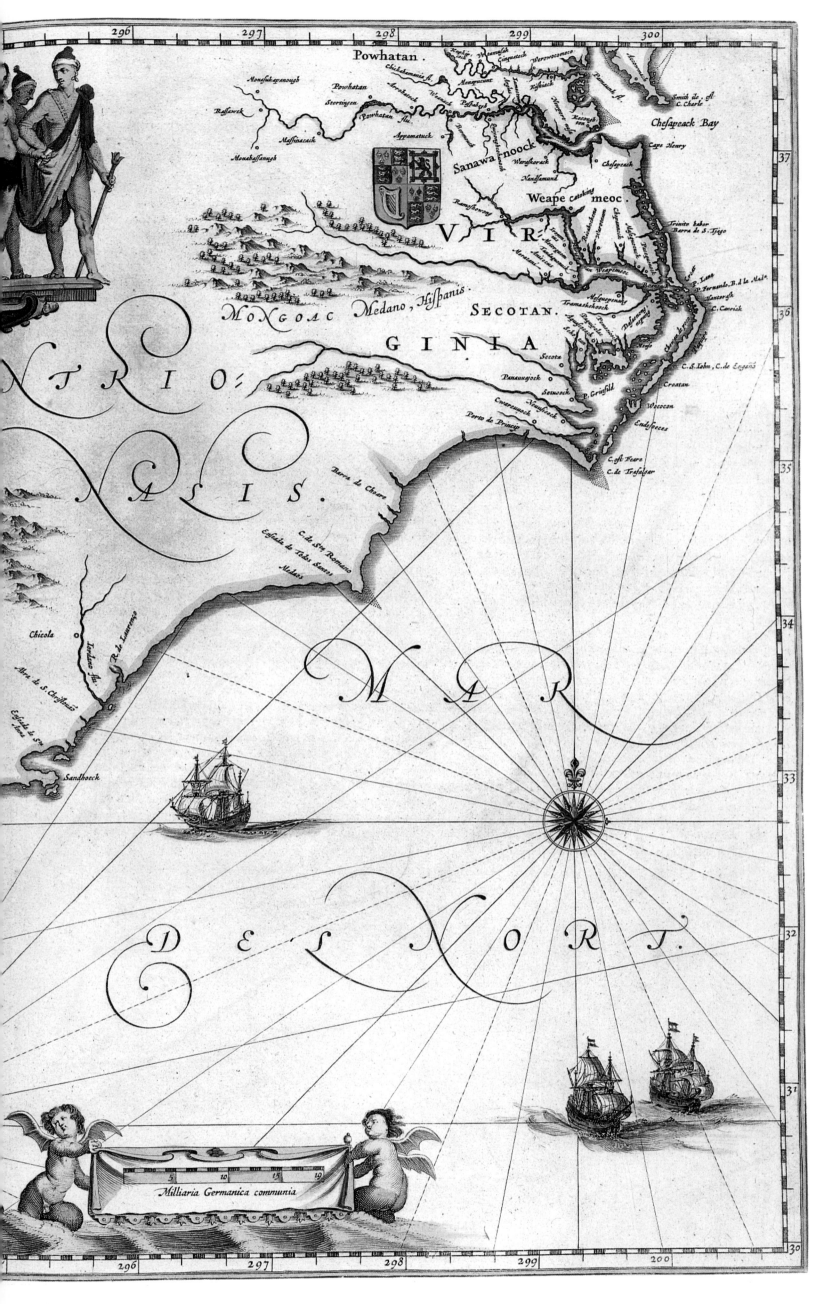

296   297   298   299   300

Powhatan.

Moneshayanough
Powhatan
Bassawek
Chickahomania fl.
Apamatuck
Steevingen
Powhatan flu.
Messinacack
Appamatuck
Monahassanogh

Sanawa- nooch

VIR-

MONGOAC Medano, Hispanis.   SECOTAN.

GINIA

NTRIO:

NASIS.

Chesapeack Bay

Cape Henry

Chesapeack

Weape meoc.

Croatan

Chicola

Iordan flu.

R. de Laurenço

Abra de S. Christoual

Sandhoeck

M A R

D E S   N O R T.

Milliaria Germanica communia

296   297   298   299   200

37

36

35

34

33

32

31

30

Nova Hispania et Nova Galicia

For this map of part of the western coastal regions of Mexico, Blaeu again took an earlier published map as his model.

By way of the Hondius map of 1606, Blaeu's map goes back to the map published by the Antwerp mapmaker Abraham Ortelius in 1579, itself probably based on a slightly earlier manuscript map. Despite the implication in the title, the map does not cover all of the province of New Spain, only a portion of modern Mexico.

At the time, the region was described as being rich in gold and silver, with pearl-fishing carried on in the coastal areas. The numerous salt lakes produced the finest salt by means of evaporation, and much was also made of the sugar cane cultivated here.

In the east of the mapped area, below the large title cartouche may be seen the city of Mexico, situated on the shores of a large lake, described as an ample city, queen of all cities in the New World. Although the mapmaker gave no clues, the small lozenge-shaped symbols to the left of the cartouche probably indicate gold or silver mines. The elaborate title cartouche is surmounted by the Spanish Royal arms.

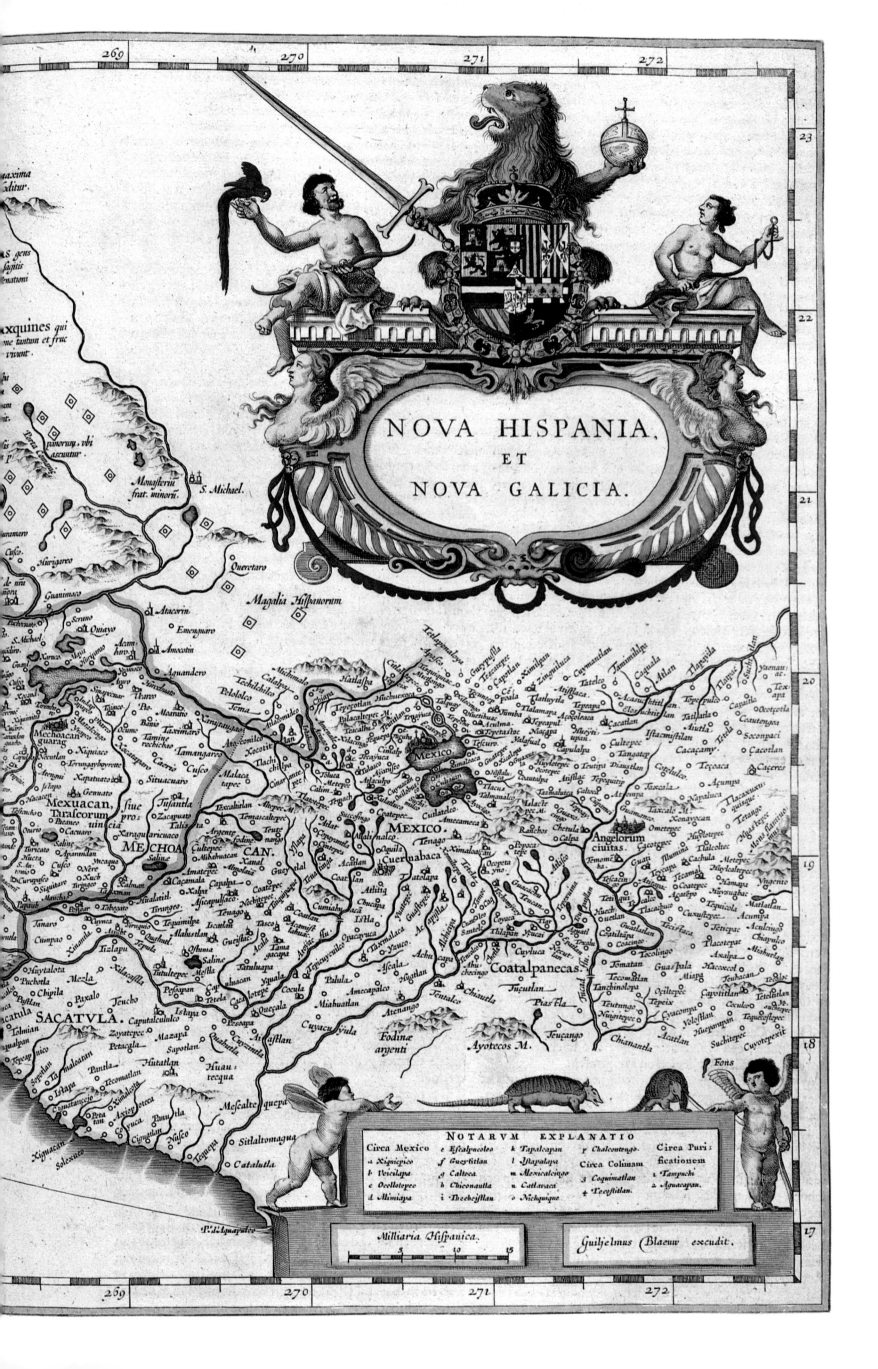

NOVA HISPANIA,
ET
NOVA GALICIA.

MEXICO.

Mexuacan, Tarascorum siue provincia

MECHOACAN.

SACATVLA.

Coatalpanecas

Angelorum ciuitas.

Magalia Hispanorum

Fodinæ argenti

Ayotecos M.

***Yucatan Conventus
Iuridici Hispaniae
Novae Pars
Occidentalis, et
Guatimala Conventus
Iuridicus***

Extending from Mexico City in the west to Costa Rica and western Panamá in the east, this map of the Yucatán peninsula and Guatemala is one of the new maps that Joan Blaeu added to the American division of the atlas in 1662.

Ever since Hernándes de Cordova's first landfall on the northern tip of Yucatán in February 1517, the region had proved difficult and resistant to subjugation by the Spaniards. The inhabitants were descendants of the Mayans, whose civilization had declined only about two hundred years before, the more accessible parts of the peninsula being taken possession of in 1528 by de Montego. De Cordova encountered 'thickly peopled countries, with masonry houses, and people who covered their persons and went about clothed in cotton garments, and who possessed gold and who cultivated maize fields', and the *Conquistadors* left accounts of the still dazzling white cities of the Maya, such as Chichén Itza and Uxmal.

By contrast, Blaeu's map of a century and a half later shows a relatively thinly settled region, with most place names concentrated in the immediate coastal areas, the interior remaining almost blank in places. The map is also characteristic of the later style of the house, showing rather less decorative embellishment and a somewhat plainer style of cartouche, here decorated with native plants, apparently tobacco and cacao.

ntrio.

23

Negrillos

Los Alcranes

CVBA.

Organes

C.S. Antonio

22

C. de Corrientes

I. de Pinos

aixo de Sisal

21

R. de Lagartes

ó Quyo

Conil

C. de Cotoche

Chuaca

Mortos de Silao

Morros de

Casqual

Sisal

20

Caiman Grande

Pta delgada

Merida

Yzaes

YVCATAN

Valladolid

Cozumel

19

Cocomes

S. Frco de Campeche

s Diabolos

18

Lago de Bacalal

Chetumal

L. de Chetumal

Quitazuenho

Pantoja

GOLFO DE HONDVRAS

Santamilla

17

zarahan

najos

Guajama

I. de Leyn

Guanaja

16

C. de 3. Puntas

Vtile

R. Guyamen

C. de Honduras

C. de Camaron

Mewen Eylanden

Hayen Eylanden

R. t Pich.

R. Baxo

R. Delht

Pta. d Cavallos

V. d' Naco

Porto de Sal

R. de Sal

Triumpho de la Cruz

Truxillo

Baya de Cartago ó Cataski

Crotoe

Bibora

15

S. Pedro

Gratias a Dios

S. Iorge d'Olancho

C. d'Gratias a Dios

G. de Nieuesa

R. de Yare

A

ONDV RAS.

Indisch dorpjen

14

Valladolid,
Comayagua

13

Chontales

R. de Yare

T

B. de Fonseca

Xeres

Segovia

Taguzgalpa ò
Tiguzigalpa

Sta Catelina

NICARA GVA.

I

Vulcan

M

12

Leon

Iaen

ys. de Perlas

S. Andero

La Posession

Realejo

Nequecheri

L. de Nicaragua

Desaguadero

I. de Manglares

11

Granada

R. do Vasquez

Monbacho

R. d' los Anzuelos

Masaya

Ncoya

Paro

Cast de Austria

A

Talamanca

Bocas del Drago

Escudo de Veragua

10

S. Iuan

Pa. de Velez

COSTARICA

Concepcion

Trinidad

C. Blanco

Gofo de Salinas

Chira

Pta. de S. Lazaro

Chomes

Cartago

Sta Fe

9

R.

El Cano

Aranjues

VERAGVA.

Panama

Carlos

8

Oriens.

Terra Firma et Novum Regnum Granatense et Popayan

This regional map of the north-eastern corner of South America belongs to the early group of plates printed by Willem Blaeu from 1630 onwards. It covers modern Colombia, part of Venezuela and Panamá.

Then, as now, this region of the Andes was difficult of access, and none more so than the highlands of modern Colombia, called Nueva Granada by the Spaniards, Granada being the home of the explorer Hernando de Quesada who was here in the 1530s. The Spaniards found the Pacific coast uninviting, with its mangrove swamps. The rivers offered some access to the interior, but after the initial attempts by Pascual de Andagoya up the San Juan River [Rio Atrato], no other explorer was tempted by this route into Popayán in western Colombia.

Equally uninviting was the Caribbean coastal area, also lined with mangrove swamps, but in 1533 the great port town of the Spanish Main, Cartagena, was founded by Pedro de Heredia to serve as a base for further expeditions into the interior in the search for gold. Farther east, on the coast of Venezuela, the town of Coro was established as a port for the shipment of Indian slaves to the Spanish islands in the Caribbean.

News of the conquest of Peru to the south stimulated interest in the possibilities of an overland connection from the Caribbean coast, followed up by Cieza de Léon among others. Such enterprises resulted in very little direct economic benefit to Spain, for most of the attempts suffered greatly from losses as a result of sickness and starvation, more so in fact than from fighting the Indians.

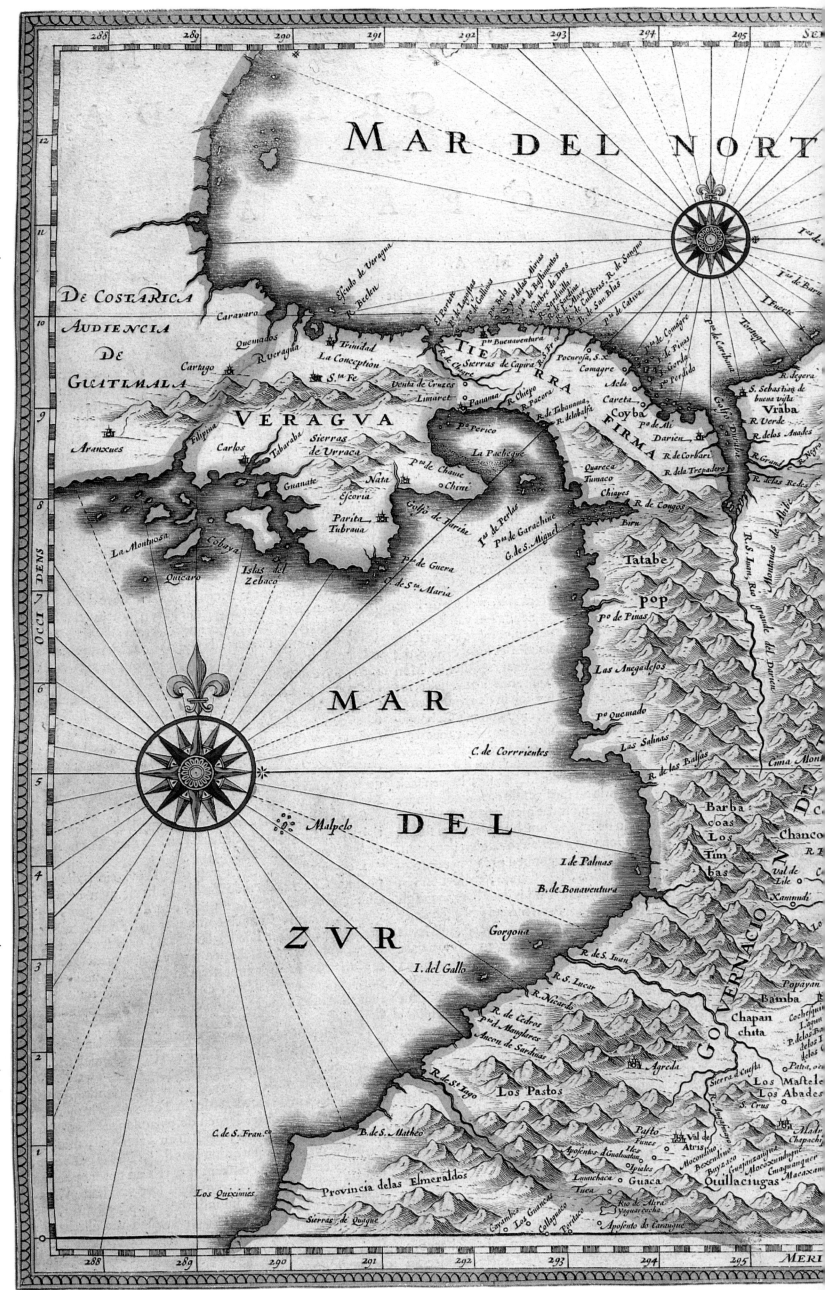

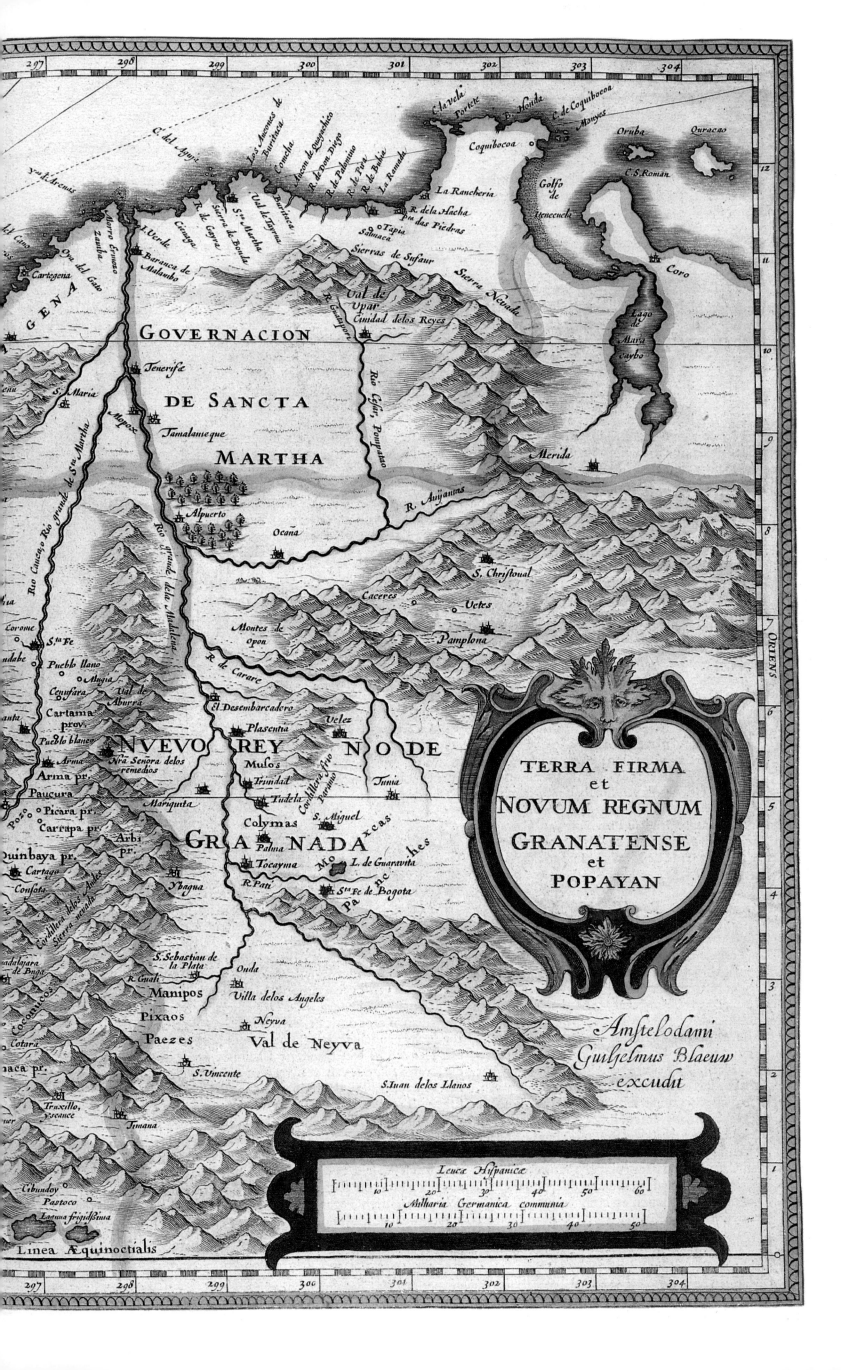

Venezuela, cum parte Australi Novae Andalusiae

This map, showing the area of modern Venezuela to the north of the Orinoco valley is another of the early group of Willem Blaeu plates of the 1630s. It extends from Lago de Maracaibo in the west to the island of Trinidad in the east and also shows the Dutch-held islands Curaçao, Aruba and Bonaire which served as a base of the *Geoctroyeerde West-Indische Compagnie* (or Netherlands West-Indian Company) since 1634.

Of the three great rivers of South America, the Orinoco was, and remains, the most difficult to navigate. It was the last to yield any of its secrets even though, on his third voyage in 1498, Columbus had noted the strong currents of fresh water from the Orinoco and believed himself to be at the mouth of one of the four rivers of Paradise.

Throughout the sixteenth century, attempts were made to search for the legendary kingdom of El Dorado, but it was not until the three Orinoco voyages of Antonio de Berrío between 1584 and 1591, all starting out from bases in Nueva Granada, that any useful knowledge of the interior was gathered. Berrío never found El Dorado, but he made several discoveries of river valleys in the interior. By a curious twist of fate, Berrío, while waiting in Trinidad for further orders from Spain, was captured by Sir Walter Ralegh, to whom he divulged his knowledge of the region, as well as a great deal of intended mis-information (see map 79).

VELA,
Auftrali
ALVSIÆ.

DEL

Dominica

Matalino

S.ta Lucia

ORTE

S.Vincente

Bekia   Vogeleylandt

Granada   Tabago

Orchilla

E.Blanco

Tortuga   Frayles   Cola

Testigos

Margarita   Flor negro   I. de Galera

Pedro

Cobana

Araij   Coetza   C.3.puntas   Boca del drago

ORIENS

adeleira   P.Salino   I. dla Trinidad

Olchie   I.de Curuçao   I.de Caribes   C.Salinar   S.Iosua

Morro d'Unare   Conuenta nueua Cordoba   I. de los Blanquisales

R.d'Ermacio   Santa Fe   Iaropas   Pta.Brac

Maniquares   Monopado   Pta.del Gallo

Comanagotha

Nueri

Maria Santa

P.Fernando

P.Gallet

Morro

Conuenta nueua Cordoba

Indios de Perito

PARIA

Indios Palenques

NVEVA ANDALV   SIA

Orinoque

Worinoque ô

Iwarepice

Rio de Paria, Yayapari, Huriapuria,

S.Thomas

Milliaria Germanica communia
5   10   15   20   25

Milliaria Gallica communia
5   10   15   20   25   30   35

AMSTELODAMI,
Guiljelmus Blaeuw excudit.

179

Guiana sive Amazonum Regio

This handsome map, another of the Blaeu plates of 1630, extends from the Isla Margarita in the north-west to the coast of northern Brazil near São Luís east of the Amazonas delta.

The interior is dominated by a large inland sea, the *Parime Lacus*, on whose north-western shore lies the fabled city *Manoa, ó el Dorado*, golden city of the Inca that travellers' tales located in the jungles of Guiana. Antonio de Berrío, explorer of the Orinoco region, and Spanish governor of Trinidad (mentioned in the notes to map 78), was captured there by Sir Walter Ralegh who represented English interests and enterprise in the early history of South America, despite his failures in Virginia and his disfavour at the court of Queen Elizabeth.

Wishing to harass Spain in the New World, Ralegh put all his energies into his Guiana project. According to contemporary thinking, South America was the cornucopia that fed the Spanish war effort in Europe. After an initial voyage into the interior of Guiana, Ralegh wrote an entertaining tract entitled *The Discoverie of the Large Rich and Bewtiful Empyre of Guiana, with a relation of the Great and Golden City of Manoa (which the Spaniards call El Dorado)*, published in 1596. It was a highly inventive work of propaganda which turned jungles and mountain wildernesses into an arcadia. He wrote, making mention of the kingdom of headless men: 'Such a nation was written of by Mandeville, whose reports were held fables for many years, and yet since the East Indies were discovered, we find his relations true of such things as heretofore were held incredible.' They were, so Ralegh had been informed, to be found in the Ewaipanoma tribe on Caura River in Venezuela.

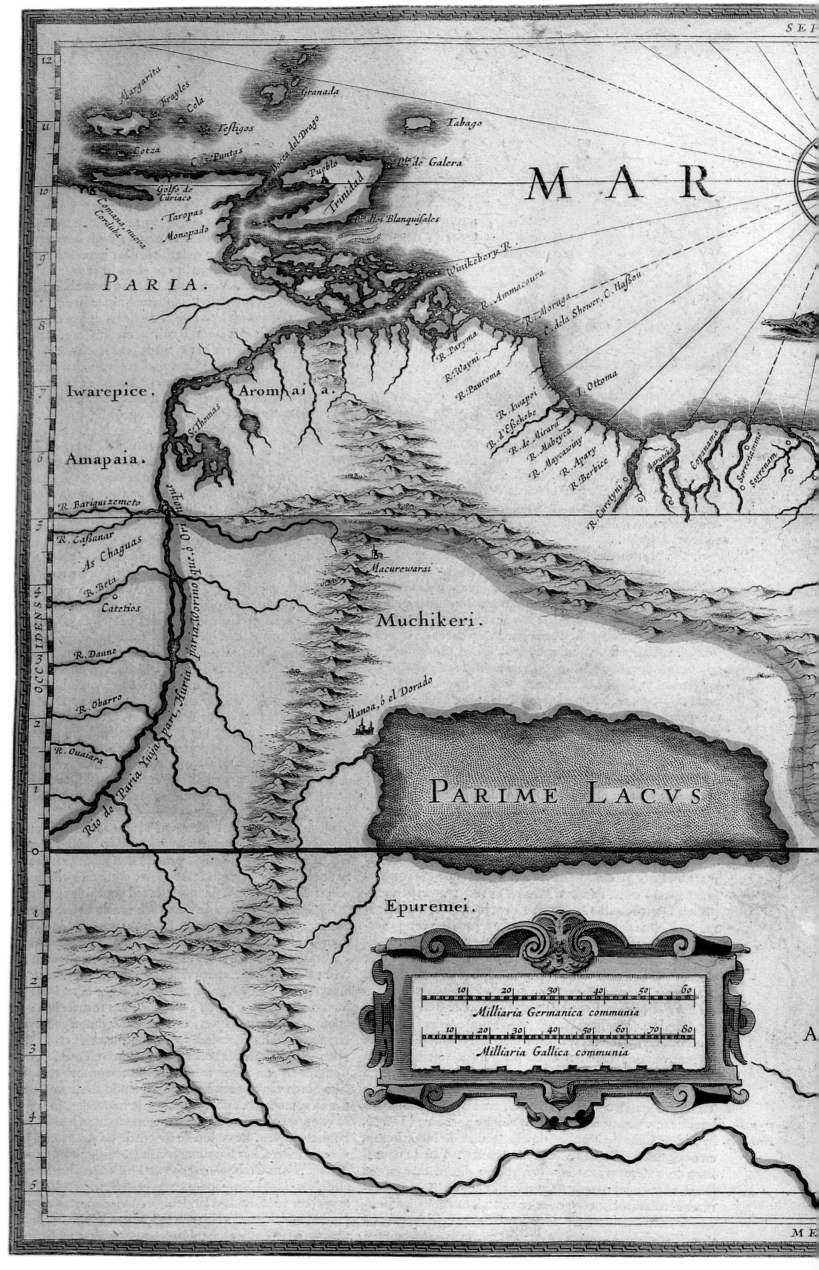

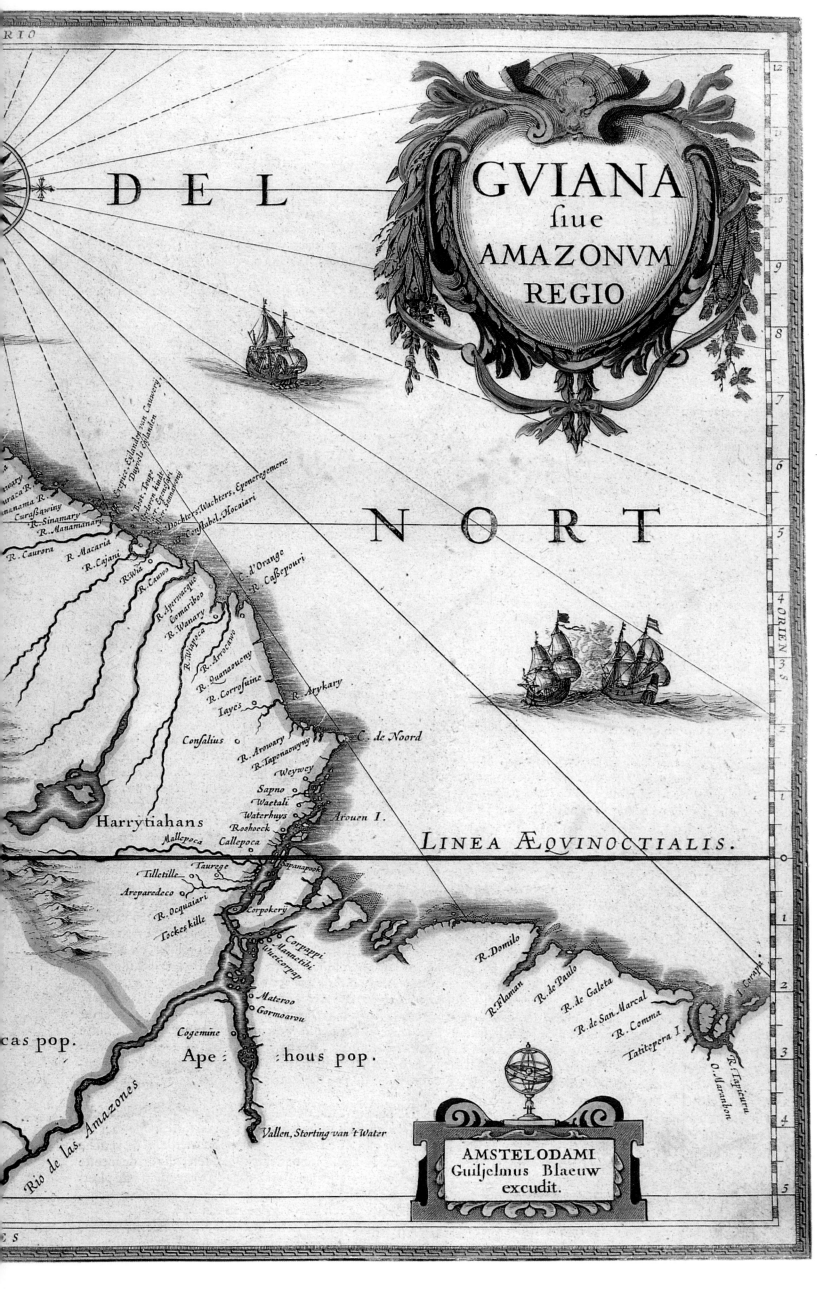

For nearly twenty years Ralegh attempted to establish an English colony here, to find El Dorado and to exploit the mines, none of which, in the end, succeeded. Ralegh was executed in 1618, partly as a result of his failure in Guiana and partly as a result of Spanish pressure on James I, for his having killed Spaniards on his last expedition to Guiana in 1617.

Blaeu's elegant map preserves at least the legend.

Brasilia

Oriented west to the top of the plate, this general map of Brazil was an early product of Joan Blaeu himself, made after he had assumed full control of the publishing house following the death of his father a few years before.

This plate was made to replace the de Laet derivative which Willem had acquired from the Hondius plate stock in 1629 and is considerably more detailed than its older namesake. At the time of the first appearance of the map in 1642, the Dutch were actively attempting to colonize the north-eastern coastal regions of Brazil. Dutch attempts to found an empire in South America began in 1624 with an attack on Bahia [Salvador], the natural harbour at Bahia de Toros os Santos. The attack was unsuccessful, and the *Geoctroyeerde West-Indische Compagnie* [Netherlands West-India Company] made another, successful, attempt in 1630, this time at Olinda de Pernambuco [Recife] farther north near the north-easternmost point of Brazil.

At the height of their power in Brazil, when the Dutch controlled or influenced four of the seven Portuguese *capitanías* (or governorships) in Brazil under the leadership of Johan Maurits van Nassau-Siegen, much of the trade of north-eastern Brazil was in the hands of the Netherlands West-India Company acting on the assumption that it had the right to trade – and make war – with Spain and Portugal in the Americas.

However, the Dutch never quite succeeded in bringing the Portuguese colonists in the region under their control. Johan Maurits, during his governorship which lasted from 1637 to 1644, never ceased to warn his superiors in The Netherlands that unless they sent out Protestant settlers from The Netherlands, or Germany,

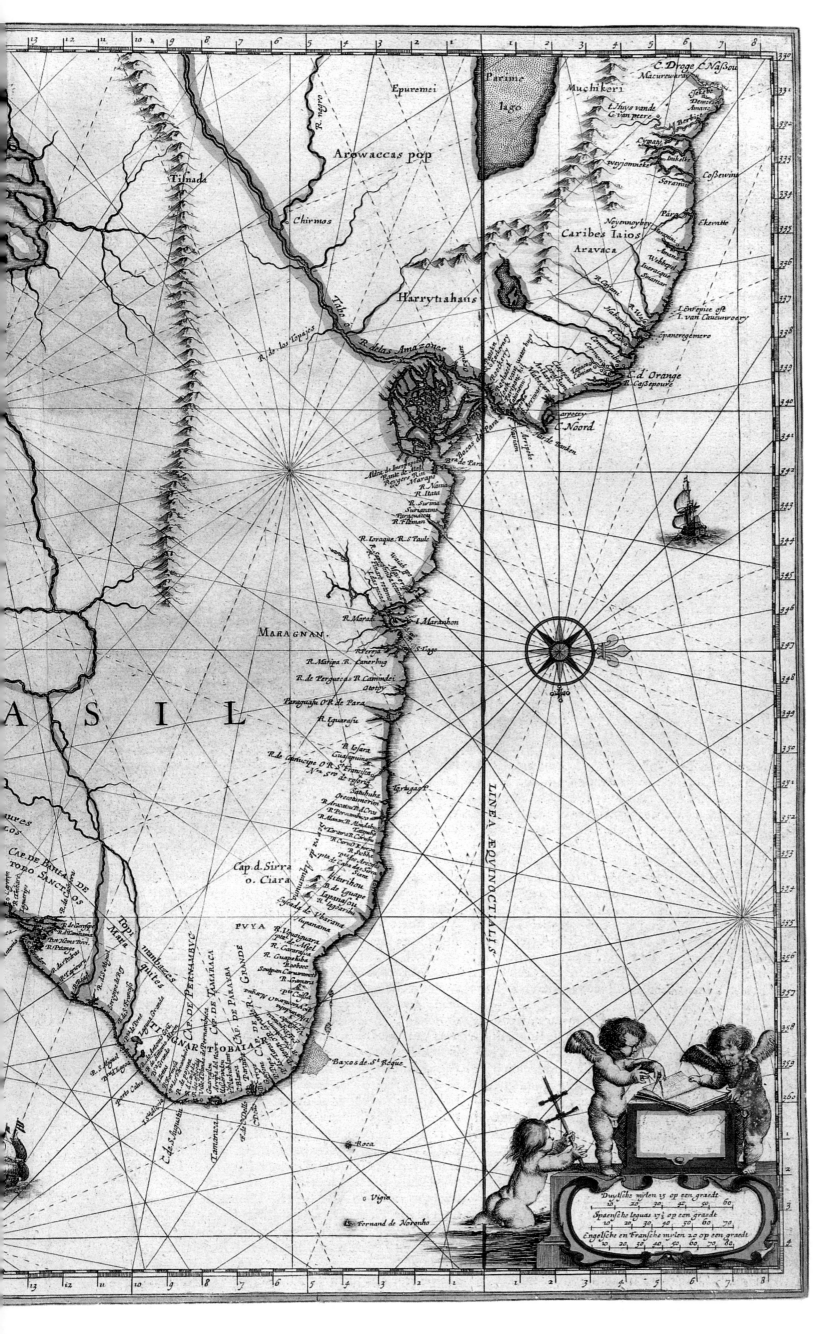

or Scandinavia, to replace the Roman Catholic Portuguese settlers, the latter would always remain Portuguese at heart, and would ultimately revolt against the Dutch at the earliest opportunity.

Johan Maurits's fears came to pass in 1645, and in the Luso-Dutch war which followed, many senior Dutch officials who had married Portuguese wives, turned their allegiance towards João IV of Portugal, leading to the final expulsion of the Dutch from Brazil in 1654.

Praefecturae de Paraiba, et Rio Grande

This beautiful map, one of a uniform group of four, is quite unlike any other map in the Blaeu atlas.

Although it first appeared in the atlas in 1662, this and its companion maps had first appeared in another earlier work published by Blaeu, the *Rerum per octennium in Brasilia* (1647) by the Remonstrant theologian Caspar van Baerle (or Barlaeus), who died very soon afterwards in 1648.

Barlaeus's great work, still one of the most valuable sources for Brazilian history, was published under the auspices of the Dutch governor in Brazil, Johan Maurits of Nassau-Siegen, whose governorship from 1637 to 1644 Barlaeus describes in a eulogistic but nevertheless impartial account compiled from official sources.

The large pictorial vignettes of this small group of maps illustrate much about local life and conditions of the time: here, a procession of Indians from a mission is illustrated after the paintings of the artist Frans Janszoon Post (*c.* 1612–1680) who was with Johan Maurits in Brazil during the years 1637–1644. The building depicted has not been identified with any certainty, but must have been in or near Pernambuco.

This and the other maps from the Barlaeus work are examples of the re-use of map plates by Joan Blaeu from non-atlas sources (see also the maps of southern Denmark, map 8 and also map 15) in order to embellish even further what was already a sumptuous atlas.

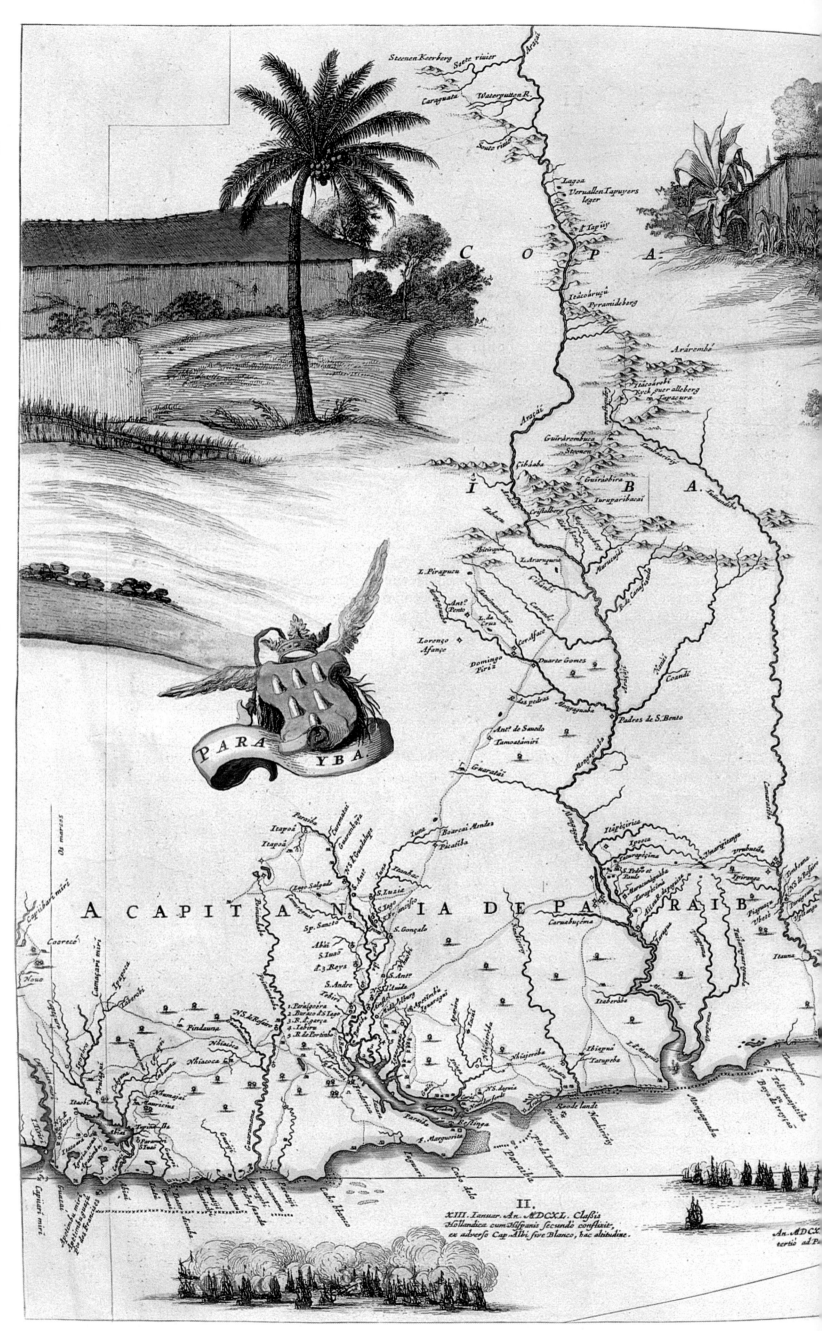

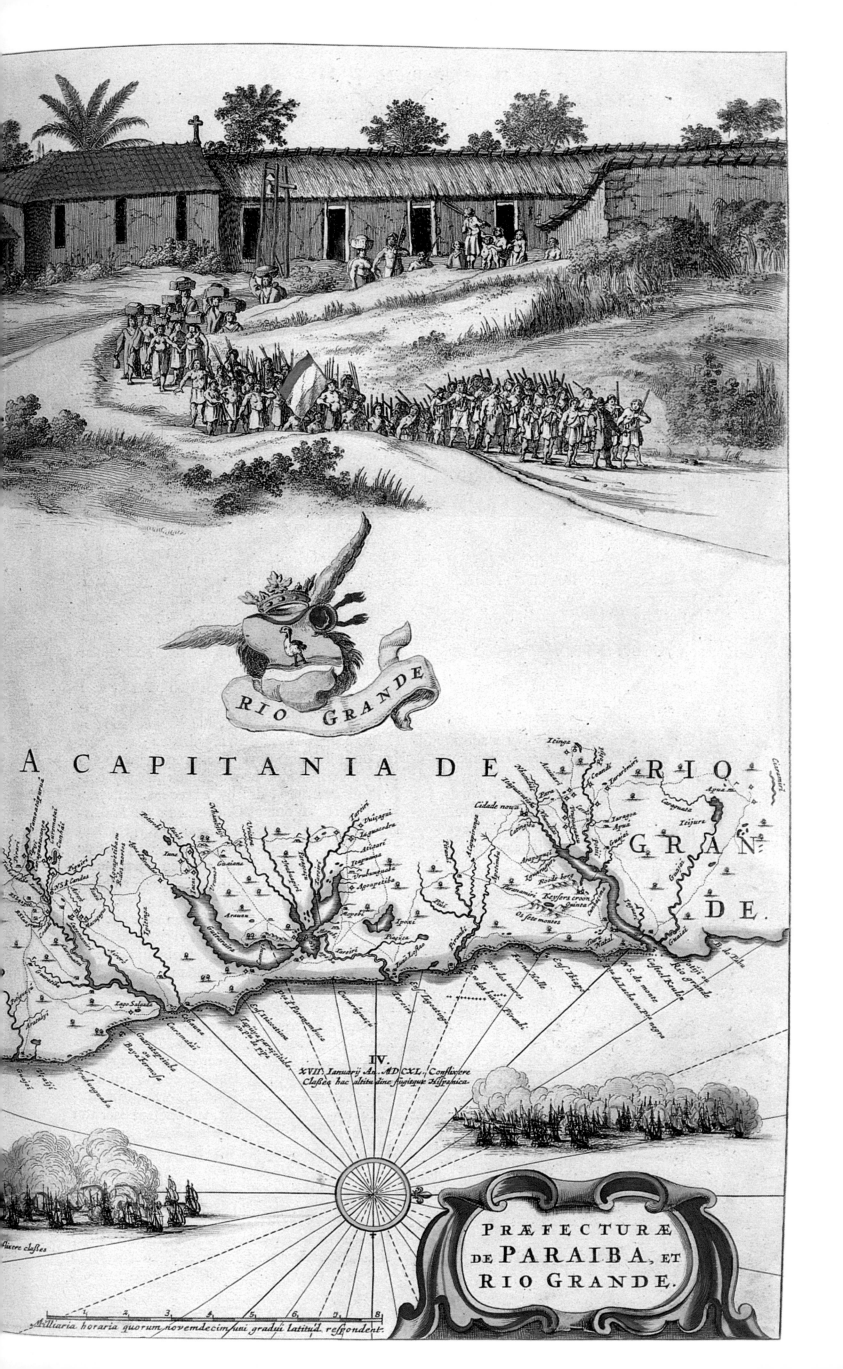

RIO GRANDE

A CAPITANIA DE RIO GRANDE.

IV.
XVII. Ianuarij A.o M DC XL. Conflixere
Classes hac altitudine, fugitque Hispanica.

PRÆFECTURÆ
DE PARAIBA, ET
RIO GRANDE.

Milliaria horaria quorum novemdecim uni gradui latitud. respondent.

Chili

This is another of Willem
Blaeu's early group of
maps, showing the coastal
region of central Chile
from Copiapo in the north
(near the left-hand margin)
as far as a point to the
south of the island of
Chiloé.

Apart from the relatively
large island of Chiloé, it is
readily apparent that little
was known of the fjord-like
nature of the coast or the
offshore islands of the
Archipiélago de los Chonos.
The modern cities of
Santiago (marked as *S Iago
dela Nueva Estremadura*),
Valparaíso (marked as a
river estuary on Blaeu's
map), Concepción and
Valdivia (spelled *Baldivia*
on the map) stand out clearly,
the latter three having all
been founded during the
mid-sixteenth century by
the then governor of
central Chile, Pedro de
Valdivia.

Valdivia encouraged
exploration by sea of the
coasts to the south, but
expeditions met with hostile
receptions from the local
peoples. A more accurate
picture of this part of the
South American coast had
to wait until the publication
in Rome of the Jesuit
Father Alonso de Ovalle's
*Historica Relacion del reyno de
Chile* in 1646.

Blaeu never revised his
map of Chile; despite the
fact that Nicolas Sanson
had issued a more up-to-
date map based on Ovalle's
researches at Paris in 1656,
Joan Blaeu remained
content to reissue this
obsolete map.

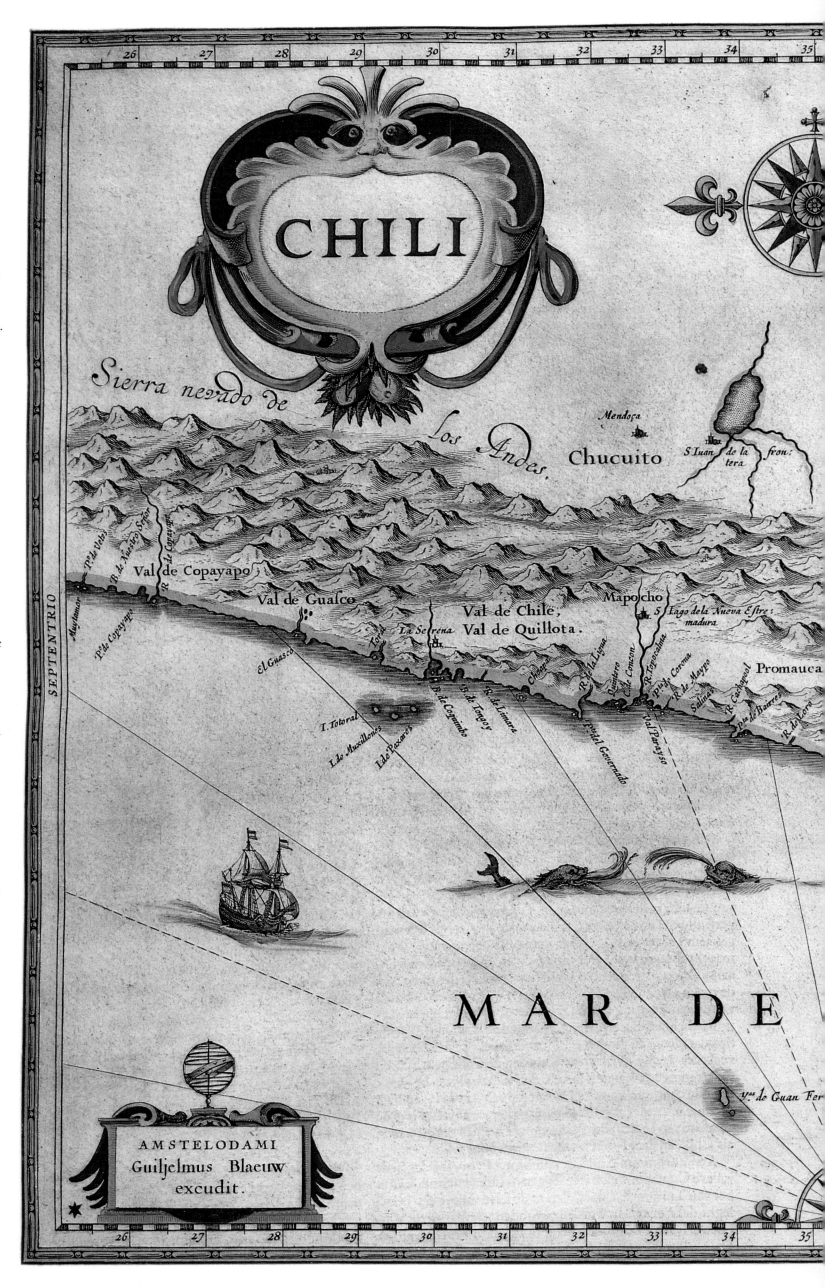

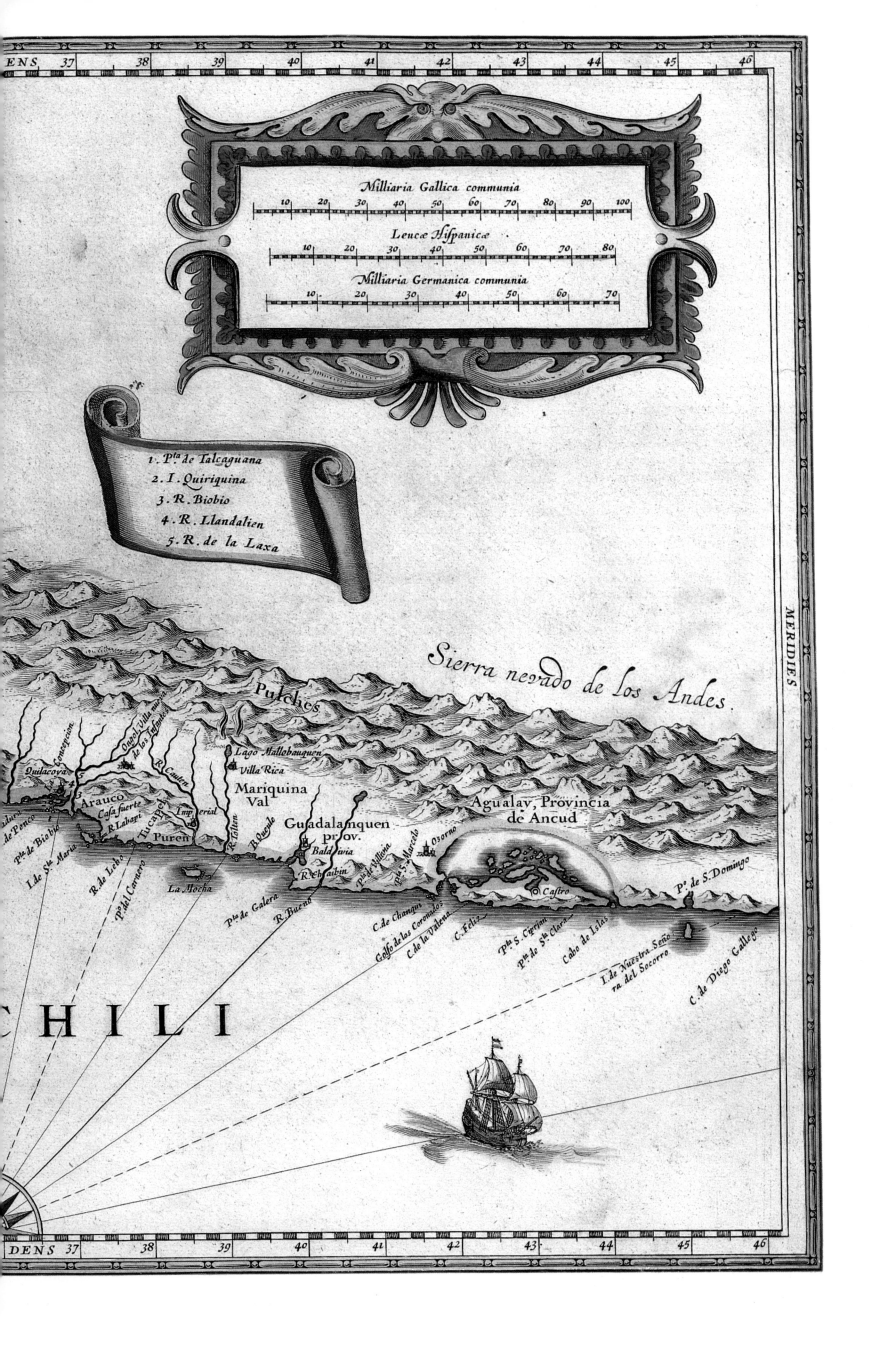

Milliaria Gallica communia

10 20 30 40 50 60 70 80 90 100

Leucæ Hispanicæ.

10 20 30 40 50 60 70 80

Milliaria Germanica communia

10 20 30 40 50 60 70

1. Pta de Talcaguana
2. I. Quiriquina
3. R. Biobio
4. R. Llandalien
5. R. de la Laxa

Sierra nevado de los Andes

Pulches

Lago Mallobauquen

Villa Rica

Concepcion

Angol Villa rica de los Infantes

R. Cauten

Quilacoya

Mariquina
Val

Arauco

Casa fuerte

Imperial

R. Labapi

R. Tolten

Agualav, Provincia
de Ancud

Pta de Penco

Tucapel

Puren

Guadalamquen
prov.

B. Quexle

Baldivia

Osorno

Pta de Biobio

R. de Lebo

La Mocha

R. Chraibin

Pta de S. Marcelo

Castro

Po de S. Domingo

I. de Sta Maria

Pta del Carnero

Pta de Galera

R. Bueno

Pta de Villona

C. de Changui

C. Feliz

Pta S. Cyprian

Cabo de Islas

Gosso de los Coronados

Pta de Sta Clara

C. de la Valena

I. de Nuestra Seño
ra del Socorro

C. de Diego Gallego

CHILI

Peru

Here, Willem Blaeu – this map being from another of the early plates – shows the Pacific coast of South America from Ecuador (at the left-hand side) as far south as the Atacama desert in the northern reaches of Chile.

Although the interior terrain is not mapped with any particular degree of accuracy, Blaeu's map nevertheless conveys a vivid impression of the difficult terrain of the Andes in Peru.

As early as 1520, Spanish settlers in Panamá had heard tales of a powerful civilization rich in gold that lay to the south, and in 1522 an expedition was organized to find this land and the people called Birú or Pirú in the south. In 1524 Francisco Pizarro led the first of his expeditions that led ultimately to the discovery and conquest of the Inca empire which extended over wide areas of modern Ecuador, Peru, Bolivia and part of Chile. Pizarro obtained from Atahuallpa, the head of the Inca empire, a huge ransom of silver and gold that made Spain rich almost beyond the most inventive dreams of the Spanish conquerors, and once the mountain city of Cuzco was captured in 1533, the Spanish hold over much of South America was virtually complete.

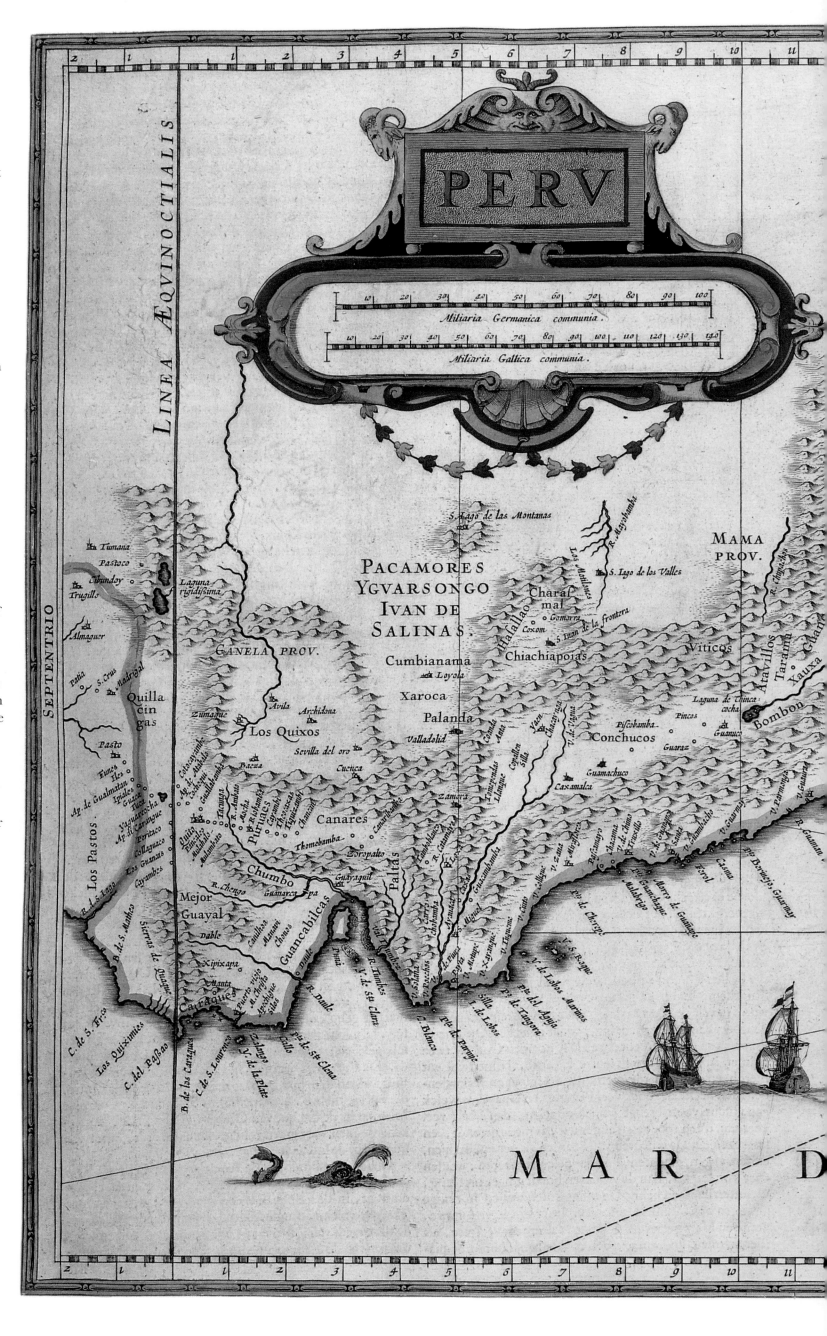

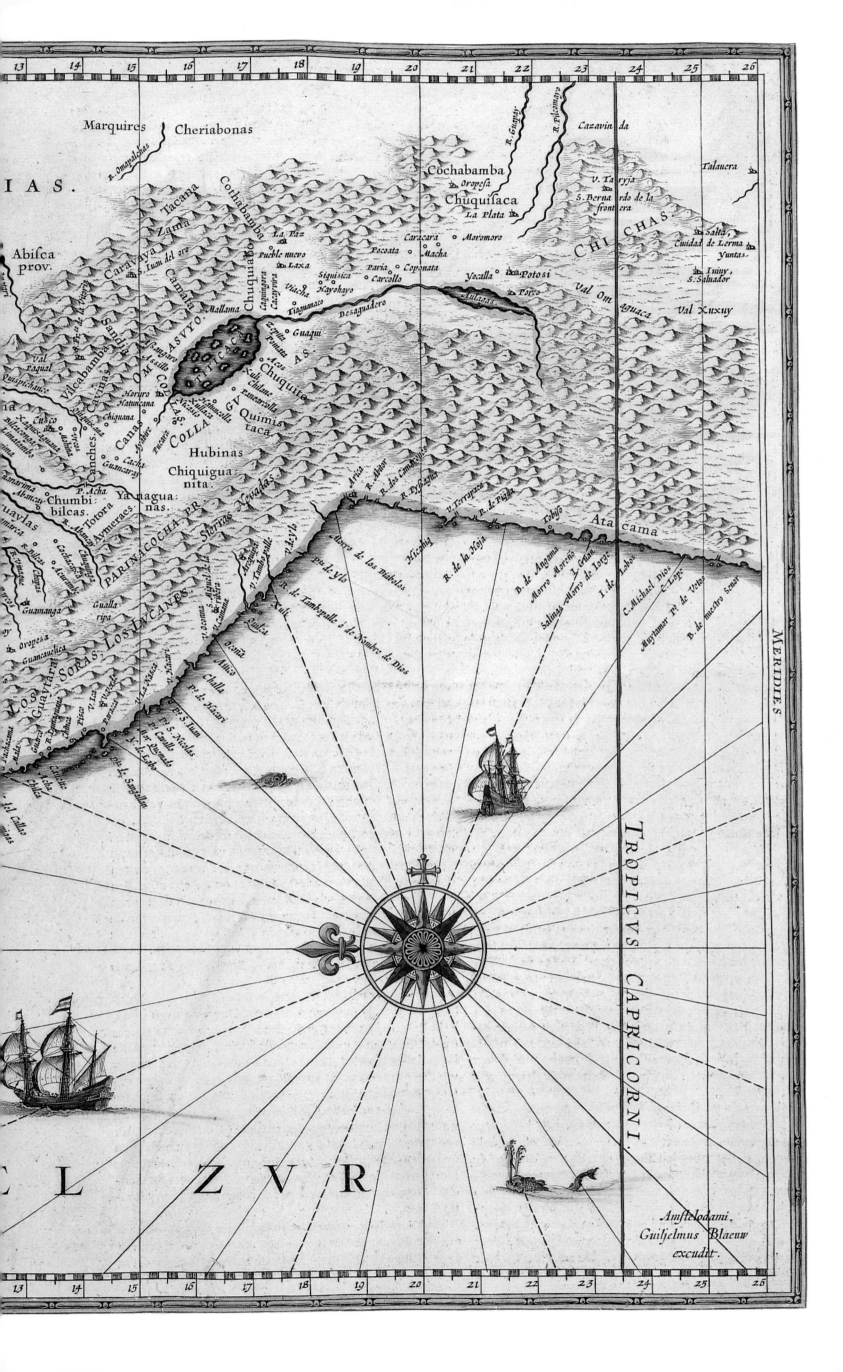

Marquires　Cheriabonas

R. Guapay　R. Pilcomayo

Cazavin da

IAS.

R. Omapalchas

Tacana
Zama

Cothabamba

Cochabamba
Oropesa
Chuquisaca
La Plata

v. Tarvja
S. Berna do de la
frontera

Talauera

CHI CHAS

Salta,
Cuidad de Lerma
Yuntas.

Abisca
prov.

Caravaya

P. de la Puerta
Iss. Iuan del oro

Camata

Chuquiau

La Paz
Pueble nuevo
Laxa

Caracara
Pocoata
Paria
Carcollo
Copanata
Macha
Moromoro

Vocalla
Potosi
Porco

Val Om aguaca

Iuiuy,
S. Saluador

Val Xuxuy

Vilcabamba
Sandia

Caravaya

Calpingora
Cacayico

Siquisica
Vtacha
Mayohayo

Mallama
Tiaguanaco

Desaguadero

Aullagas

Horuro
Hatuncana
chiquana

Assillo
Nicasio
Cepita
Pomata

Guaqui
Acas

Cusco
Xaquixaguana
pilcoconga
Limatambo

Canas
Cacha
Guancaray

Quibre
Xullilaca
Huacilla
Zepita

Xuli
Chilane
Tancarvilla

AS.
Chuquite
GV
Quimis
taca.

Canches

Combapata

COLLA

Hubinas
Chiquigua
nita.

TI
TI
CA
CA

Chumbi
bilcas.
Ya nagua;
nas.

Sierras Nevadas

Arica
R. Abior
R. de los Camaroxes
R. Lysbagha

v. Terragraca
P. de Pisha
Tobyso

Ata cama

PARINACOCHA PR.

Guaviarai

LOS SORAS LOS LVCANES

v. Ionabopalle
Asylo

v. Timbopalle
Tomana

R. de Timbopalle i de Nombre de Dios

Morro de los Diabolos

Hicapha

R. de la Hoja

B. de Angama
Morro Moreno
Salinas Morro de Iorji

I. Grand
I. de Loba

C. Michael Dios
C. Lope

Guamanga

Gualla
ripa

v. Ocoina
Sr. ribera
Ilo
Xuli

Pta. de Ylo

Muytamar Pt. de Velos
B. de nuestro Senor

MERIDIES

Oropesa

Guancavelica

v. Ilo
Victoria
Pisco

Challa
Pto. de Hacari
P. de S. Iuan
v. S. Nicolas

Atiko
Ocoita

v. Iza
v. de Lobo

TROPICVS CAPRICORNI.

EL　ZVR

Amstelodami,
Guiljelmus Blaeuw
excudit.

Asia noviter delineata

The origins of this general map of the Asian continent go back as far as 1617 when Willem Blaeu issued it as a separate publication. It was then included in the atlas series from 1630 to the 1660s, essentially unchanged in spite of more up-to-date information appearing on several of the regional maps of Asia issued by the Blaeus.

Like the other general continental maps, this stunning map is embellished with five pairs of costumed figures in the side border vignettes and nine small town views in the frieze along the top. These include Calicut, Goa, Damascus, Jerusalem, Hormuz, Bantam and Aden.

In contrast to the map of China (see map 93), Korea is drawn as an island marked *Corea Ins.* There is no hint at all of Australia to the south of the East Indies, but there is a strong suggestion of a sea passage from Europe via a north-east passage through the Strait of Anian [*Fretum Anian*] between north-eastern Asia and America.

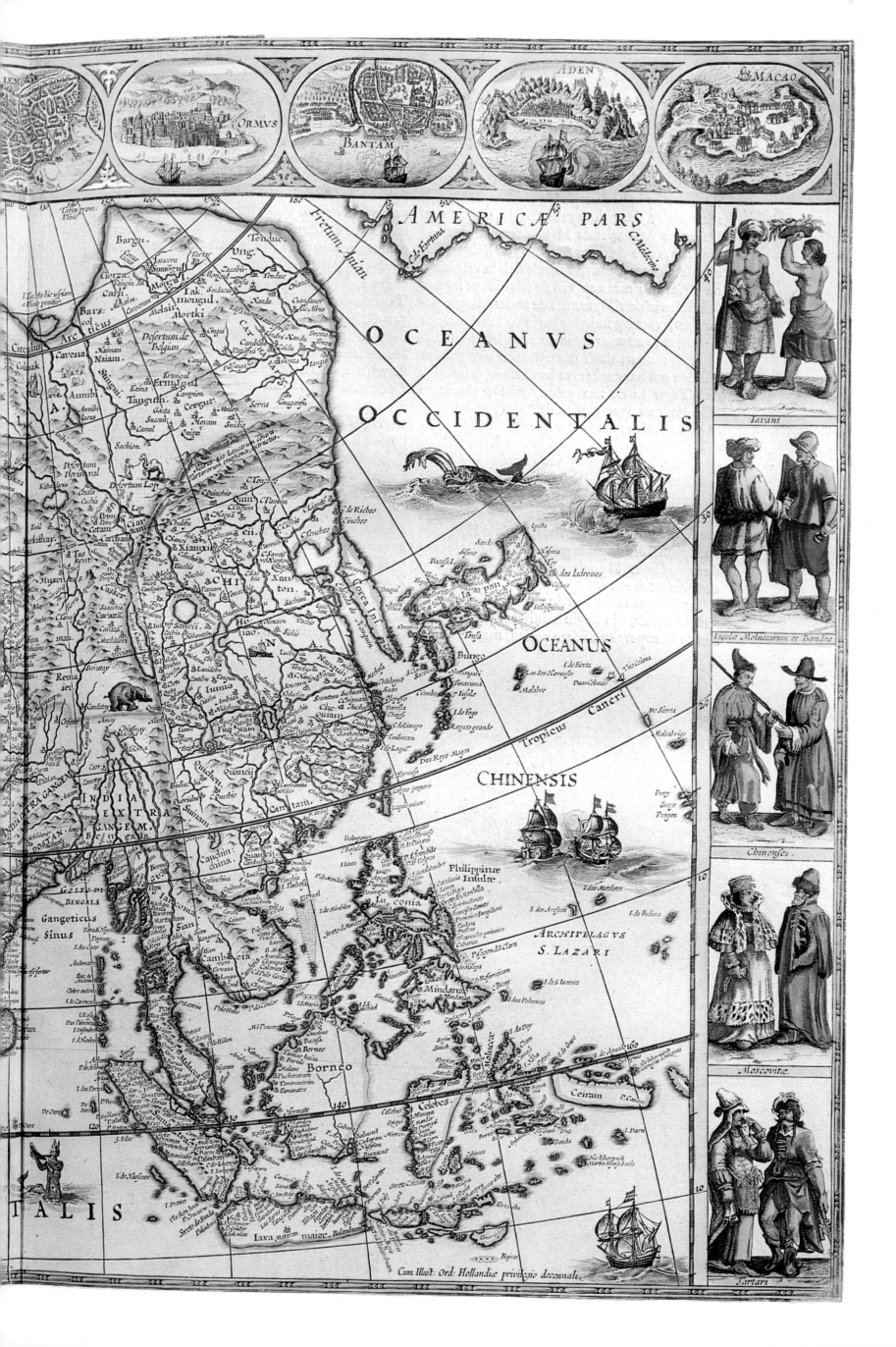

India quae Orientalis dicitur, et Insulae adiacentes

Willem Blaeu's map of the East Indian archipelago, extending from India to Japan, shows some of the Dutch discoveries in Australia, in the lower right-hand corner, as two short stretches of coastline corresponding to the west coast of the Cape York Peninsula and part of the coast of Western Australia.

Blaeu's map is one of the first printed maps to show any part of Australia. It continued to be issued, unchanged after its final state, from 1635 up to the atlas of 1662, long after some of the information it contained had been superseded. This was despite the fact that Joan Blaeu, as cartographer to the *Verenigde Oost-Indische Compagnie* (VOC) [Dutch United East-India Company] from 1638 to 1673, had access to the latest information concerning the extension of Dutch maritime power in the East Indies, publishing the results of such discoveries (especially in Australia) on large World maps, such as that of 1648.

In other words, Blaeu's atlas map of the East Indies and part of Australia ignores the results of Abel Janszoon Tasman's discoveries made during the voyages of 1642–1644. In 1642, Tasman was appointed commander of an expedition to the South Seas, during which he discovered the island later named after him as well as part of the coast of New Zealand. His voyage of 1644 coasted along the shore of the Gulf of Carpentaria and along the northern coast of Australia as far as the Tropic of Capricorn.

Tasman's discoveries were published very soon afterwards on Blaeu's large World maps, rendering it all the more curious that the atlas map was never revised.

In effect, this map remained an historical map of the archipelago, showing

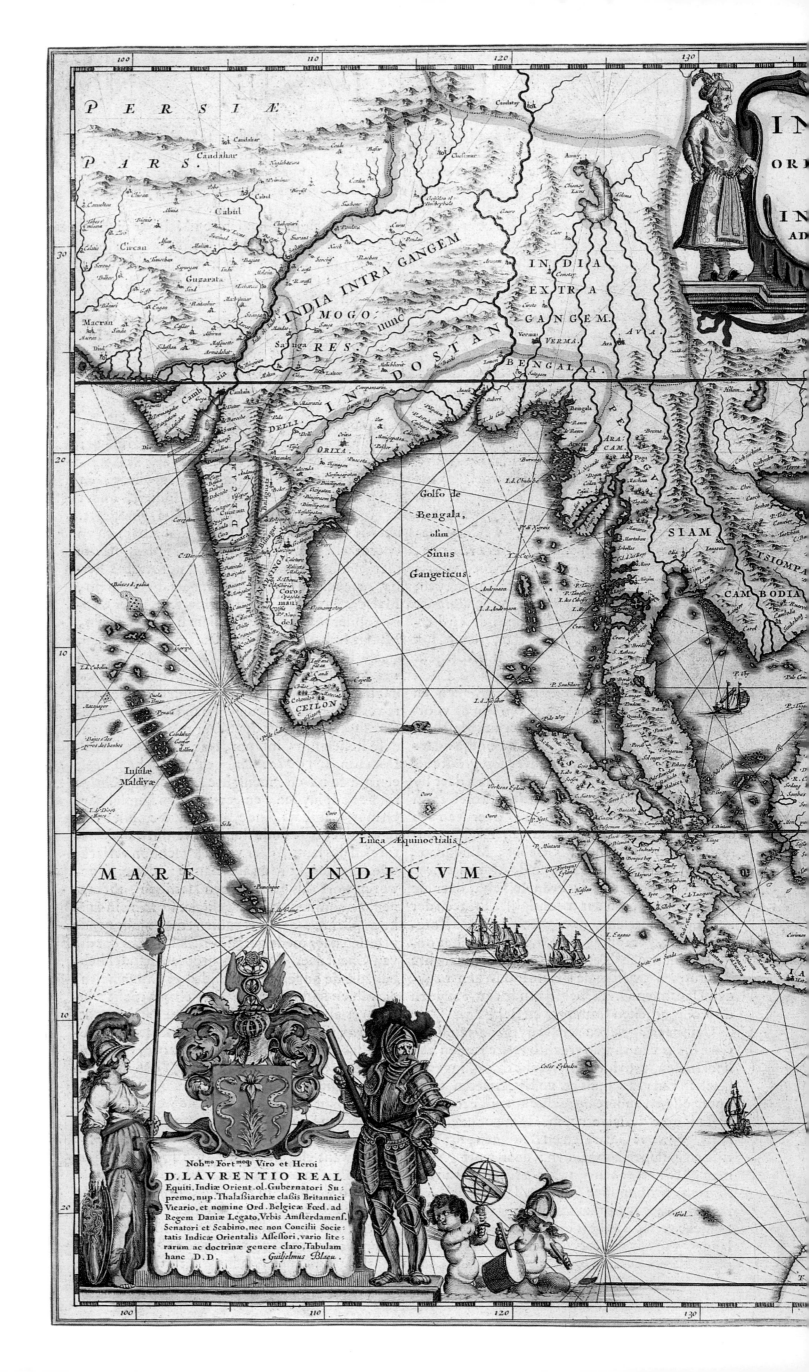

discoveries made, albeit in a rather haphazard and fortuitous manner by the Dutch, between 1606 and 1623.

The design of the map emphasizes the importance of the commercial interests in the East Indies, centred as it is on the heart of what was to become The Netherlands East Indies and later Indonesia. This is further underlined by Blaeu's dedication (seen at the lower left-hand corner) to Dr Laurens Real, who had been the Governor-General of the East Indies at Batavia [Jakarta] in Java from 1616 to 1618.

Magni Mogolis Imperium

'The Empire of the Great Moghul', in northern India, as mapped by Joan Blaeu and his brother Cornelis in 1638.

The fascination of seventeenth-century Europe with this great empire in the East created a demand for maps that was fulfilled largely by Dutch mapmakers, even though Dutch commercial interests in the East were concentrated elsewhere. Blaeu's map stretches from Persia to China and shows lands travelled by the embassy of the Englishman Sir Thomas Roe to the Moghul emperor Jahangir in 1615, derived from a map published by William Baffin in London in 1618.

Curiously, Blaeu and his rival mapmaker in Amsterdam, Jansson, included only one map of India in their atlases, and this Dutch version of Baffin's map remained the standard Dutch view of the north part of the subcontinent and central Asia throughout the seventeenth century.

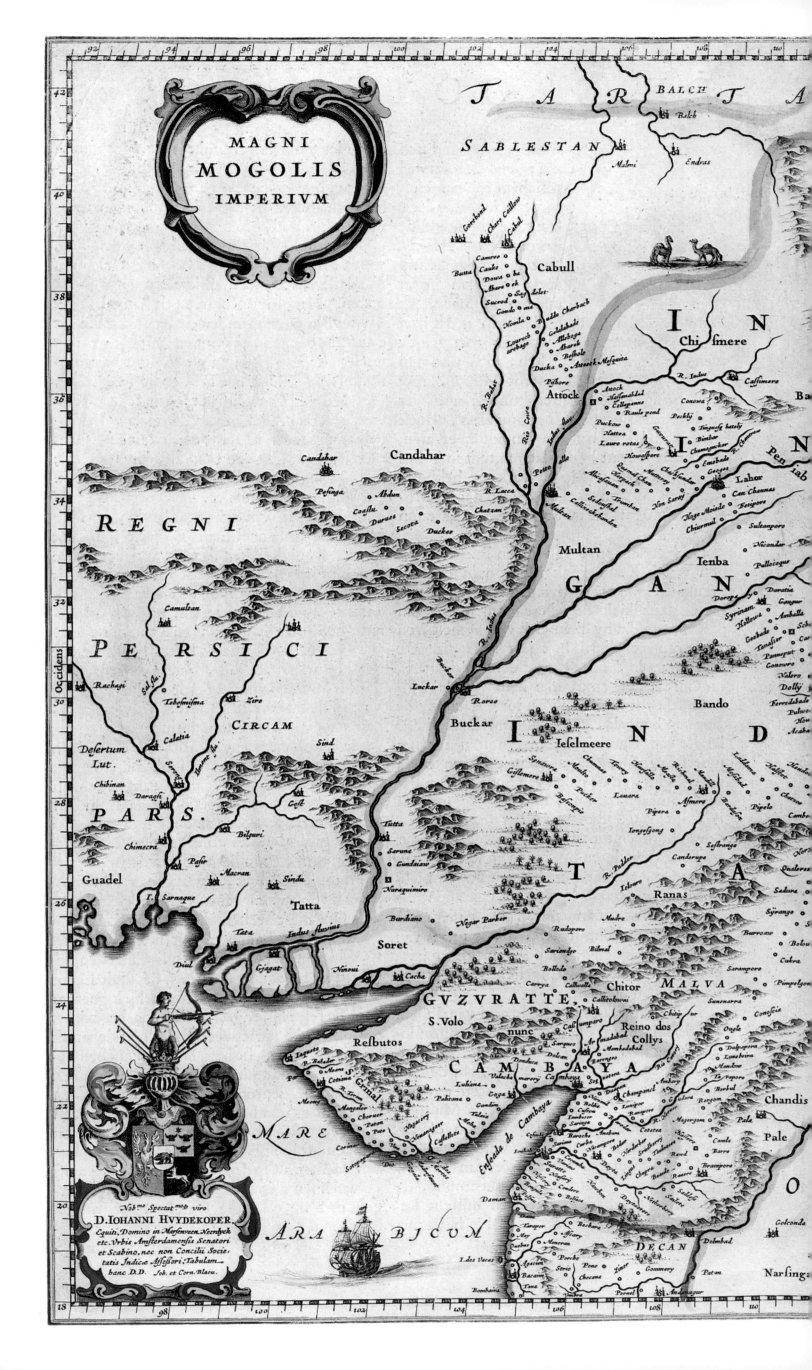

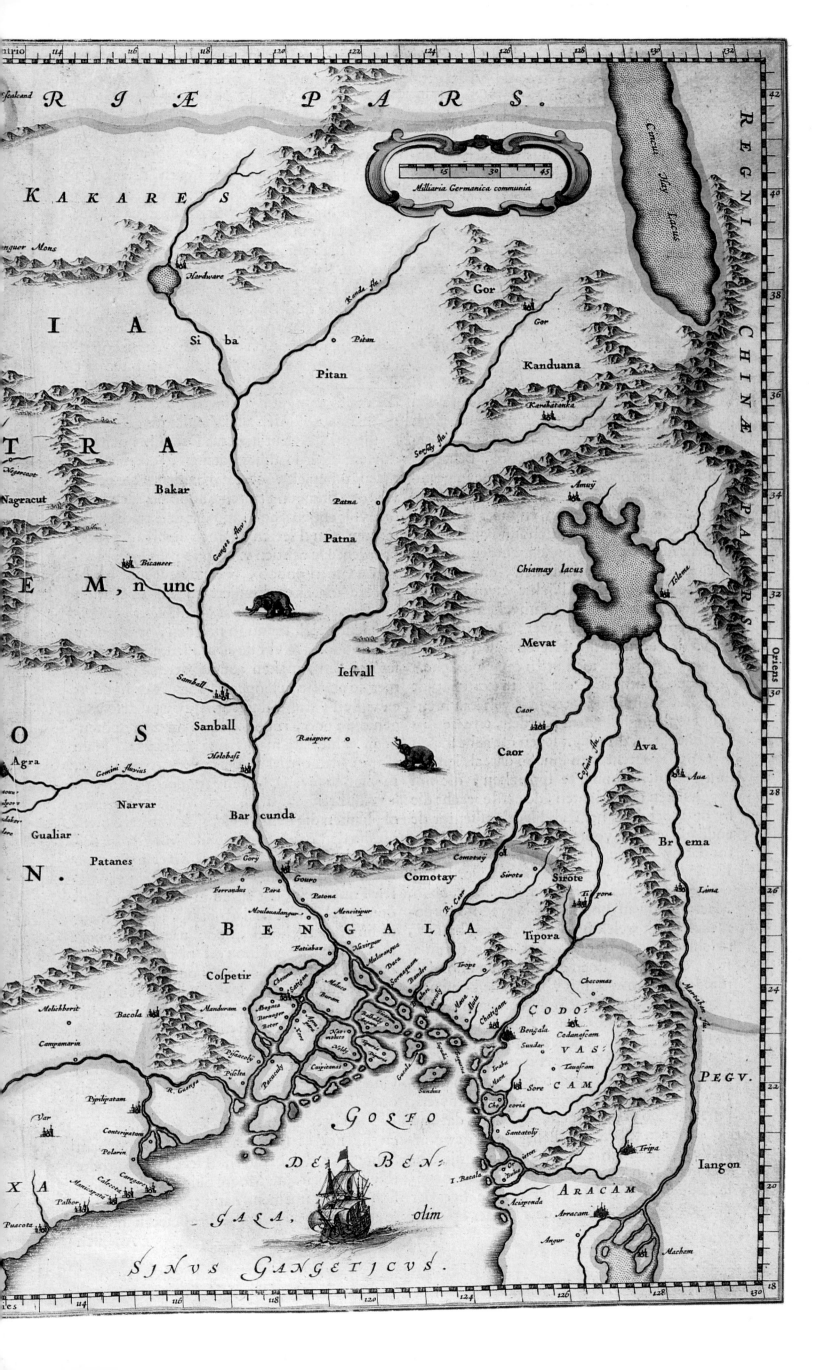

R I Æ   P A R S.

KAKARES

Milliaria Germanica communia

CHINÆ PARS

REGNI

Oriens

I A

nquer Mons

Hardware

Si ba

Pitan

Pitan

Konda flu.

Gor

Gor

Kanduana

T R A

Nagracut

Nagracut

Bakar

Serssiy flu.

Karahatanka

Amuy

E M, n unc

Bicaneer

Patna

Patna

Ganges fluv.

Chiamay lacus

Telema

Samball

Iesvall

Mevat

Sanball

O S

Agra

Holobass

Gemini fluvius

Raiapore

Caor

Caor

Caor

Ava

Aua

Eginin flu.

Narvar

Bar cunda

Br ema

N.

Gualiar

Patanes

Gory

Gouro

Comotay

Comotay

Sirote

Sirote

Lana

Tipora

Ferrandus

Para

Patona

Moulenadangue

Menevipur

R. Caor

Tipora

B E N G A L A

Fatiabas

Navirpor

Trops

Colspetir

Chuna

Scotigon

Malaca

Baram

Deca

Sornagum

Bander

Moua

Mui

Charigam

Chocomas

CODO:

Melichberit

Bacola

Manduram

Abgada

Bernager

Beter

Angeli

Iran

Nas mahuca

Addy

Bandel

Buttali

Gracili

Benigala

Sunder

Codanescam

VAS:

Tanascam

CAM

Campamarin

Pisacoly

Pisolta

Pecinely

Cavitanss

Goal

Irabu

Moen

Sore

R. Guenga

Sundua

PEGV.

Pipilipatam

Cha coria

Chorion

Var

Conteripatam

Santatoly

Tripa

Tripa

Iangon

GOSFO

Polarin

DE BEN:

I. Ratala

X A

Calcota

Manicapata

Palhor

Mani

Acisponda

A R A C A M

Puacota

GAEA,   olim

Arracam

Angur

Macham

S I N V S   G A N G E T I C V S.

Moluccae insulae celeberrimae

Willem Blaeu's map shows the Spice Islands of the East Indian archipelago, islands described by one sixteenth-century voyager, Jan Huyghen van Linschoten, as possessing cloves 'in so great abundance, that as it appeareth, by them the whole world is filled therewith…'.

Ever since the first Portuguese expedition under Dalboquerque from Malacca in 1511, the Spice Islands, or Moluccas, had been the great prize to Europeans in the East. Great attention was therefore paid by navigators and mapmakers to the accurate depiction of the islands and routes to them, both from Europe as well as from other European strongholds in the East. The early Portuguese navigators soon found that the most important of the Spice Islands were Ternate, Tidore (*Tidoro* on Willem Blaeu's map of 1630), and Halmahera (part of which is shown along the bottom of this map by a rendering of its native name as *Gilolo*) for cloves, and Amboina and the Banda Islands for nutmeg and mace.

However, there was no real threat to Portuguese supremacy in the archipelago until the first arrival of a Dutch fleet under van Linschoten and his subsequent description of the Portuguese stations in the East which was published in Amsterdam in 1595–1596. Shortly after, the first Dutch voyage to the East Indies set out destined for Java and Bali. Another Dutch voyage set out in 1598, to be followed in 1602 by the establishment of the *Oost-Indische Compagnie* (Dutch East-India Company). Within the short span of ten years, the Dutch established for themselves a virtual monopoly in the highly lucrative trade with the Spice Islands, gradually extending their influence and control over large parts

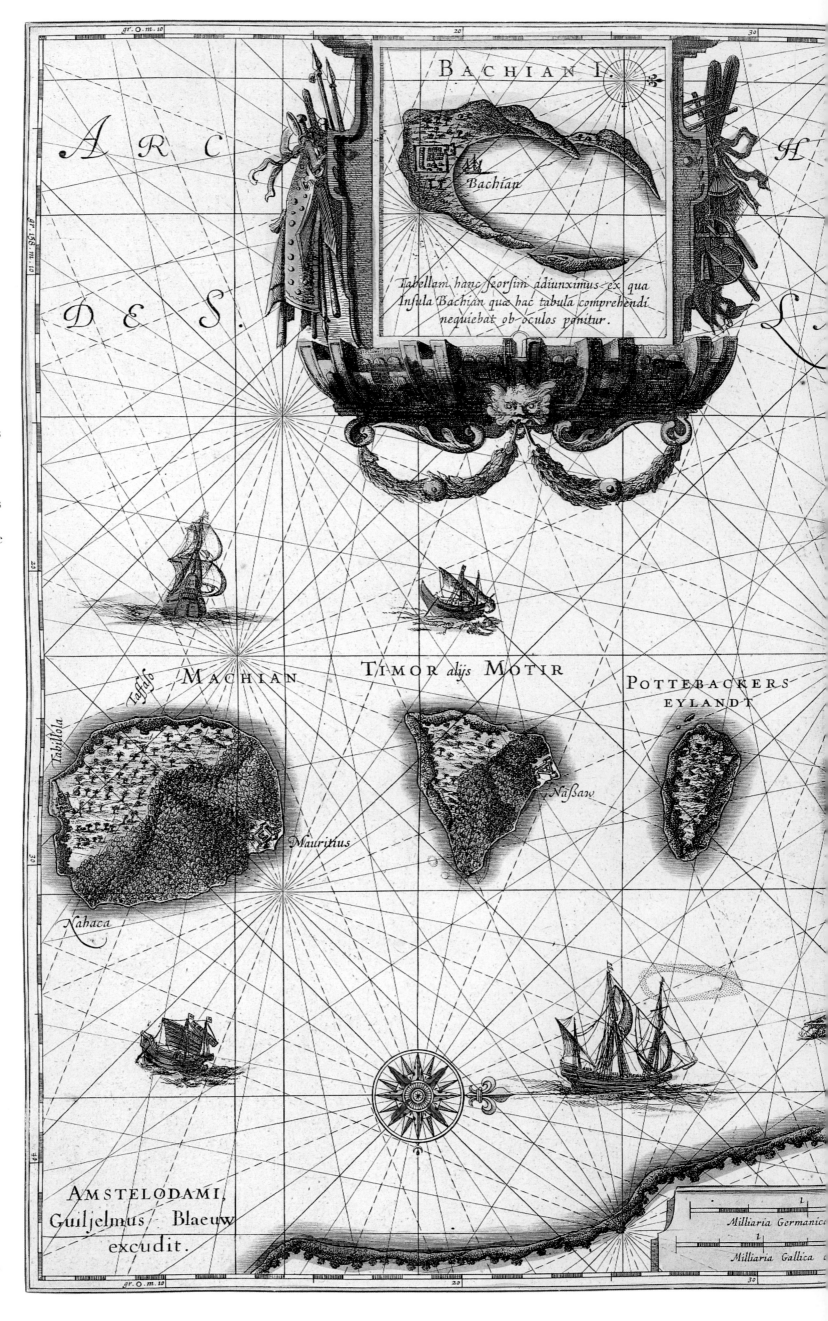

MOLVCCÆ
INSVLÆ
CELEBERRIMÆ

Gammalamme

Tacòmma

Hærij

TERNATE

Hooge dory

MITERRA

Marieco

Malayo

Taliao

Bay van
Gilolo

TIDORO

GILOLO I.

of the East Indian archipelago.

From north to south respectively, the little islands shown on this map – the earliest large-scale atlas map of the region – are known today as Ternate, Tidore, Mot and Makian and lie off the middle west coast of Halmahera in the northern part of the East Indies archipelago.

197

Tartaria sive Magni Chami imperium

This handsome map shows all of eastern Asia between the Caspian Sea and northern China and Manchuria outside the confines of the Great Wall.

Blaeu's map of north-eastern Asia is not signed, but it dates from 1635, when Tartary vaguely meant those regions to the north of Persia and China. The name Siberia only began to be applied with the gradual eastward expansion of the Russian cossacks into those areas hinted at in the accounts of Marco Polo from three centuries earlier.

The mythical and legendary nature of the geography of this vast interior is emphasized by the inclusion of devils and dragons in the *Desertum Lop* to the west of the Great Wall.

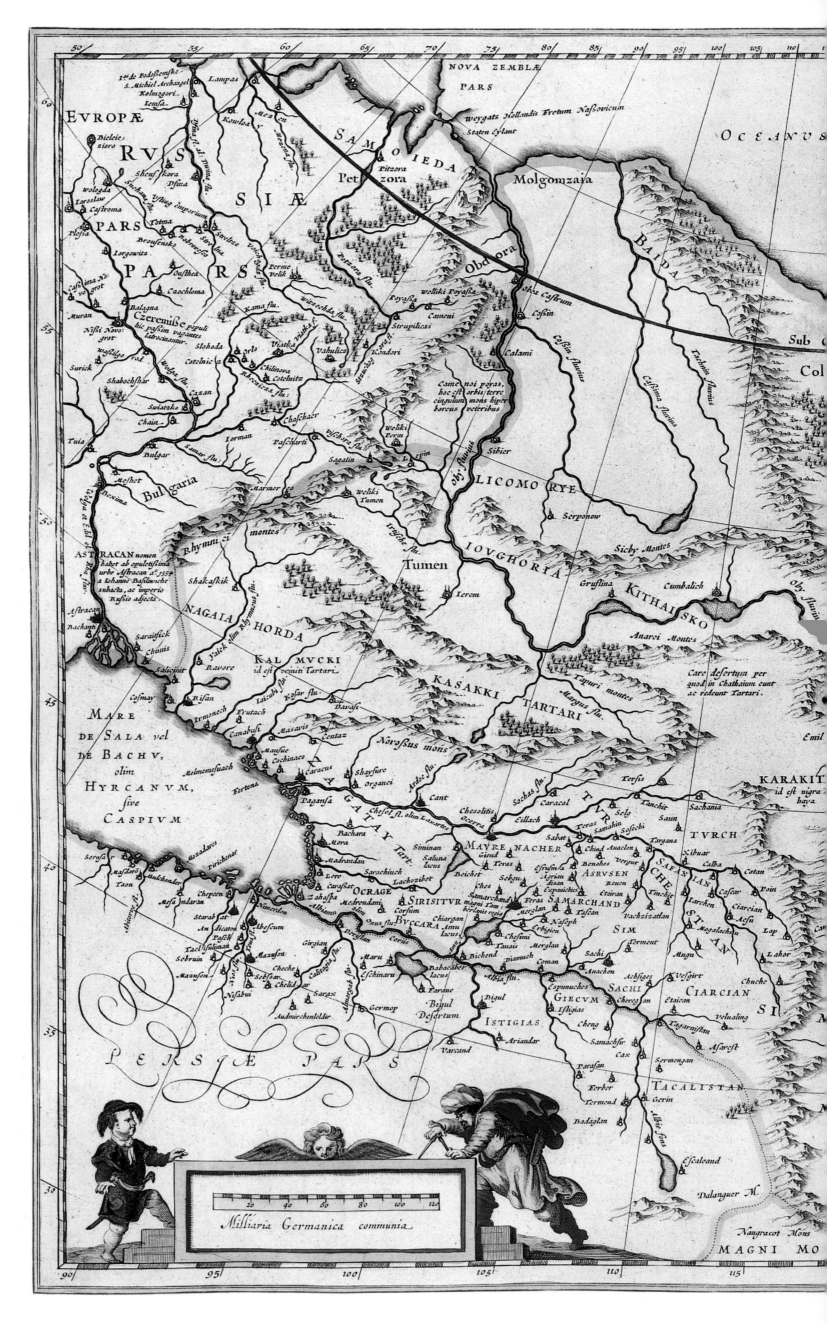

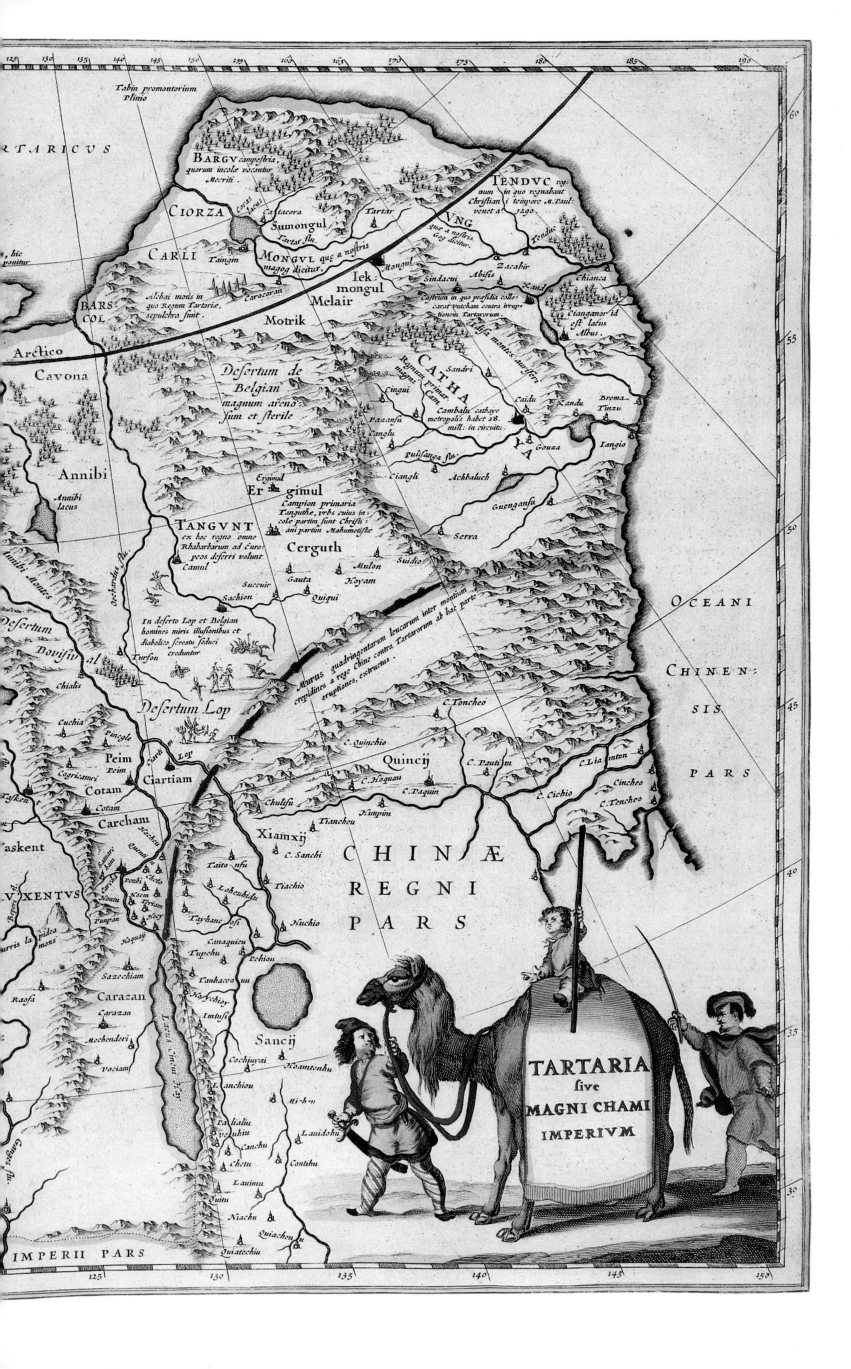

RTARICVS

Tabin promontorium
Plinio

BARGV campestria,
quorum incole vocantur
Mecriti .

CIORZA
Castacora
Sumongul
Tartar.flu.

CARLI   Taingin

Alchai mons in
qua Regnum Tartarie,
sepulchra sunt.

BARS:
COL

Arctico
Cavona

Annibi
Annibi
lacus

MONGVL que a nostris
magog dicitur.

Iek-
mongul
Melair

Motrik

Carocoran

TENDVC reg
num in quo regnabant
Christian i tempore M.Paul
venet a° 1290

Tartar

VNG
Que a nostris
Gog dicitur.

Mongul

Sindacui

Abisis

Tenduc

Zacabir

Castrum in quo praesidia collo=
carat vutcham contra hirup=
tionem Tartarorum.

Desertum de
Belgian
magnum areno=
sum et sterile

Xandu

CATHA
Regnum primar
magni Cam

Cingui

Pazansu

Canglu

Ciangli

Sandri

Cambalu cathaye
metropolis habet 28.
mill: in circuitu.

Pulisanga flu.

Achbaluch

Chianca

Cianganor id
est latus
Albus.

Caidu

Xandu

Brema-
Tinzu

Iangio

Gouza

Guengansu

Eximal
Er gimul

TANGVNT
ex hoc regno omne
Rhabarbarum ad Euro=
peos deferri volunt
Camul

Cerguth

Campion primaria
Tanguthe, urbs cuius in=
cole partim sunt Christi=
ani partim Mahumetisae

Serra

Mulon

Suidio

Desertum
Dovisu al

Chialis

In deserto Lop et Belgian
homines miris illusionibus et
diabolico screatu seduci
creduntur

Gauta
Sachion

Succuir

Quiqui
Hoyam

OCEANI

CHINEN=

Turfon

Murus quadringentarum leucarum inter montium
crepidines a rege chine contra Tartarorum ab hac parte
eruptiones, extructus.

SIS

Desertum Lop

C.Toncheo

PARS

Peim
Peim

Piaegle

Cuchia

Cogricamri

Cotam
Cotam

Ciartiam

Lop

C.Quinchio

Quincij

C.Hoquau

C.Pauti.m

C.Paquin

Chulisu

Tiancheu

Humpim

C.Lia nton

C.Cichio

Cincheo
C.Toncheo

Carcham

askent

XENTVS

Xiamxij

Taito nsu

Tenki Cheto

C.Sanchi

Loheuhisu

Tiachio

Huchio

CHINÆ
REGNI
PARS

urris la Pidea
mons

Hoey

Punpan

Hochau

Sazechiam

Tayhane

Canaquieu

Tupehu

Pehiou

Raosa

Carazan
Carazan
mechenderi

Vociam

Sancij

Kosschioy

Imtusi

Cochiuyxi

Hoamtenhu

Lanchiou

Mi-hn

Lawidoshu

TARTARIA
sive
MAGNI CHAMI
IMPERIVM

Ganges flu.

Palialiu
veJuhiu

Canchu

Chetu

Lauimu

Contihu

Quitu

Niachu

Quiachen

IMPERII PARS

Quiatechiu

199

Persia sive Sophorum regnum

Covering an area of southern Asia still largely recognizable today as modern Iran, Blaeu's map shows an empire astride the overland trade routes to the East. Persia itself was the source of fine carpets, tapestries, diamonds, turquoise and pearls, the latter coming from the Gulf island of Bahrain.

The Portuguese, and later the English, established factories at Hormuz in the south, and during the reign of Shah Abbas I, towns were opened to foreign traders and merchants, principally English and Dutch, the latter obtaining a monopoly in the silk trade in 1645.

The cartouche is decorated with three figures in the Court costume of the period.

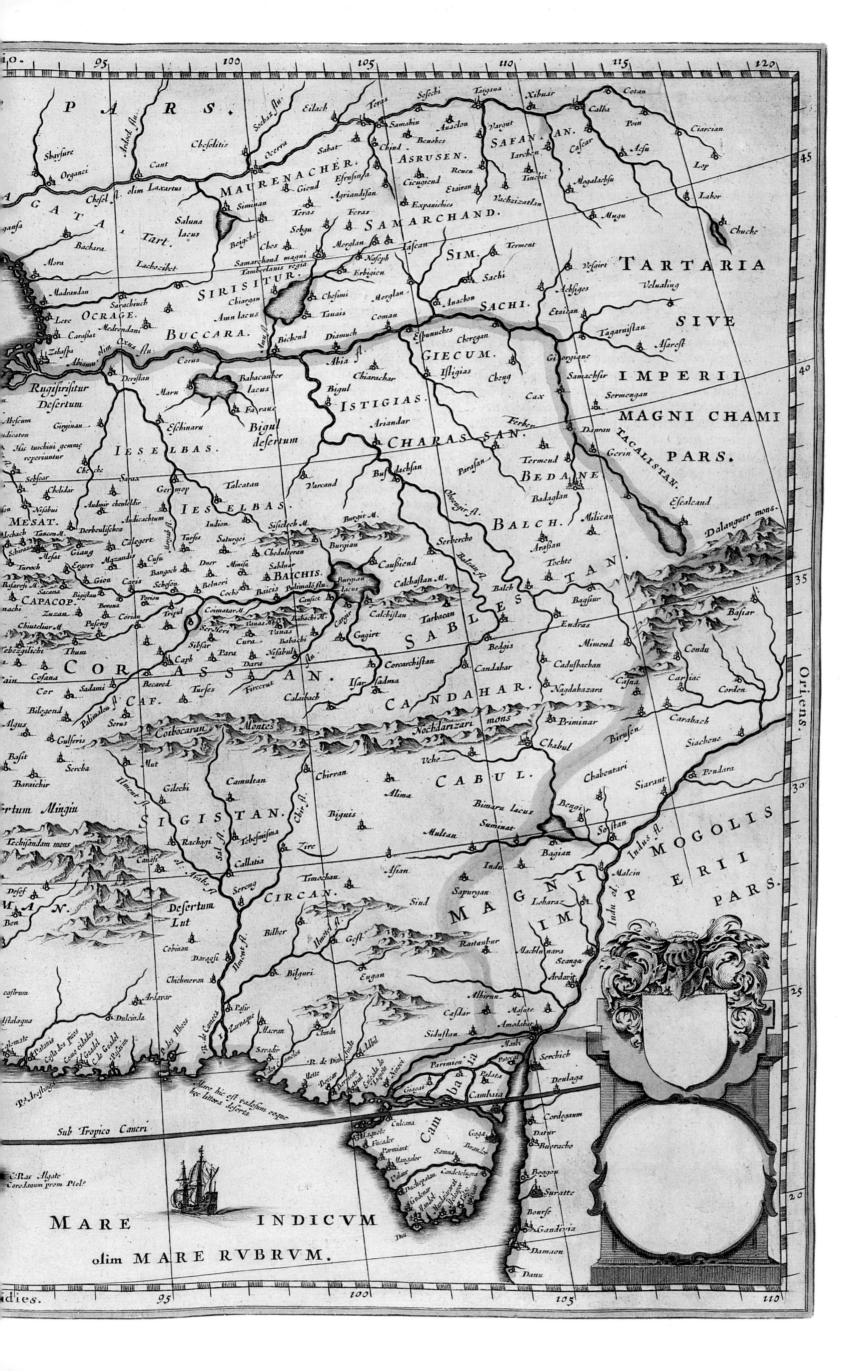

Turcicum Imperium

This is the standard seventeenth-century picture of the Turkish Empire, including the Balkans in south-eastern Europe, the North African littoral, the Levant and the Arabian peninsula in addition to the area of modern Turkey.

Much of the place name information on this map is derived from maps published in 1561 by the Italian mapmaker, Giacomo Gastaldi, whose maps exercised great influence over later European mapmakers, even throughout the seventeenth century.

Formidable though the barrier presented by the Turkish Empire in the Near East was, by the early years of the seventeenth century it was beginning to show signs of decadence and weakness, especially after the defeat of the Turkish navy at the hands of the combined Christian forces of Western Europe at the Battle of Lepanto in 1571, from which Turkish naval power never fully recovered.

Centred on the palace of the Sultans at Constantinople, the administration of the empire was passed down through local rulers, the *beys*, *deys* and *pashas*, who never lost an opportunity to enrich themselves and to develop often considerable powers of their own.

Further defeats of the Turks occurred in 1669 when Candia [Crete] was taken by the Venetians, and in 1683 when they suffered a humiliating defeat outside Wien at the north-western extremity of European Turkey.

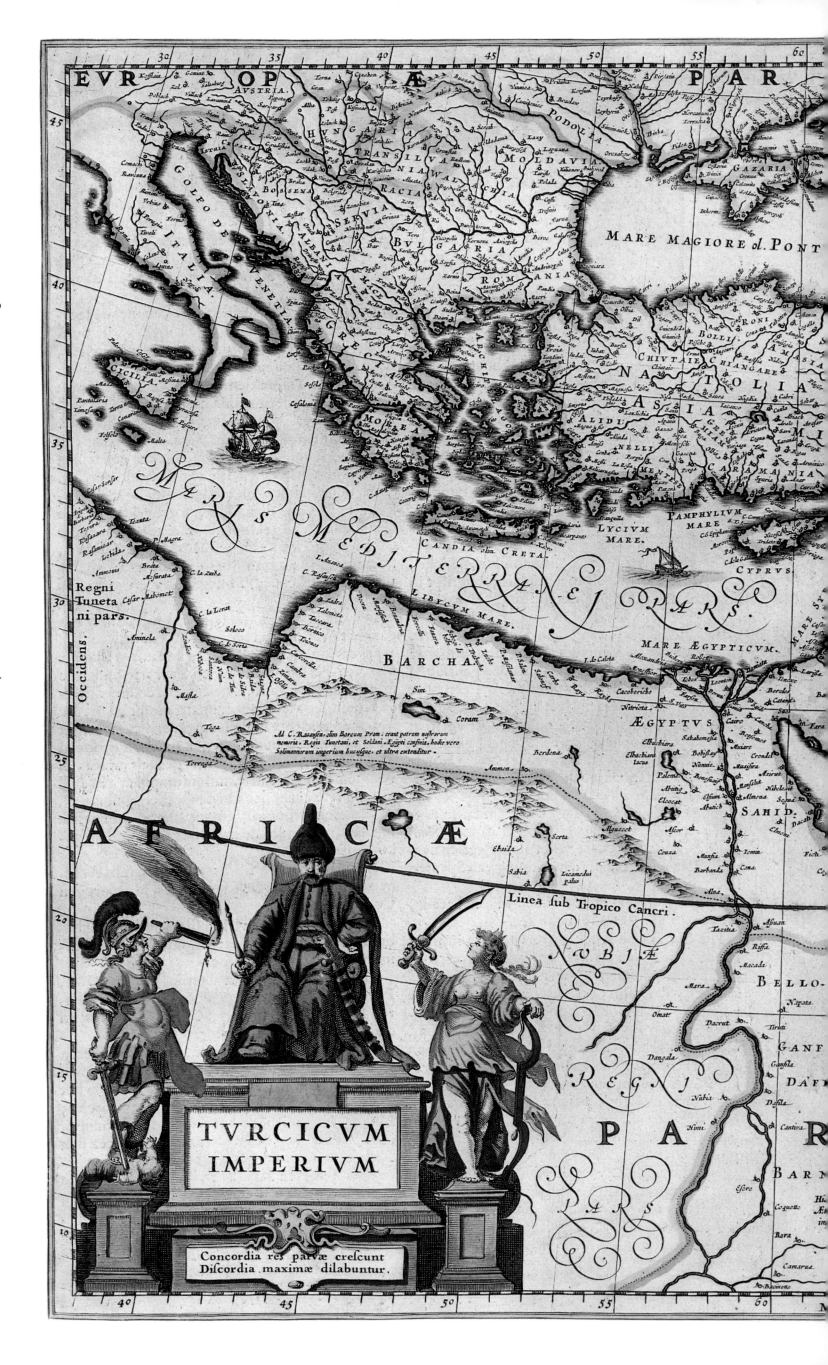

TARTARIÆ PARS.

Magni Ducis
Moſcoviæ confinia.

ASTRACAN NOVA.

GIVRGVRA.

MARE DE BACHVI. CASPIVM MARE
ET HYRCANVM.

GAZARA

MENGRELIA

GIORGIA.

DAIBVT

ARMENIA

TVRCO MANIA

CVRDI

SERVAN.

GILAN.

MEDIA

PERSIÆ

BINGIVL

SARCH

ASYRIA

RABIA

BOTAN

MESOPOTAMIA

DIARBECH.

CVSISTAN

FARCI

ARDEN.

CALDAR

ARABIA DESERTA.

CALDEA.

ARAC

ELARAN

ORMVS

MARE ELCATIF.

SINVS PERSICVS.

AYAMAN,

ANNA.

ELCATIF.

olim ARABIA

MASCALAT.

FELIX.

AMAN SIRIF DIN.

ALIBINALI.

SINVS ARABICVS MARE DE MECCA

THEAMA

GVBEL AMAN.

IRMIN.

ZIBIT

HERIT.

MAMIR.

MARE ARA:
BICVM
et
INDICVM

ADEN.

SO.

Milliaria Germanica communia.

Magnifico Prudentmo Spectatmoq; Viro
DAVIDI DE WILHEM
IVL. Curiæ Brabanticæ Senatori,
et IIItris Arauſionenſiū Principis Con:
ſiliario, viro Orientalium linguarum
peritiſſimo, ſtudiorumq; quotquot
ſunt, elegantiorum fautori ſerio,
Tabulam hanc D.D.D.
Guilielmus et Iohannes Blaeu.

PARS.

Oriens.

Willem Blaeu's beautiful map of Cyprus first appeared in 1635. Although, it must be admitted, Blaeu shows no new geographical information on the island (for the map is based entirely on that published more than sixty years previously by Abraham Ortelius of Antwerpen in 1573), it is, from an aesthetic point of view, perhaps the finest atlas map of Cyprus so far published. Many of its decorative features were copied by later mapmakers: the coat of arms at the top centre is that of the House of the Lusignans dating from 1393, that in the upper left-hand corner is the Turkish arms. But the eye is drawn to the dominant figure of Aphrodite at the lower right, sailing towards Paphos drawn by swans.

An anonymous sixteenth-century commentator wrote of Cyprus: 'Cyprus doth iustly challenge his place amongst the greater Ilands of the Mediterran sea…It is inferior to no Iland that I know: for it yeeldeth plenty of wine and oile: it hath also sufficient corne to find it selfe…This Iland sendeth ouer divers commodities into other countries, whereof they yearely raise great profit and gaines; it doth not much stand in need of any forrein commodities or merchandise.'

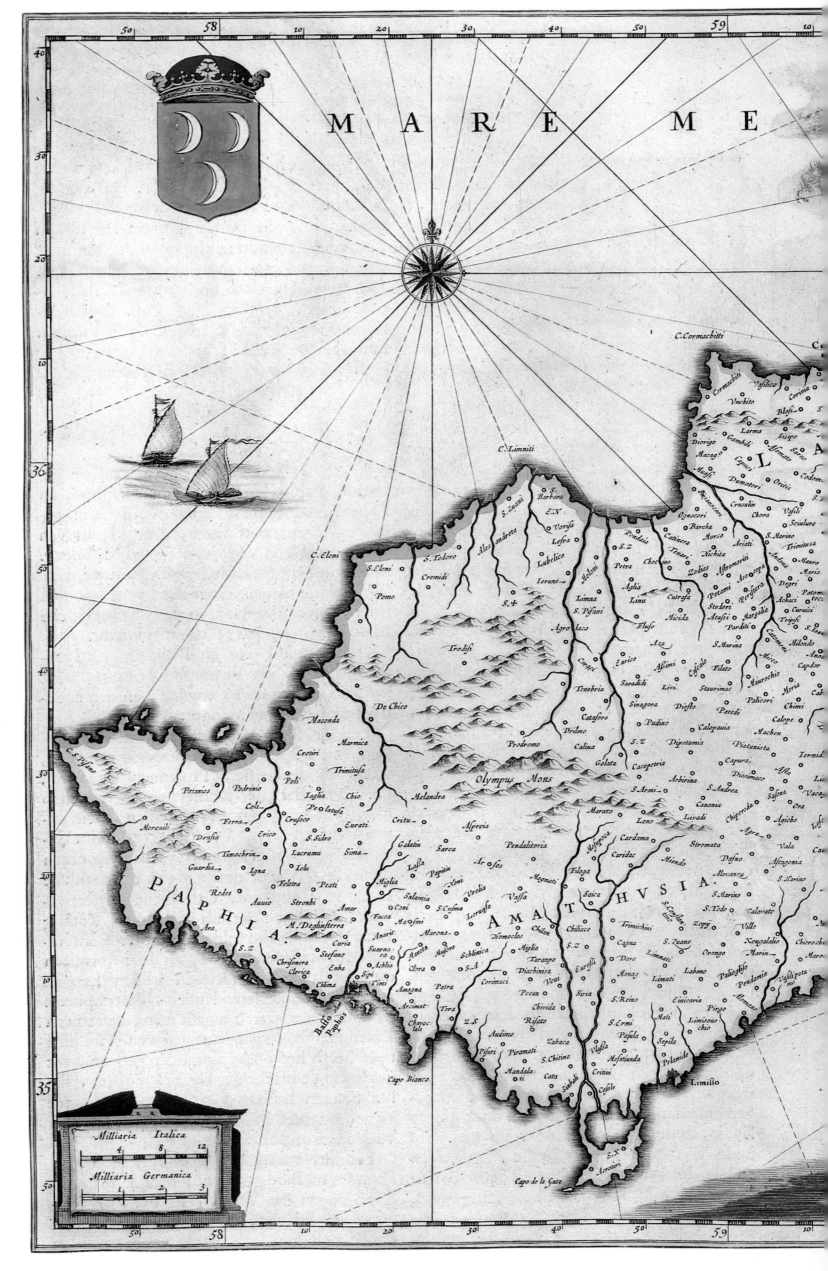

Terra Sancta quae in Sacris Terra Promissionis olim Palestina…1629

This is one of the very few maps published in Blaeu's atlases that bears a date. It was actually made by Jodocus Hondius the younger in 1629, but was not printed until after the purchase of the plate by Willem Blaeu (who added his imprint in the lower part of the cartouche).

At this time, many of the maps of Palestine were oriented to show east at the top to focus on Jerusalem. Here, the orientation is inverted so that Blaeu's map shows Palestine as it might have been viewed by Moses from the top of Mt Pisgah. The decorative features are Old Testament in inspiration: Moses holding the Tablets of the Law, stands to the left of the cartouche, Aaron to the right, while in the Mediterranean Jonah is about to be swallowed by the whale and in Sinai is shown the route of the Exodus. In the Red Sea at Yam Suf, Pharaoh's armies are shown drowning. The lands of the Twelve Tribes are shown straddling both banks of the Jordan, and the city of Jerusalem can be seen occupying a place of honour in the upper centre of the map.

The geographical detail of the map itself is taken from an inset on a large map of Palestine by the traveller Pieter Laicksteen and the mapmaker to Philip II of Spain, Christian 's-Grooten, published at Antwerpen in 1570. This inset map, its importance recognized by Hondius and by Blaeu, was unorthodox in its treatment of the outline of the Red Sea and its triangular outline for the Sinai peninsula – long before either was finally admitted by mapmakers as more accurate than traditionally accepted versions.

The Blaeus retained this map for all editions of the firm's atlases for more than

thirty years from 1630, even
though the rival publisher
Joannes Jansson issued a
more detailed seven-sheet
map of the region in his
own atlas.

orum, 1000 Passuum

21   24   27   30

Occidens

Septentrio

MEDITERRANEUM

Meridies

Oriens

MARE SYRIACUM

Tripolis

Ioppe

Lidda

Cæsarea Palestinæ

Turris Stratonis

Carmeli

Ptolomais

Belus

Sion

Acuba

Tyrus

Sarepta

Sidon

Gabala prom.

Biblium

Berithus

Philistæorum Terra

DAN

Terra Syro Phœniciæ

Terra Gibilitarum

ASER

NEPTALIM

EPHRAIM

MANAS

SABULON

SE

HAR

Samaria

Mare Galilææ

REGNUM BASAN

Cæsaria Philippi

Heliopolis

BENIAMIN

Ierusalem

Iericho

GAD

Hesbon

Terra Gilead

Terra

TERRA TRACONITIS

Terra Aram

Regnum Zoba

Damascus

RUBEN

Pella

Rabba

AMMONITÆ

Terra Tob

CELESYRIA

MOABITÆ

ARABIA PETROSA

Cademoth Desertum

Moabitarum Desertum

BETANIA

Gerra

TERRA SANCTA
quae in Sacris
Terra Promissionis olim
PALESTINA

Amstelodami
Ex officina Guilielmi Blaeuw 1629

Arabia

Up to 1662, the Blaeu atlases had had no separate map of the Arabian peninsula; Arabia was shown as a large part of the Turkish Empire (see map 89). This map by Joan Blaeu (but unsigned) made its debut in the atlas of 1662.

It demonstrates a tradition going back to the time of the second-century AD geographer, Claudius Ptolemy, in giving a threefold division of Arabia: *Arabia Petraea* (Rocky Arabia) in the north-west, *Arabia Deserta* (Desert Arabia) in the north, and *Arabia Felix* (Fertile Arabia) occupying the bulk of the peninsula, with many towns quite impossibly located in the middle of the desert.

When Blaeu issued this map, Arabia was a dangerous and mysterious place for non-Muslims, entrance resulting in certain death, or, as Richard Burton put it two hundred years later, 'a choice thrice offered between circumcision and death.'

That is not to say that trade was not carried out with Arabia. Dutch traders were attempting to gain the trade in coffee at the port of Mocha [Al Mukhā] in the far south at the entrance to the Straits of Bāb al Mandab. At the time coffee, like tea, was becoming highly regarded in Europe for its medicinal and healthful properties, and the ever-resourceful Dutch traders saw a perfect opportunity for great profit by securing such a trade.

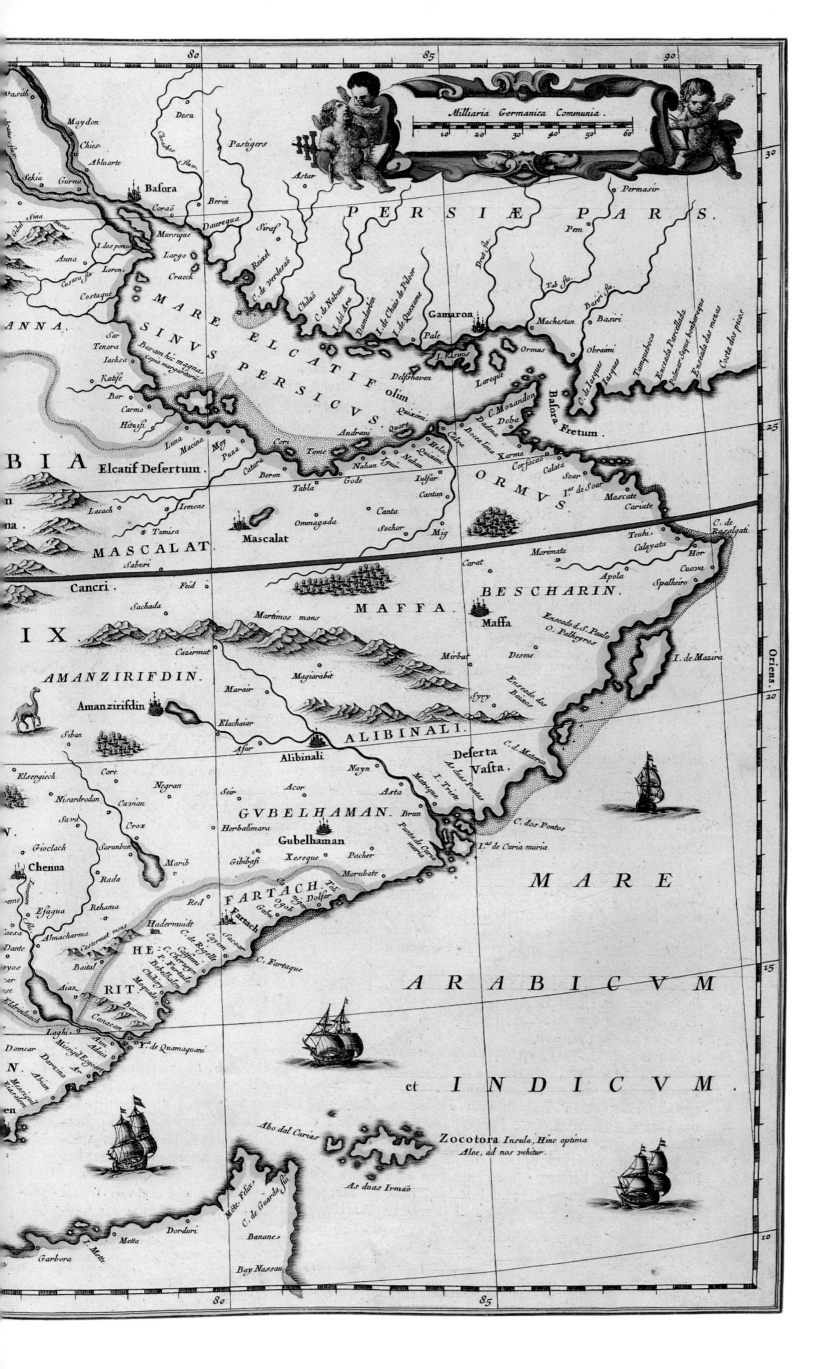

Milliaria Germanica Communia.

10   20   30   40   50   60

30

Vasith

Maydon

Desu

Chies   *Abluarte*

Sekia   *Gurna*

Choebas   *Flex*

Pastigers

Permasir

Basora

Beron

Astar

PERSIÆ PARS.

Corao

Daurequa

Murrique

Siraf

Pen

Largo

I. dos porcos

Anna

Loron

Craeck

Reael

C. de Verdexao

Drek. Siu.

Cosara Ra.

Costaque

Chilao

C. de Naham

I. del Ara

I. de Chaia de Pdoor

Damalabin

I. de Quexome

Tab. flu.

Basri. flu.

Basiri

Gamaron

Machestan

Tanquebaca

Enciada Parvellada

Polmer. feque bubarque

MARE

Sar Tenora

Bar-am hic magnæ copia margaritarum.

Pale

Ormus

Obrami

Bareda das meras

Costa dos picos

Iachea

SINVS

I. Kisius

Lareque

C. de Iasques

Iasques

Katfe

Bar

ELCATIF

Delfshaven

Quiximi

C. Mozandon

Carmo

PERSICVS.

olim

Quare

Doba

Hitasfi

Andrani

Tonte

Quiximi

Basora Fretum.

Luna   *Macuna*

Mey

Puza

Cori

Hola

Caxem

Dudena

BIA   **Elcatif Desertum.**

Catara

Beron

Nahan

Eguar

Nahan

Quiximi

Xarma

Corfacaõ

Calata

Soar

Lacach

Temene

Tabla

Gode

Iulfar

Cantan

ORMVS.

I. de Soar

Mascate

25

Tumisa

Canta

Cariate

MASCALAT

Ommagada

Sochor

Mig

Teuhi

C. de Rasalgati

Saberi

Mascalat

Marimata

Calayata

Hor

Cancri.

Feid

Carat

Apola

Cuova

MAFFA.

BESCHARIN.

Spalheiro

Sachada

Martimos mons

Maffa

Enseada d. S. Paulo

O. Palheyros

IX.

Cazirmut

Mirbat

Desme

AMANZIRIFDIN.

Maraur

Magiarabit

Enseado dar Baixos

I. de Mazira

Amanzirifdin

Elachaiar

Eyry

Siban

Afar

ALIBINALI.

20

Elsergiech

Core

Negran

Alibinali

Nayn

Deserta

C. d. Materca

Nisardrodan

Seir

Acor

Asta

Vasta.

I. Trite

Oriens.

Savd

Casnan

Crox

Brun

Marequa

GVBELHAMAN.

Gioclach

Sarunbum

Herbalimara

C. dos Pontos

Rada

Marib

Gubelhaman

Punta de Curia

I.as de Curia muria

Chenna

Gibihafi

Xeseque

Pacher

Esaqua

Rehama

Morubate

MARE

Red

FARTACH.

Toli.

Dolfar

Almacharma

Hadermuidt

Gabu

HE-

Castermut mons

C. de Rex. Ille

Osob

Baital

C. Chequen

Fartach

Aiaz

C. Furtado

Sacour

RIT.

Dekchalim

Chibeger

Meyulla

C. Fartaque

15

Baram

ARABICVM

Eldrindluach

Laghi.

Aim Alaia

Damcar

Canacam

Ar.

Y. de Quamaquani

Abian

Maeyigui

Xiaraden

N.

et **INDICVM.**

Abo dal Curias

Zocotora *Insula, Hinc optima*

Aloe, ad nos vehitur.

I. Metta

As duas Irmaõ

Mette

Dorduri

Mõte. Felix.

C. de Guarda fui

Garbora

Banane

Bay Nassau

80   85

Imperii Sinarum nova descriptio

This and the following six maps form part of a series of detailed general and regional maps of China and Japan published by Joan Blaeu in 1655 based on the compilations of the Jesuit Father Martino Martini.

Martino Martini (1614–1661) was born at Trento in Italy and entered the Jesuit College at Rome where he studied mathematics under Athanasius Kircher, the mathematician and scientist. Martini embarked for the East Indies in 1640 with twenty-two other missionaries, arriving at Goa in India in November of that year. He entered China in 1643 in Zhejiang province during a time of great internal unrest and upheaval in China. He was, however, able to travel throughout the country as far into the interior as the Great Wall, collecting and sorting materials for a survey of the Chinese Empire. In so doing, Martini determined for the first time with any degree of accuracy the astronomical position of many towns and geographical features. He returned to Hangzhou in 1646, founded a new missionary church at Lanxi, also in Zhejiang province, remaining there for four years until he chose to return to Rome on behalf of the Jesuit Mission. On the way back to Europe, his ship was blown a long way off course and Martini was forced to land in Norway.

His travels to Rome then continued via Amsterdam where he met Joan Blaeu and was able to assist with the production of the *Atlas Sinensis*, in which these maps were first published, and which later formed a part of the great 1662 atlas. Martini thence proceeded to Rome to conduct his mission business with the College of Cardinals, eventually returning to China in 1657, where he remained for the rest of his life, dying at Hangzhou in 1661.

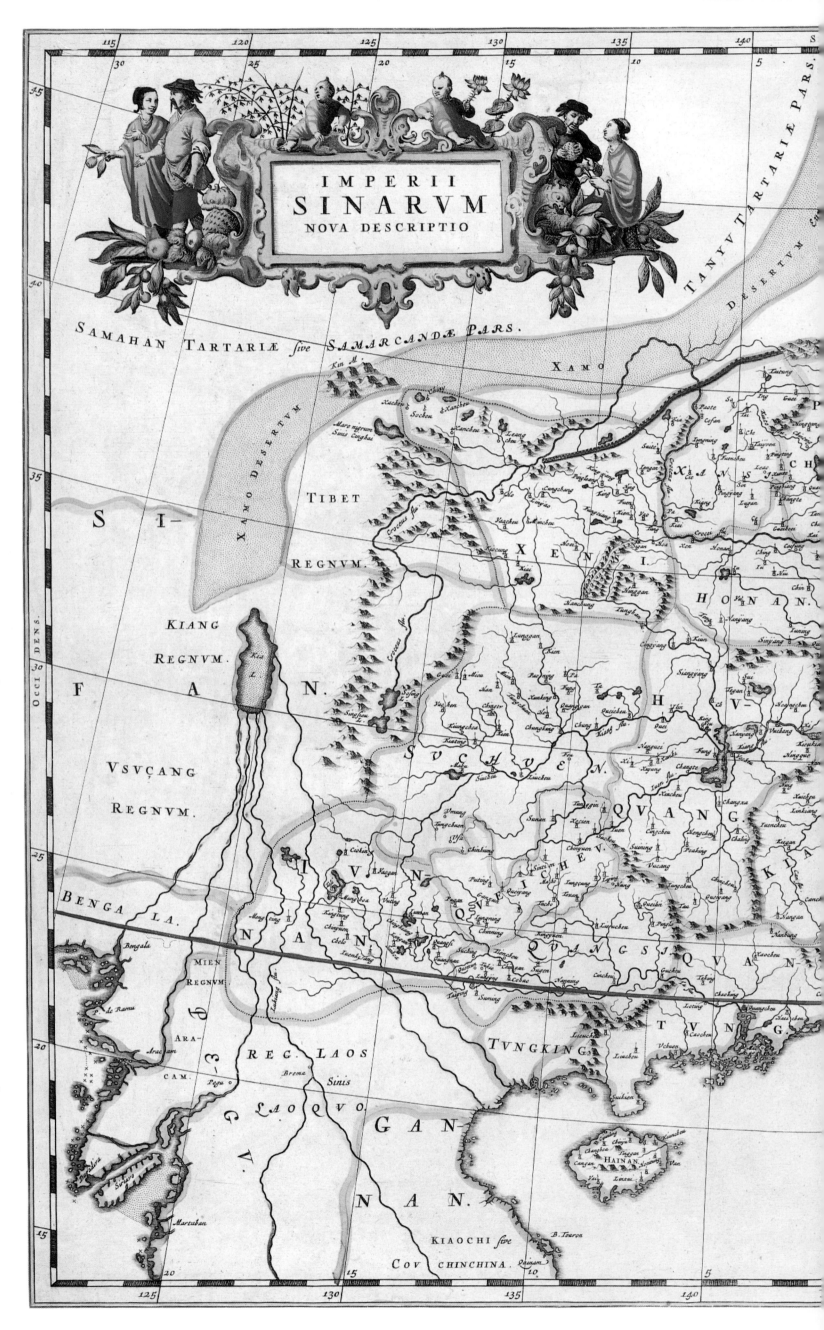

Martini's description of China was also published concurrently with the regional maps as a work entitled *Sinicae historiae*, the text of which Blaeu reprinted almost in its entirety as the descriptive text to accompany the maps of the *Atlas Sinensis*.

The maps were produced at about the time the Ming dynasty was toppled and the country came under Manchu control. It is interesting to note that the provinces of modern China retain most of their seventeenth-century divisions, and a detailed comparison between Martini's view and the modern outlines of the provinces shows very many close similarities, making a lasting tribute to the skill both of Martini himself and the Chinese maps to which he must have had access.

For the first time on any non-Chinese produced map, Korea is shown as a peninsula instead of as an island, as had been the case with the map of China produced by Blaeu's predecessor Hondius, who had used sixteenth-century Portuguese sources. In addition, Martini was able to produce an accurate and highly influential map of Japan, an influence that could still be detected in maps produced at the end of the eighteenth century.

Pecheli sive Peking, Imperii Sinarum Provincia Prima

Hebei, the First Province of China, includes Beijing, and is suitably the most decorative of the series of regional maps in the Martini series. The title is enclosed within a charming set-piece composed of two Chinese elders seated in ornamental chairs, with their servants and a pair of extremely flamboyant birds, their form delightfully emphasized by the rich colouring. It is not known why Beijing (thus named since the fifteenth century, after a short period as Kublai Khan's 'Cambaluc') should here be called *Xuntien*. Note the detailed key to the categories of towns given by Martini to the left of the title ornament.

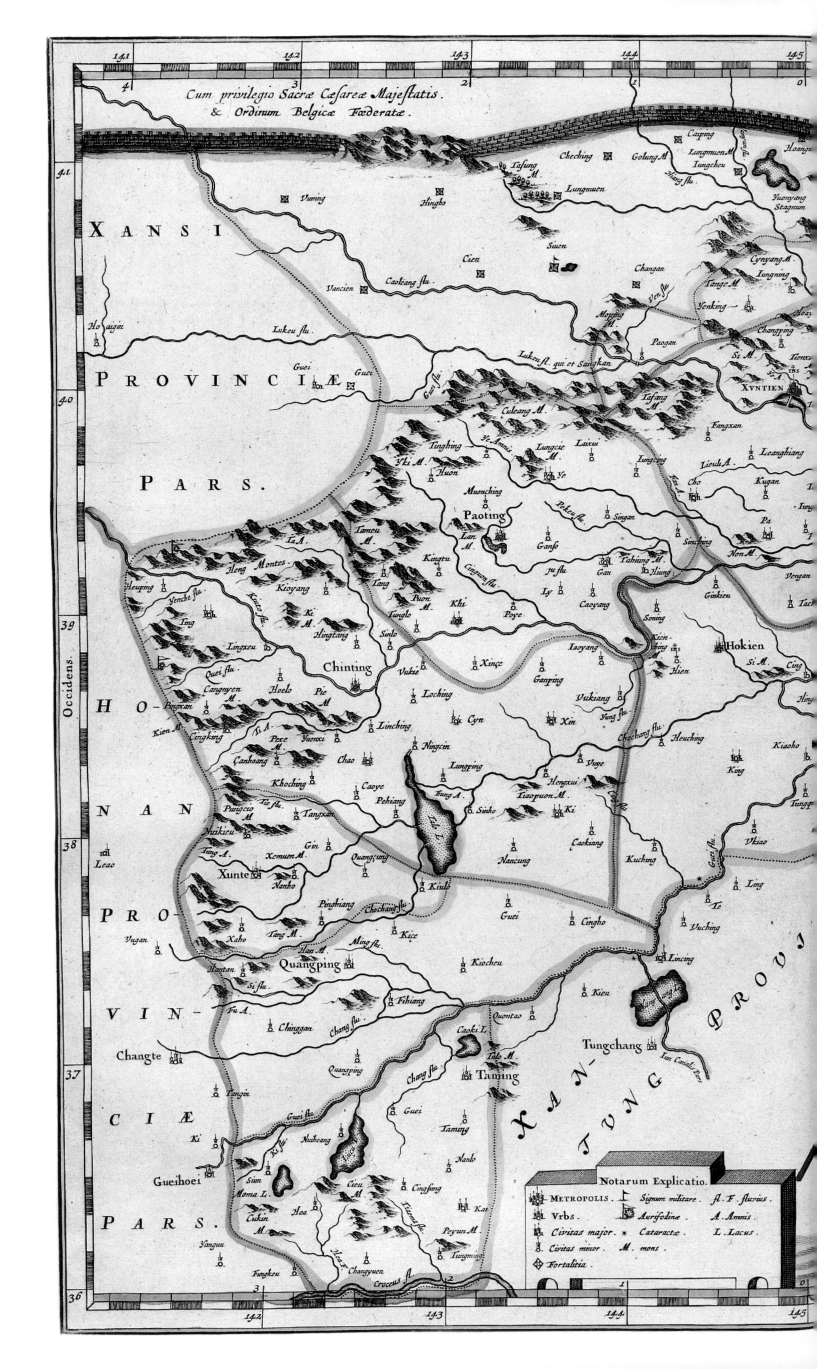

Hoangfu.

Hoeccheu

Fuüing

Pet-an M.

Cie fla.

Cziun

Quh Ki

Cunhoa   Yen

Iotien

Ciengan

Tu M.

Mon

Lo

Iungping   Vuning

Iungping

ngho

Paote

Yang M.

Heng M.

Loting

Cu M.

Fungxang

Changli

Yu

Tiencin

Xanghai

Salinæ

xan

Chungtiao M.

Stadia Sinensia, quorum 250 uni gradui respondent

50   100   150   200   250

Milliaria Germanica, quorum 15 unum Constituunt gradum.

5   10   15

Ningyuen

L E A O T V N G

Quangning

P A R S.

40

Chekiao   Co

Chehai   Quangning

Xintung   Cinagni

Ç A N G   S I N V S

Taoyuen

39

Mixe

Sungtao

Oriens.

P A R S.

38

37

PECHELI,
SIVE
PEKING,
IMPERII SINARVM
PROVINCIA PRIMA.

36

Xensi, Imperium Sinarum Provincia Tertia

Shaanxi, the Third Province of China, to the south-west of Beijing and including the western end of the Great Wall, depicted on the map in greatly exaggerated form. The provincial capital, Xi'an (*Sigan* on Martini's map) is the resting place of the celebrated army of terracotta soldiers guarding the tomb of the first Emperor of China, Qin Shi Huangdi.

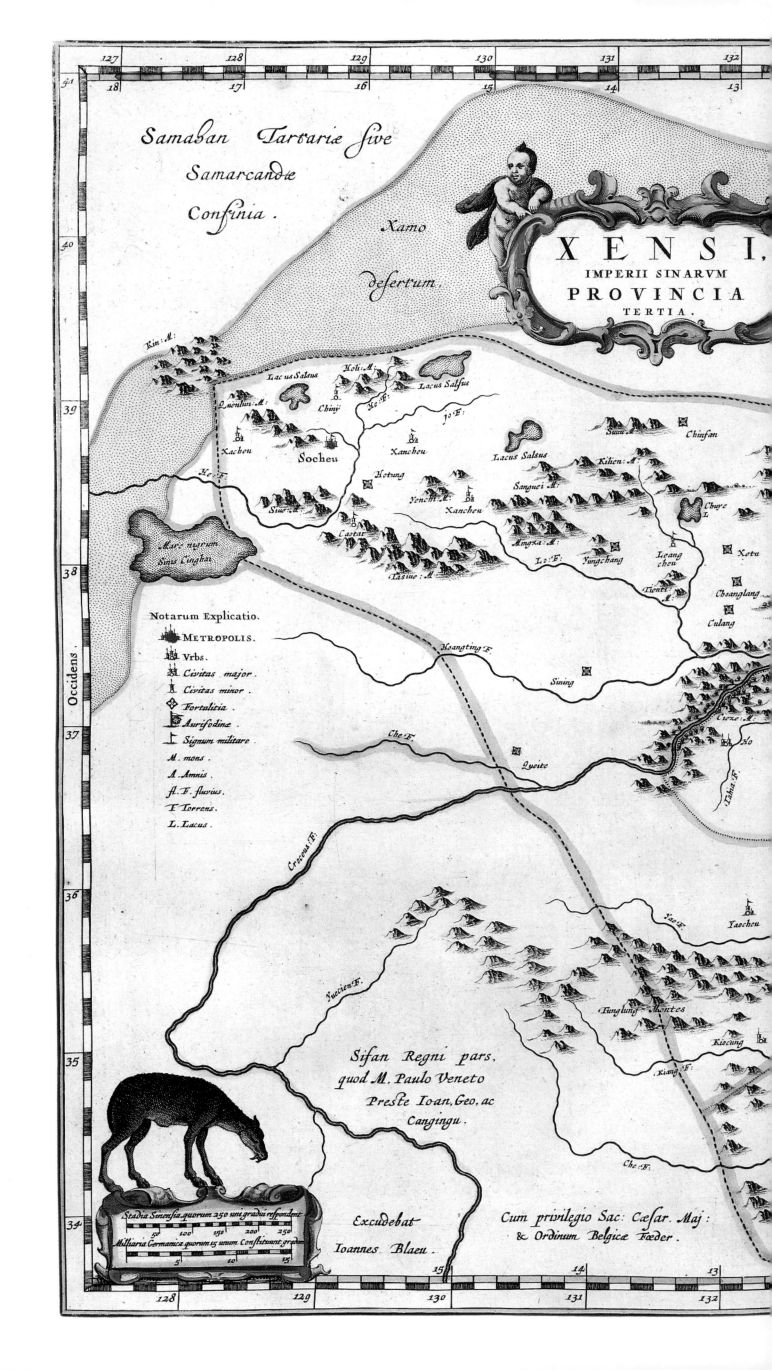

Samaban Tartariæ sive Samarcandæ Confinia.

Xamo

desertum

XENSI,
IMPERII SINARVM
PROVINCIA
TERTIA.

Kin: M.

Lacus Salsus
Holi: M.
Lacus Salsus
Quonlun: M.
He: F.
Chini
Jo: F.
Suui: M.
Chinfan
Xacheu
Socheu
Xancheu
Kilien: M.
Hotung
Lacus Salsus
Sanguei: M.
Yencui: M.
Chuye L.
Siue: M.
Xancheu
Caotar
Mingxa: M.
Leangcheu
Xotu
Lo: F.
Yungchang
Tasine: M.
Tientu: M.
Choanglang
Mare nigrum Sinis Cingha
Culang

Notarum Explicatio.
🏰 METROPOLIS.
🏯 Vrbs.
🏯 Civitas major.
🏯 Civitas minor.
◇ Fortalitia.
🏯 Aurifodinæ.
⊥ Signum militare.
M. mons.
A. Amnis.
fl. F. fluvius.
F. Torrens.
L. Lacus.

Hoangting F.
Sining
Cexe: M.
Che F.
Queite
Ixhu: F.

Crocena: F.

Yao F.
Yaocheu

Yaecien F.

Tunglun Montes
Kiocung

Sifan Regni pars,
quod M. Paulo Veneto
Preste Ioan. Geo. ac
Cangingu.

Kiang: F.

Che: F.

Stadia Sinensia quorum 250 uni gradui respondent.
50   100   150   200   250
Milliaria Germanica quorum 15 unum constituunt gradum
5   10   15

Excudebat
Ioannes Blaeu.

Cum privilegio Sac: Cæsar. Maj:
& Ordinum Belgicæ Fœder.

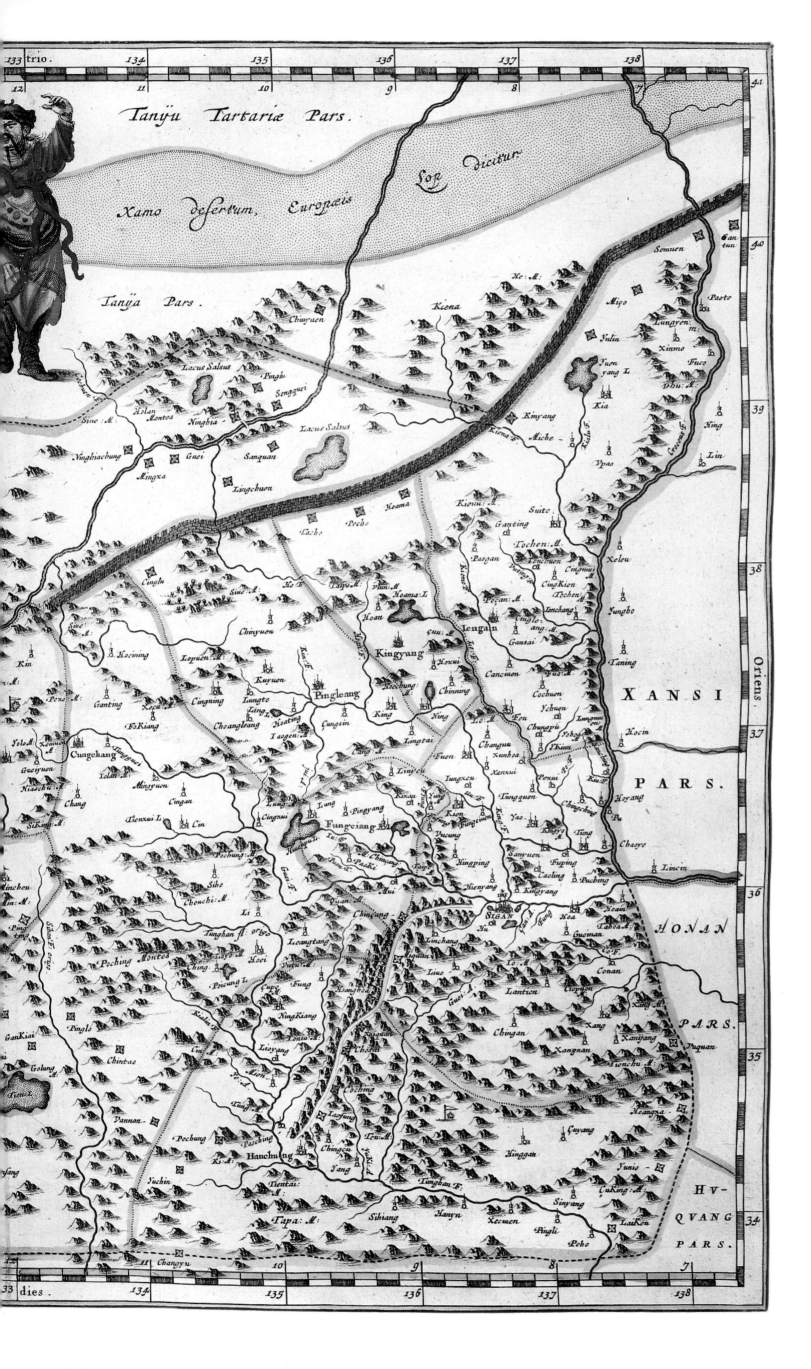

12 11 10 9 8 41

Tanÿu Tartariæ Pars.

Xamo desertum, Europæis Lop dicitur 40

Tanÿa Pars.

He: M:
Kiena
Migo
Semuen
Santun

Chuyuen
Yulin
Lungyen: m:
Xinmo
Fuco
Paoto

Yuen yang L
Kia
Dhu: M:
King 39

Lacus Salsus
Pinglu
Senggvei
Kinyang
Miche
Kialo F:
Ypao
Lin

Holan Montes
Siue: M:
Ninghia
Lacus Salsus
Kiena fu
Kiou: M:
Suite
Ganting
Xelou

Ninghiachung
Guei
Sanquan
Hoama
Pecho
Lacho
Plan: M:
Hoan
Hoama L:
Lenchuen
Cingmui
Cing Kien
Tochen fu
Yungho
38

Mingxa
Lingchuen
Taiye: M:
çuu:
Iengan
Cinglo
ang: M:
Pecan: M:
Lenchang
Taning

Cinglu
Siue: M:
He F:
Chinyuen
Gansai
Oriens

XANSI

Kin
Siue: M:
Hocining
Lopuen
Kuyuen
Kingyang
Hoxui
Cancuen
Cochuen
Ychuen
Lungmui en:
Hocin
37

Pexo: M:
Ganting
Xecu
Cingning
Lungte
Pingleang
Kiechung
Chinning
Lo:
Feu
Chungpu
Yohoa
Yola: M:
Lecmuen
FoKiang
Jing
King
Ning
Changua
Xunhoa
YKiun
PARS.

Cungchang
Tolan: M:
Choangleang
Hoating
Taogen:
Cungsin
Cang:
Langtai
Fuen
Xanxui
Tungquon
Pexui: M:
Chingchug
Hoyang
Pu

Gueiyuen
Niachu:
Mingyuen
Cingan
Lung:
Linÿu
Kiao
Yung
Kien
Hu:
Yao
Kinÿa
Tang
Chaoye

Chang
Tienxui L
Cin
Cingxui
Pingyang
Fungtuen
Sanyuen
Fuping
Lincin
36

SiKing: M:
Huechui: L:
Fungciang
Yucung
Hienping
Caoling
Puching

Pechung
Pao Ki:
Iaÿ
SIGAN
Xsa
Haim
Tahoa: M:
HONAN

Incheu
Min: M:
Siho
Chenchi: M:
Li
Mui
Hienyam
Kingyang
Hu
Fu
Gueman
Co F:

Ping yang
SiHan F: arigo
Tunghan fl: arigo
Leangtang
Chincang
Iuan: M:
Linchang
Iiquan
Io: M:
Conan
Lantien
Cleyuen
Xang: M:
PARS.

Pocung Montes
Taiye: M:
Hoei
Yufun
Liuo
Gui:
Chingan
Xangnan
Xanfang
Paquan
35

GanKiai
Poicung L:
Pingli
Cucy
Fung
Ningkiang
Hoangheu
Xiggan
Chosan
Ionchu: M:
Hoangxa

Golung
Lioyang
Tonia:
Guyang

Yunli L
Chintao
Mien
Cuching
Hanchung
Lasfung
Ten: M:
Xinggan
Yunis:
CuKing: M:
HV-

Yuchin
Pechung
Paoching
Chingcu
Yang
Tunghan F:
Sinyang
QVANG

Tapa: M:
Tientai:
Sihiang
Hanÿn
Lecmuen
Pingli
LaiKeu
PARS.

Peho

215

Shandong, the Fourth Province of China. For the first time on a printed map, the Shandong peninsula is mapped in a more or less correct form, together with Laodong and the Bohai Sea. Near the upper edge can be seen the eastern end of the Great Wall, again greatly exaggerated, while the western shores of the Korean peninsula are found along the right-hand margin.

XANTVNG, SINARVM IMPERII PROVINCIA QVARTA.

Stadia Sinensia, quorum 250 uni gradui respondent

Milliaria Germanica quorum 15 unum Constituunt gradum

Cum privilegio Sacr. Cæsar. Maj:
& Ordinum Belgicæ Fœderatæ.

A O T V N G.

S I N V S.

C O R E A

P E N

I N S V L A.

Notarum Explicatio.

METROPOLIS		Aurifodinæ
Vrbs.		Signum militare.
Civitas major.		M. mons.
Civitas minor.		A. F. fluvius.
Fortalitia		L. Lacus.

Vcheu
Chungtun
Cientun
Puho
Chungui
Quangningco
Quanningyuen
Tanyang
Tingleao
Caiyuen
Fung hoang
M.
Samuen
Quangning
Saline
Focheu
Leaoyang
Lien
M.
Tieling
Vanxeu
M.
Vansung M.
Taichou
Kincheu
Ganlo
Liuxun
Pieyang
Hoicheu
Eaicheu
I. Lieniun

Tung I.
I. Xamuen
Cheug M.
Xechin
Chin
ng
teu
Panglai
Kixan
Chiteu
M.
Gueihai
Chaoyuen
Hoang
Ninghai
Siaoye
Hiyang L.
Texan
Venteng
Chingxan
aicheu
Layang
Kiochang
Leuhia
Tasung M.
Tamao M.
Cieme
Ningcin
Cinghai
Sanxan
Tenheng
iaolao
Talao
Suifo
I. Yoxa

Holan
Tangleu
Yalo flu.
Iaoyflu.
Hiaoflu.
Hunking
Pinggan
Kingki
Huanghai
Chungceng
Ceuenlo
Fungma

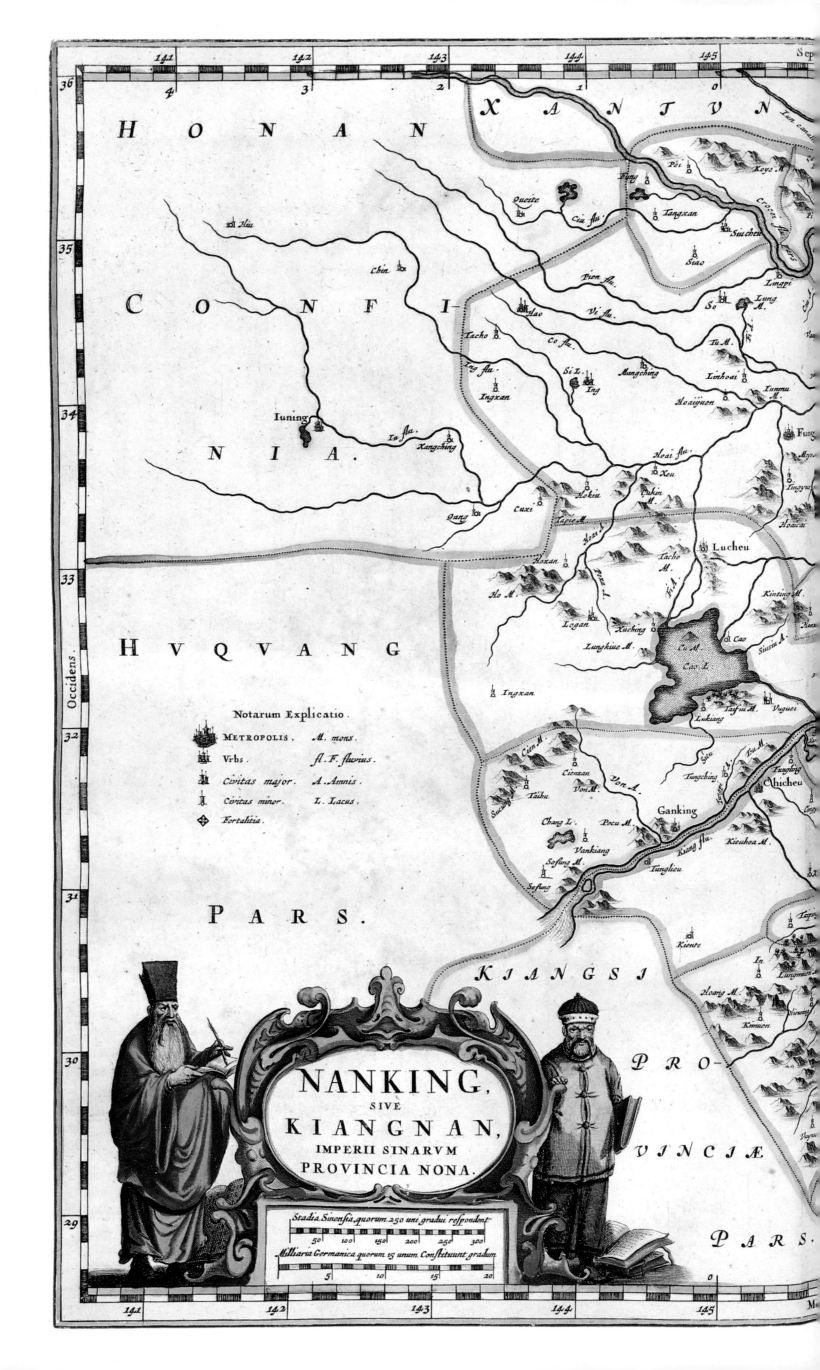

Nanking, sive Kiangnan, Imperii Sinarum Provincia Nona

Nanjing, or Jiangnan, the Ninth Province of China. The old province of Nanjing is now divided into the modern provinces of Anhui and Jiangsu. Particularly prominent is the lower course of the Chang Jiang [Yangtze River], with the large lake Tai Hu immediately south. This province also includes the site of Shanghai, marked on the map as the small fishing village of *Xanghai*. Also of interest on this map is the relatively large number of Jesuit missions, each indicated by the letters 'IHS' surmounted by a cross.

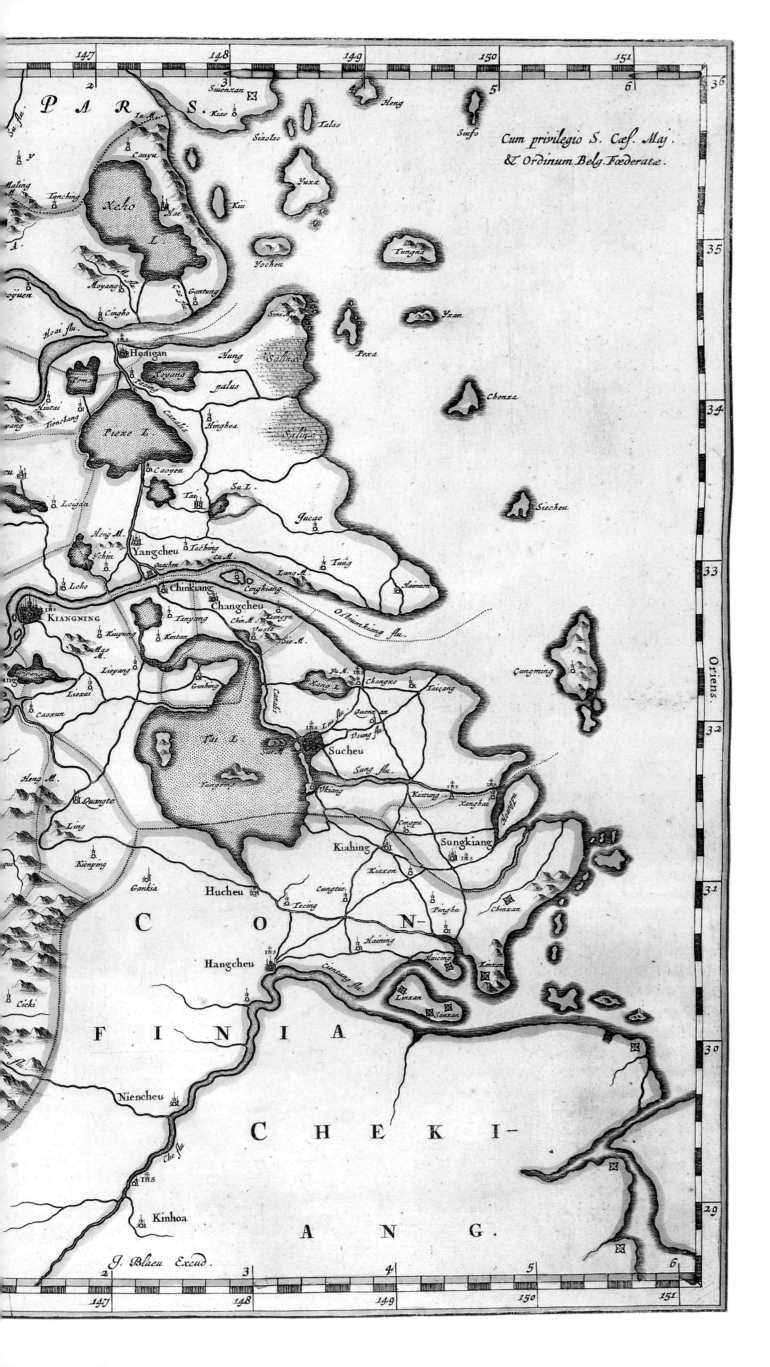

P A R S.

Cum privilegio S. Cæs. Maj.
& Ordinum Belg. Fœderatæ.

Suenxan
S. Kiao
Heng
Siaolao   Talao
Iu M.   Canyu
Siufo
Maleng
M.
Tanching
Yuxa
Kiu
Xeho
L.
Moyang   Ma fu.
Cae fu.   Gantung
Yochen
Tungan
Cingho
Sini.
Yxan
Hoai flu.
Hocigan   Aung
Salina   Pexa
Sayare
Paning
galus
Chenxa
Tienchang
Piexe L.
Hinghoa
Salina
Caoyen
Su L.
Loyan   Tao   Iucao
Siechea
Heng M.
Ichin   Taching   Cu M.
Yangcheu   Ouchen   Tung
Loho   Cu M.   Lang M.
Chinkiang   Cengkiang   Haimen   O. Takimkiang flu.
KIANGNING   Changcheu   Chin M.   Kiangxn
Tanyang   Vusie
Kiuyung   Kintan   Sie M.
Mao
Lieyang   Yu M.
Cushing   Venxo L.   Changxo   Çangming
Liexui   Taicang
Caoxun   Iua fu.   Quenxan
Tai L.   Tfung flu.   Vsung flu.
Heng M.   Sucheu
Quangte   Sung flu.
Ukiang   Kiatung   Henghai   Ciang flu.
Ling   Tuxin   Cingpu
Kienping   Kiahing   Sungkiang
Gankia   Kiuxen
Hucheu   Cungtie   Pinghu   Chinxan
Tcing
C O N -
Haining
Haicing   Kinxan
Hangcheu   Cienteng flu.
Linxan
F I N I A   Sanxan
Niencheu

C H E K I -

Che flu.

Kinhoa

A N G.

J. Blaeu Excud.

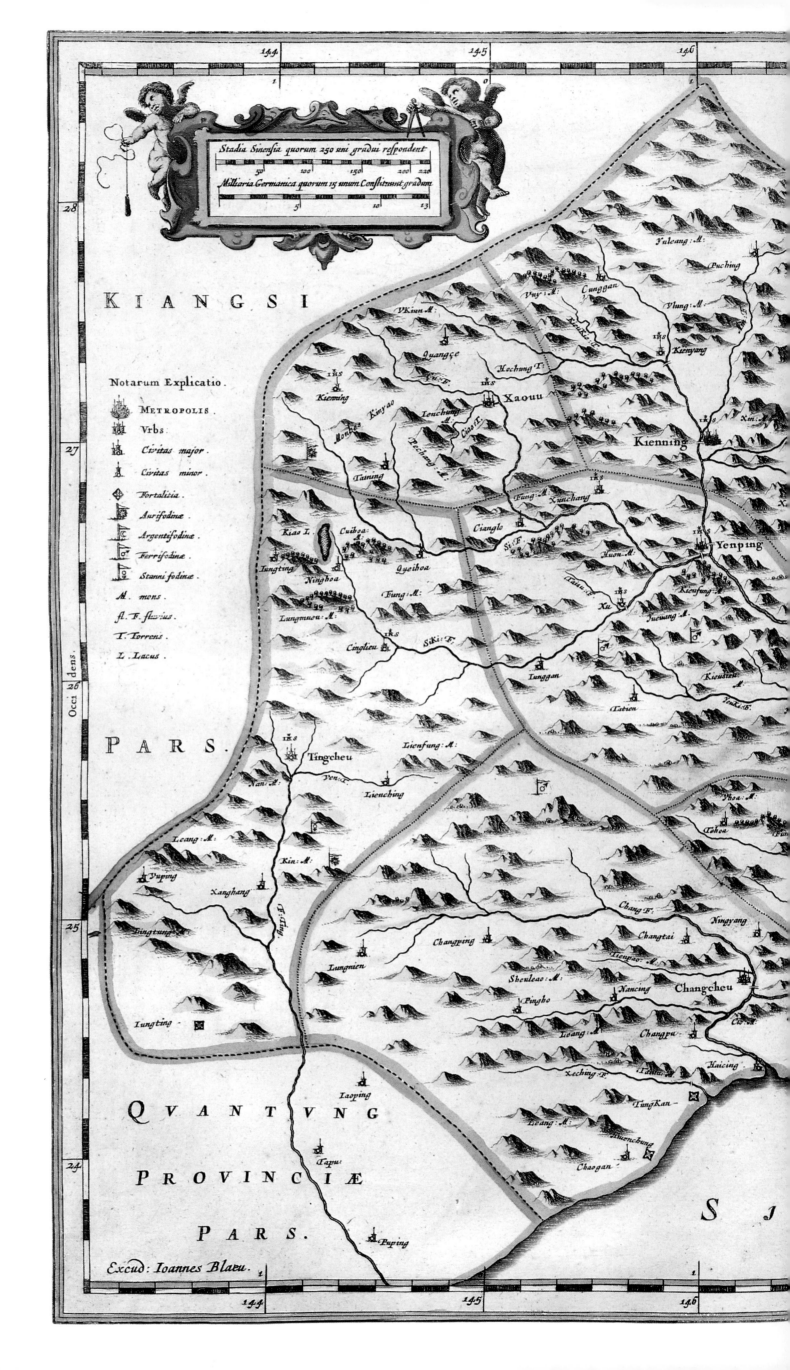

Fokien, Imperii Sinarum Provincia Undecima

Fujian, the Eleventh Province of China. This coastal province faces the island of Taiwan and includes the port city of Fuzhou (*Focheu* on the map), and the site of one of China's new Special Economic Zones at Xiamen (marked *Hiamuen*).

KIANGSI

Notarum Explicatio.

Metropolis.
Vrbs
Civitas major.
Civitas minor.
Fortalitia.
Aurifodinæ.
Argentifodinæ.
Ferrifodinæ.
Stanni fodinæ.
M. mons.
fl. F. fluvius.
T. Torrens.
L. Lacus.

PARS.

QVANTVNG

PROVINCIÆ

PARS.

Excud: Ioannes Blaeu.

FOKIEN
IMPERII SINARVM
PROVINCIA
VNDECIMA.

Cum privilegio Sacræ Cæf. Maj.
& Ordd. Belgicæ Fœderatæ.

P A R S

Tungchi

Locing   Hoigan

28

Vencheu

Sining

Xuigan   Iungnoen   Haifung

C H E K I A N G

Pingyang

Kingyuen   Toixun

27

Kinxan   Pumuon

Yingche   Xening

Fogan   Lungxeu

Chingho

Foning   Xung

Hoangpic   Heiruing   Ningte

Cutien   Stuefung   Sienmai   Lieyuen

XuiKeu   Lienkiang   Tinghai

Ori

ens.

Fuyung   Kiao F.

26

FOCHEV   Longquen   Muihoa

Caocai   Cantai   Keutai   Changlo

Xeching   HaiKeu

Tachaug   Tangfo

Focing

Kieusien

Hinghoa   Hoasiu   Vangan

Sienyeu   Hocung

Nangan   Leyang   Siaoco

Ciuen
cheu

O C E A N V S

25

Paocu

Tunggan   Ganhai

Salinæ

I. FOR-

MOSA,

incolis

I. Quemoi

PEKAN,

Sinis

24

E N S I S.   SIEVKIEV.

Iaponia regnum

This comparatively modern-looking map of Japan was the seventeenth and last of the maps provided by Martino Martini for Joan Blaeu's *Atlas Sinensis* of 1655.

Martini's map was to provide the most accurate depiction of the general outlines of the principal islands of Japan – Honshu, Kyūshū and Shikoku – for more than a century. The map was copied extensively by other mapmakers throughout the remainder of the seventeenth century and was replaced during the eighteenth century by maps that were in nearly all respects considerably inferior, albeit rather more flamboyant in design. Martini's first-hand knowledge of the Chinese mainland enabled him to draw Korea correctly, for the first time on a printed map, as a peninsula even though little interior detail is shown. However, what lay to the north of Japan was a mystery, not only to Europeans, but to the Japanese and Chinese as well. Only a hint of the north island of Hokkaidō is given at the upper right-hand corner as *Eso*, but it remained uncertain, until the second half of the eighteenth century, whether *Eso* (also know as *Yèzo*) was an island or part of the Asian mainland. The traveller Engelbrecht Kaempfer, who went with a Dutch embassy to Japan in 1690, wrote that geographers were as yet uncertain whether Yezo 'confines on Tartary or America, consequently where they are to place the streight of Anian, or the so long wished for passage out of the North [that is, Arctic] Sea into the great Indian Ocean'. This was not mere academic speculation, for the correct answer depended on the possibility of a north-eastern sea passage from Europe. Even as early as 1613, William Adams, an Englishman domiciled in Japan for many years, had

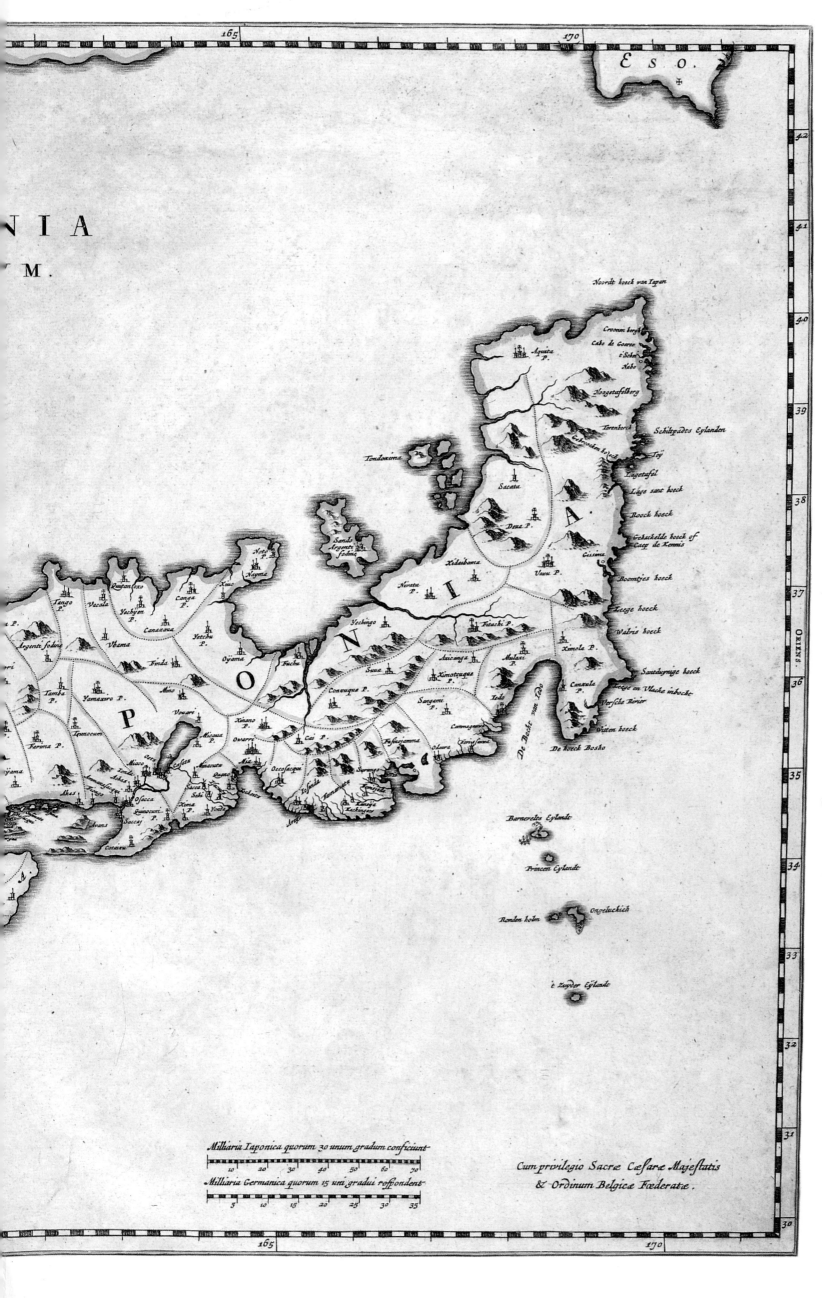

Noordt hoeck van Iapan

Croonen hoeck

Cabo de Goree

t'Schee

Nabt

Aquita P.

Hoogetafelberg

Schildpades Eylanden

Tondoxima

Terenhoris

Ioy

Lagetafel

Sacata

Lage sant hoeck

Roock hoeck

Dena P.

Gehackelde hoeck of

Caep de Kennis

Xidaibama

Gissima

Nivata P.

Uaxu P.

Boomtjes hoeck

Yechingo

Fitachi P.

Letse hoeck

Walris hoeck

Aricanga

Malaci P.

Ximola P.

Suua

Ximotzuque P.

Iedo

Santduynige hoeck

Conuuque P.

Sangami P.

Canxula P.

Heetge en Vlacke inbocht

Catmagaru

Versche Revier

Witten hoeck

De Bucht van Cabo

De hoeck Bosho

165 · 170

NIA
M.

Noto P.
Nayma
Quitanexo
Tango
Vacola
Yechyen P.
Canga
Xaro
Argenti fodine
Vbama
Yetchu
Cananoua
Finds
Ojama
Fuchu
Tamba P.
Yamaxiro P.
Alno
Vouari
Xnano P.
Ozuwa
Farima P.
Tesmocuni
Misao
Ogamu
Ishu
Misca
Cesta
Cay P.
Ixi
Lis
Macuta
Ofacca
Xima P.
Sacca
Schi
Qua
Fasaujamma
P.
Saura
Forisi
Kumocuni
Saccai
Yoda
Icange
Cocaire
Conga P.
Yetchu P.
Sando
Argenti
fodina

P
O
N
I
A

Barnevelts Eylandt

Princen Eylandt

Ronden holm
Ongeluckich

t'Zuyder Eylande

42
41
40
39
38
37
36
35
34
33
32
31
30

ORIENS.

Milliaria Iaponica quorum 30 unum gradum conficiunt

10 20 30 40 50 60 70

Milliaria Germanica quorum 15 uni gradui respondent

5 10 15 20 25 30 35

Cum privilegio Sacræ Cæsaræ Majeſtatis
& Ordinum Belgicæ Fœderatæ.

165 · 170

written back to England recommending Japan as a base for 'discouerie to the northward…neuer hath bin better menes to discouer'.

Rumours of landfalls to the north of Japan led to the Dutch based at Batavia in the East Indies to send two expeditions, one in 1639 under Matthijs Quast and Abel Janszoon Tasman, the other in 1643 under Maarten Vries, to explore the region. Their reports merely added to the confusion among mapmakers, no doubt providing a reason for Martini not to attempt an outline for any coast to the north of Honshu other than *Eso*.

As with his general map of China, Martini here provides information on the internal administrative divisions in Japan: each of the feudal fiefdoms is shown, with the chief town in each, while some evidence of the activity of Jesuit missions, since the arrival of Francis Xavier in 1549, can be gathered from the town symbols surmounted by a small cross.

A SELECTED LIST OF
FURTHER READING

EEGHEN (I. H. van) 'The printing-house of Dr Joan Blaeu behind the New Church', in: *Theatrum Orbis Librorum* (*ed.* T. C. van Uchelen, K. van der Horst and G. Schilder) (Utrecht 1989), pp. 402–415.

FONTAINE VERWEY (H. de la) *Uit de Wereld van het Boek III. In en om de 'Vergulde Sonnewyser'* (Amsterdam 1979).

KEUNING (J.), *ed.* M. DONKERSLOOT-DE VRIJ. *Willem Jansz. Blaeu. A biography and history of his work as a cartographer and publisher* (Amsterdam 1973).

KOEMAN (C.) *Atlantes Neerlandici. Bibliography of terrestrial, maritime and celestial atlases and pilot books, published in The Netherlands up to 1800. Volume I* (Amsterdam 1967).

KOEMAN (C.) *Joan Blaeu and his Grand Atlas* (Amsterdam 1970).

SCHAMA (S.) *The Embarrassment of Riches. An Interpretation of Dutch Culture in the Golden Age* (London 1987).

SEIFERT (T.) *Bayerische Staatsbibliothek. Die Karte als Kunstwerk. Dekorative Landkarten aus Mittelalter und Neuzeit* (München 1979).

SKELTON (R. A.) *Decorative Printed Maps of the 15th to 18th Centuries* (London 1965).

STONE (J. C.) *The Pont Manuscript Maps of Scotland. Sixteenth century origins of a Blaeu atlas* (Tring 1989).

VRIJ (M. de) *The World on Paper. A descriptive catalogue of cartographical material published in Amsterdam during the seventeenth century* (Amsterdam 1967).

WHITEHEAD (P. J. P.) and M. BOESEMAN. *A portrait of Dutch 17th century Brazil. Animals, plants and people by the artists of Johan Maurits of Nassau* (Amsterdam, Oxford and New York 1989).

WOODWARD (D., *ed.*) *Art and Cartography. Six Historical Essays* (Chicago and London 1987).

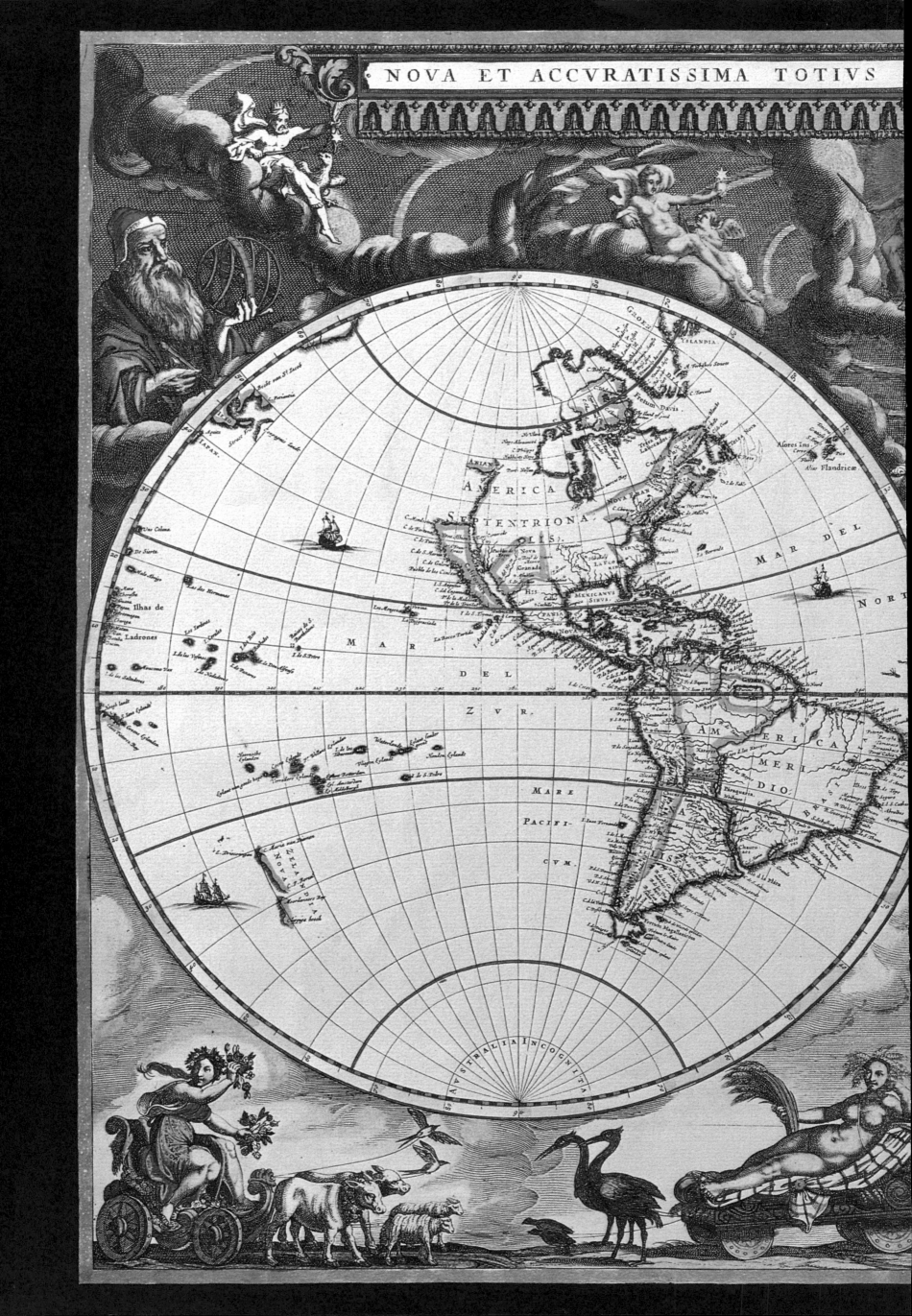